To

" Best

Ron WATTS

Heroes Publishing

HUNDRED WATTS
a life in music

RON WATTS

First published in Great Britain in 2006 by
Heroes Publishing.
P.O. Box, Perry Barr,
Birmingham B42 1UZ.
www.heroespublishing.com

The rights of Ron Watts to be identified as author of this work has been asserted by him in accordance with the Copyright, Design and Patents Act 1988.

All rights reserved. No part of this publication may be reproduced, stored in a retrieval system or transmitted in any form or by any means electronic, digital, mechanical, recording or otherwise without the prior permission of the publisher.

ISBN 0-9543884-4-5

Cover Photo - Bucks Free Press

Printed by Bookmarque

Acknowledgements

First of all, thanks to Dave Woodhall, for transcribing my thoughts into a readable form. To Glen Matlock for kindly providing a foreword, Michelle Brigandage and Sylvia Pitcher for photographs. Tom Robinson, John Otway and Dylan Jones for their kind words. Rachel Wakefield of the Bucks Free Press for her help.

During my career there have been many people who have helped me, and I'd like to thank as many of them as I can remember:

Mike Leadbetter, Simon Napier and John Broven of Blues Unlimited, for all their help when I was starting out as a promoter. Steve Kane, Keith Welch and Nimrod Ping for keeping the Brewer's Droop show on the road in the face of much adversity. Ron Saunders and Mick Fitzgibbons for their co-operation at the Nag's Head. Roger and Jeff Horton for keeping alive the 100 Club, a fitting tribute to their abilities. Shakey Vick, Bruv Sawney, Trevor 'Spike' Jones and Bobby Walker for their practical assistance and wise counselling.

All the ladies I've know, and I'd better say no more about that.

The musicians I've played and worked with, even the ones who were a pain. Everyone else who thinks they deserve a mention. I'm sure you do.

And finally Terri, Marie, Stuart and their children.

Some of the people I've mentioned above are no longer with us, and I'd like to pay particular tribute to them.

A couple of final points – there are times during the book when I've described events out of chronological order for the sake of clarity, while 'Wycombe' and 'High Wycombe' are one and the same place.

Foreword
by
GLEN MATLOCK

Throughout the history of popular culture, certain locations have been synonymous with the vanguard of youth ideologies and musical movements.

From jazz in New Orleans in the early part of last century, the Mississippi Delta for country blues and later Chicago with its city blues, from Memphis as the birthplace of rock and roll and over to England and the Beat Boom in Swinging London in the 1960's. We can then go back across the Atlantic to Haight Ashbury in San Francisco for the first stirrings of the hippy movement.

Skip forward to the seventies and we will find the eerily simultaneous first awakenings of punk rock in both London and New York, then if we travel a little further in time to Seattle we find grunge.

It would appear that if there is going to be something going on, then quite naturally, there has to be somewhere for it to be going on in.

We can further narrow this down to specific venues in these places, whose names can be written almost as large as the acts for whom they provided the maternity ward. Andy Warhol's Factory and Max's Kansas City in New York - the Velvet Underground. The Crawdaddy and Eel Pie Island - the Rolling Stones and the beat explosion. The UFO club – Syd Barret's Pink Floyd. The Hacienda – the Madchester scene. And of course the Cavern for the Beatles.

After playing seemingly every art school in the Home Counties and a slew of particularly weird and wonderful Conservative clubs, bingo halls and chicken in the baskets in the north of England, the Sex Pistols, by a stroke of good fortune, found themselves wandering equipment in hand through the stage doors of the 100 club in early 1976. We had been invited to this (at the time) august jazz venue by the promoter, one Ron Watts. Ron had witnessed a particularly ramshackle support slot to Screaming Lord Sutch and I think, the Savages (I don't remember there being too many Heavy Friends there at the time) at a technical college gig in High Wycombe where I believe, as they say, he used to 'knock around'.

What he saw in us at that stage I shudder to think, but as he explains in this book, he had had an ear to the ground as to what the word on the street was (we had already begun to build a following at that stage - albeit a miniscule sized one). He put two and two together to come up with five, although somehow miraculously making the figures work.

Our show at the 100 Club was far from an instant success but Ron's never say die attitude encouraged us to persevere, culminating a good few months later in the now legendary, although not as you will discover for necessarily all the right reasons, Punk Festival in the autumn of that year. Punk Rock was fit and ready to be unleashed upon the Western World.

There's a whole host of facts and behind the scenes stories of shenanigans which I have only discovered on reading the relevant pages and have found them fascinating – and I was there at the time! I feel that the Sex Pistols owe a debt of gratitude to Ron Watts for his foresight and assistance in giving us the chance to take a big step up the ladder of success.

Yes, the Pistols may well have been the right thing at the right time, but to finish the phrase, Ron Watts provided the right place...

Glen Matlock

HUNDRED WATTS
a life in music

Introduction

"That tosser from the Damned's here. If he wants a fight he can have one."

That was my first reaction to the arrival of Captain Sensible at the 100 Club one afternoon in early 2005. We were celebrating the life of Dave Goodman, punk producer and the man who had brought some professionalism to the Sex Pistols' early performances. Glen Matlock was there, so was Mick Jones of the Clash, and a host of semi-remembered faces I hadn't seen for more than twenty years had also turned up.

The Captain's arrival took me back to those pioneering days, when punk was threatening the moral fabric of society and I was playing a leading part in the most exciting musical revolution this country has ever seen. But it wasn't the first time I'd been involved in something like that.

In the fifties, rock'n'roll was the devil's music while ten years later the blues would surely eat away at the moral fabric of the country. Then there was my own small speaking part in the Permissive Society, and plenty of other ways in which I was beyond redemption, if the moral guardians of our nation were anything to take notice of.

Not that I took much notice as I continued enjoying myself, immersed in doing something I loved for thirty years and more. As you'll see as my story unfolds, that afternoon at the 100 Club was honouring just one chapter in a never-ending story. It began before any of us were born, and it'll continue after we're long gone. I'm proud of my contribution, and I'm privileged to have met so many of those who did the same, whatever label their music came under.

As is the nature of such gatherings, the Captain and I were chatting away like old mates within minutes, enmities forgotten in a haze of nostalgia for the time when just walking down the street was a political act. That was when I realised that the musicians who were creating that revolution were hardly more than schoolboys at the time, and although they might not act it, they're middle-aged men now. It was also when I realised that I'd got to get this story of mine down in print.

The bits that I can remember, that is.

Chapter 1

We`ll Meet Again

For someone who's spent most of his adult life living and working in the south-east of England, I come from a family with surprisingly widespread roots.

My mother, for example, Jeannie Winspear Harkness, was born in the mining village of Hetton le Hole, in Durham, in 1921. Along with the rest of her family, mum moved down south during the thirties. Like many others who had been trying their hardest to scratch out a living in the north-east during the depression, they figured work would be easier to find in the comparatively prosperous south.

By this time she was living with Maria and Ted Whitfield, her mother's sister and her husband. They'd got no children, so I suppose they had a bit more money than my grandparents, who had another daughter and two sons. Because things were tight mum moved in with the Whitfields and they raised her as their daughter. It was a common practice at the time, and a practical solution for all concerned. My natural grandparents had their financial burden eased a bit, Ted and Maria had the child they'd longed for and mum grew up perfectly content. Everyone's happy, even though social services wouldn't let such a thing happen nowadays.

Both families moved into adjoining houses in Placket Way, Cippenham, which is a part of Slough, and Jeannie later got a job as a cashier and bookkeeper at a butchers' shop in the town. If she hadn't taken the position things might have worked out differently for a lot of people, the entire cast of what became known as punk included, because the manager of the shop was one George William Watts, later referred to by me as 'dad'.

The Watts family were old Wiltshire yeoman stock, honest sons of the soil, although my paternal grandfather, Albert, is worth a book of his own. Albert was in the Royal Navy for many years; in the First World War he took part in the Battle of Jutland and then served in the Dover Patrols, when they would be out every night keeping the English Channel open to shipping against everything the Germans could throw at them. Albert rose to the rank of Lieutenant Commander before leaving the navy when the war ended. Later on, he opened a company that constructed wells, became Head Waterman at Eton College, which must have been a dream job for someone who loved sailing as he did, then founded the Slough Naval Club and the Sea Scouts in the town.

The family were living in the village of Vernham Dean, on the border of Wiltshire and Hampshire, when my father was born in 1910, although they moved to Slough, which was easier for the Chatham dockyards where granddad was based, in 1924. Dad became a national hero a few years later, after saving three girls from drowning in the Grand Union Canal at Slough. He was riding his bike along the towpath when he saw them in the water and dived in to rescue the girls one at a time. The incident made headline news and he was presented with a handsome carriage clock, which still has pride of place in my house.

Mum always reckoned that when she met dad it wasn't so much love at first sight as fear, as she was intimidated by this big man, eleven years her senior, but she soon changed her mind and after a few years events got more serious between them. War broke out, and dad volunteered for the navy when the phoney war ended with the invasion of Belgium and France in 1940. As often happened at that time, they got married just before he embarked, although he must have had at least one bout of leave because some two years later, on the 13th November 1942, Ronald Watts was born. Mum was left with the task of bringing me into the world and helping me grow up, while my dad had the far easier task of escorting the North Sea convoys, bringing coal down from the coalfields of the northeast to the Thames dockyards. He was in the peculiar position of being an ordinary seaman while his father was a serving

Lieutenant Commander, granddad having been recalled to teach divers at the navy college in Gosport, Hampshire, before he went back to Eton, where he worked until he was well into his eighties.

I was fated to be an only child, my mother losing a daughter in childbirth, although there was some suspicion that dad got up to something he shouldn't have done with a Greek refugee when he was serving in Egypt during the war. It would be nice to think that her name was Onassis and the product of their liaison went on to make something of himself in the shipping business, but I don't suppose it's any nearer me even if it were true. He probably ended up working in a bar in Corfu.

With the war being such a vivid time, I can remember much more of what happened to me when I was a toddler than most people nowadays can. The first memory I have was when my mum went away for a week to have what we thought would be my little brother or sister. I can remember sitting on the bench seat we had, looking out of the front window towards the garden gate, wanting to know where my mum was. She'd been gone a week, then my nan said, "They've put her through the roller," which didn't make me feel very happy but was as good a way as any of telling me that my mum would be returning minus her bump and also, sadly, minus her daughter.

We were living in Slough now, and with Windsor Castle a mile away, the town became the target for more than its fair share of bombing raids. John Bejeman once wrote, "Come friendly bombs and fall on Slough." He wasn't around during the war.

One afternoon, it must have been in the late autumn of 1944 because it was a lovely hot day, we could hear the drone of a V1 doodlebug. Everything went quiet as we waited for the noise to die down, because that was when they dropped out of the sky, and suddenly there was silence. Pandemonium, my mum gathered me up, threw me onto the bed and laid the pillows and blankets on top of me as we waited for the explosion. Not knowing what was going on, I thought she was trying to suffocate me. There was an almighty bang as the bomb went off two hundred yards away. Chunks of shrapnel came though our roof and ruptured the water tank, but that was soon sorted out. The school down the road wasn't so lucky, though. They suffered a direct hit and the caretaker was killed, although no children were about at the time otherwise there would have been carnage.

We used to have a lot of planes flying overhead, and my mum would always get very worried when they were around and usher me indoors even when it was the RAF or the Americans who were above us. I always thought she was worrying about nothing, but then years later during the Gulf War all the stories started to come out about friendly fire, so maybe she was ahead of her time. Another time, and again I was only about eighteen months old but I was still able to remember it all, there were so many planes flying around that I was getting excited about them. We were used to the noise of the planes flying overhead so there must have been lots around all day. A couple of days later the Normandy landings took place, and they must have been taking troops and supplies to the landing stages.

When I was three, my mum and the rest of the family started telling me about this strange thing I was going to have called a dad. "Your dad's coming home," they told me, as I thought, "What's a dad?" and wondered if you could eat it, play with it or stick it up your nose. Like many children my age, I had no recollection of any man around the house apart from really, really old ones such as my grandfathers. But anyway, one afternoon I was sitting at the table with the rest of the family, when there was a knock on the door and this mysterious 'dad' figure I'd heard so much about had arrived. It was the strangest thing – he just stared at me for what seemed an eternity. I know that time can stand still in these situations, but to this day I don't know if he was looking at me for a couple of minutes or an hour. It may have been that he was stunned by the sight of his little lad again, but even when he eventually picked me up I couldn't feel any real affection coming from him.

With dad back home and working as a butcher, life soon got back to its normal idyllic state. We could see Windsor Castle out of the back window, the woods at Burnham Beeches were a short walk from home and the River Thames flowed a couple of fields away. It was a hell of a playground for a little lad. I had a delightful childhood – plenty of friends at school, cousins around all the time, aunts and uncles in plentiful supply. My father had two brothers and a sister, all of whom had their families living locally, while my mom's family were still around. We had the usual rounds of football in the winter, cricket in the summer – the road outside was so quiet we'd play cricket out there and only have one or two cars an afternoon to disturb us – and swimming in the Thames, in which, of course, our mothers were convinced we were bound to drown or catch some unspeakable disease.

I often read about people who had the most extraordinary time as children, with excitement galore and famous people popping up all over the place. Nothing like that happened to me, apart from my first few years being spent at war, and even that, of course, was the same as for millions of my contemporaries. I had a perfectly normal upbringing, for which I apologise to anyone who reads this book expecting tales of boyhood intrigue and early meetings with school friends who went on to become household names, and feels short-changed.

Towards the end of the forties I started to take an interest in music. For as long as I could remember, the women of the family had been listening to American Forces radio and music could always be heard in the house. When dad returned from the navy, he and my mum used to attend the local ballrooms, where some real top line acts played. The likes of Duke Ellington and Fats Waller. Mum was really into it, but dad suffered with deafness as a result of what happened during the war, so he wasn't all that interested. "Them darkies," was his disparaging opinion of some of the greatest musicians to have ever toured this or any other country.

Then one day in what must have been 1947 or 1948, I was sitting in the garden and what I later found out was 12th Street Rag by Walter 'Pee Wee' Hunt started to play on the BBC. "What's that?" I asked my nan. Her reply, although I wasn't to know it at the time, was to have a stunning effect on my life. "That's jazz," she said.

I suppose that my contemporaries, born during the war and brought up in the early fifties, were the last generation to have enjoyed hobbies. There was little or no television, and sex was something that happened on another planet. As a result we looked for ways of passing the time. There was night school, youth clubs and organisations such as the scouts and Boys Brigade. I fished and was interested in fretwork, a type of wood carving that almost every young lad of the era took up before realising that it was utterly pointless. I liked music of course, but my great passion was sport. I played cricket and football for the school, and I was always winning trophies for athletics. 100 yards, 220 yards, long jump, triple jump, even the shot putt if the bigger lads weren't around.

By now we were living in Burnham, in a semi-detached house with a huge garden. I failed the eleven plus, but in those days you could take the exam again two years later, so I got to the newly-founded Langley Grammar School in 1956, when I was thirteen. It was a fantastic place and I still remain friends with my old form master, Mel Jones.

That was the time when I got my first job, although I soon wished I hadn't. My dad was part-owner of a string of butchers shops and also owned an abattoir. He got me a position cleaning out the slaughterhouse, and it was my job to wash away all the blood, guts, entrails, everything that comes out of a dead animal and isn't going to be sold. I was determined not to be sick on my first day and I just about managed that, but I went back home and demanded to know why I couldn't have a job in the shop. My dad looked up and said, matter of fact, "We've already got a Saturday boy." A man who stayed a naval rating while his father was a high-ranking officer was in no mood to bring nepotism into his business affairs. Luckily though, the other lad soon left and I was promoted to head of transport and distribution, and presented with my own company vehicle. Or, as it was then known, I was the delivery boy and here was the shop's bike.

It was my job to make sure everyone got their meat for the weekend. Usually it took me all of Saturday, but if I was playing football in the afternoon I'd make a start on Friday and be delivering up until nine o'clock some evenings, then start again at the crack of dawn the following day. Still, I was well-paid compared to most thirteen year-olds, with wages of 15 shillings (75p) and sometimes that much again in tips from grateful customers. I might not have had much spare time, but my record collection was beginning to grow.

By now the new phenomenon known as rock'n'roll had reached Buckinghamshire. When you're young you notice things when they're happening even if you might not be taking part in them. I'd heard the older kids talking about Chris Barber, and then about these strange Americans called Bill and Elvis. Hickie's music shop in Slough had two branches on the High Street, selling instruments, sheet music and records. I'd get in there just after four o'clock, once I'd been let out of school, and they'd be playing the music that was becoming infamous. You weren't encouraged to hang around if you weren't a paying customer, so I'd find myself buying records most days, just to be able to stay in there and listen. Naturally, I can remember the first record I bought – Chuck Berry's Schooldays on a shellac 78. It was soon followed by Fats Domino's Blue For Love EP, which proved to be a wise investment, as it cost me 2/6 (12 1/2p) and I sold it many years later for £80. I don't often sell my records, but I showed this one to a group of rock'n'roll fans at a gig and they started making me offers for it. When they reached silly money, knowing that I could get it on CD I agreed to the sale.

By the late fifties, the initial electric surge of rock'n'roll had blown itself out and popular music's driving force was now the wimpy, pretty boy pop of Bobby Vee, Bobby Darin and Dion. Disillusioned, I started getting into a different kind of sound. Fats Domino was a big favourite, some of his stuff was so unusual for the time. One track he'd recorded in 1954, Don't You Hear Me Calling, sounds more like something from the mid-sixties Swinging London era, with congas and a horn section.

Of course, the newspapers were full of outrageous stories about how rock'n'roll was the devil's music and would cause the destruction of Western civilization. My mother, who a few years earlier had been convinced that the American air force would bomb our house, was only slightly less concerned about this latest import from the other side of the Atlantic. If we ever saw a teddy boy walking down the street, I'd be told not to look at him, and she'd very often cross the street rather than walk past anyone she considered unsuitable. In her defence, the teddy boys were quite different to anything that has been around either before or since, and unlike their successors in the fashion outrage stakes, they couldn't really be termed a youth cult. Whereas most skinheads, mods or punks were teenagers and very often still at school, teddy boys were older, usually in their twenties, and therefore more threatening.

Of course, in the face of such parental displeasure I saved my wages to buy a drape suit. Dark blue jacket with velvet collar and sixteen-inch trousers, topped off with a pair of brothel creepers. I had to sneak it home, but eventually my parents calmed down enough to let me admit that their son was a teddy boy, even though mum insisted that the collar was fake velvet. My mum and dad tried so hard to make me a nice middle-class lad, I suppose it was because they'd had such hard upbringings and they wanted me to be better off than they were. In the end I didn't so much join the middle classes as play a part in destroying their influence on society, but that was much later.

Chapter 2

Mannish Boy

By now, I'd gravitated to the Saturday night hop at the Cippenham Essoldo cinema. Like many similar venues there was a dance suite upstairs, which during the day gave lessons, although there was a good deal of local outrage when it was discovered that rock'n'roll dancing was being taught as well as the more respectable waltz and cha-cha. The Saturday night band was later to become known as the Tremeloes, who are still going almost fifty years later, and although they had plenty of success in the sixties and still work the cabaret circuit now, they've never been afforded the respect they deserve for being one of the very first British rock'n'roll groups. They were fantastic; great musicians and they always seemed to be enjoying themselves. I used to ignore my date – at least, until later in the evening – and watch them from start to finish, although I still wasn't interested in making music. At this time, it was enough just to listen.

I didn't realise it, but I was getting increasingly into the blues. I was buying more records by vocal groups, and although it was still called rock'n'roll, it was in fact rhythm & blues, a term I'd never heard then. In 1958 I bought a copy of Little Walter's 78, My Babe; I wish I still had that one now, and then What Am I Living For? by Chuck Willis, which could be called the first soul record.

I was still attending the Saturday nights at the Essoldo, and one time vocal group the Delvikings played what I still say is the best gig I've seen. They were stationed at West Drayton USAF base, so played under a false name, with the future Tremeloes backing them. They had the lot – bass, mid tenor, high tenor. It was unbelievable stuff, even allowing for the nostalgia factor. And yes, the summers were always warmer then as well.

Being just half an hour from London, and with trains still running through the night, I could get to all the big shows. I managed to see Jerry Lee Lewis on the tour that was cancelled after just three dates, when it came out that he'd married his 13 year-old cousin. Jerry Lee was the best showman I'd seen up until then. He had long hair and he was forever combing it. He'd finish one number, and while the audience were screaming he'd pull out his comb, grinning and ignoring the mayhem all round while he was combing his hair, then suddenly stand up, kick the piano stool away and launch into another rocker. He was good, but for me the support band were better. The Treniers were another American r&b act. There were eight or ten of them, they did these amazing dance routines and they could play their instruments, as well as putting over some amazing vocals.

I also made my one and only visit to the legendary 2is coffee bar. It was 1958, and we'd gone on a school trip to London. Four of us stayed over and ventured into darkest Soho, where the 2is stood on Compton St. We paid our two shillings admission money each and entered this room where there was no stage, and which, contrary to what I'd expected, wasn't packed to the rafters with screaming rockers. It was reasonably full, and, happily, there were a lot of girls present, although none of them were interested in a smalltown sixteen year old. Vince Taylor, one of the earliest British rock'n'rollers, was playing and the audience were appreciative rather than enthusiastic. I got the impression that Vince was a regular and the crowd were used to him. It was a small place and I wondered how the owners could make money, as the audience weren't big spenders. Not for the last time I came away from a legendary venue distinctly unimpressed.

The music business certainly seemed a hard way of making a living, particularly as the venues were invariably unlicensed. Whether it was a small bar or cafe such as the 2is or larger enterprises like High Wycombe Town Hall and the Court Gardens at Marlow, both of which were trad jazz haunts, there seemed a belief that the audiences must be kept away from the temptations of alcohol, for fear of the mayhem that would follow. The local publicans loved it that way, of course. In fact, they probably encouraged teetotal venues so that they could take the trade before and after the show. I wonder if breweries used to 'encourage' the licensing justices to refuse applications from such places?

I went to see Eddie Cochran and Gene Vincent in 1960, at the Adelphi in Slough, on the tour when they had the crash that killed Cochran and left Vincent severely injured. They were another couple of showmen with charisma that reached out from the stage to the back row; Eddie was a great blues player and knew how to get the audience going. At one point he'd lean his guitar up at the side of the stage and make as though he was shagging it, all the time firing out some of the greatest teen anthems ever written – Summertime Blues, Somethin' Else, C'mon Everybody, 20 Flight Rock. Both he and Gene were regulars on Saturday Club, a BBC radio show that was essential listening for music fans in the fifties. Musicians would play live in the studio, and it was the best way of getting information about the music scene.

I also saw Chuck Berry, and although he was great, even back then he would play as short a set as he could get away with. The promoters got wise to this, and started making him do two or three venues on the same night. You'd see him booked to perform in Wolverhampton at seven in the evening, Birmingham at 8.30 and Coventry at ten. It was the only way they could afford to bring him over. Bill Haley was another great night. By the time I saw him the initial success had faded and he was obviously frustrated at having to play the old hits – Rock Around The Clock, Shake Rattle & Roll, and the others that had changed the face of music – when he wanted to be doing the r&b material he'd started out playing.

Wee Willy Harris; there was another performer, one of the first British rockers. Totally nuts, but with an ego to match and bright pink hair, which was brave for England in the fifties. He wasn't the greatest singer, which was probably why he never had any hits, but he could perform. And Cliff Richard, who I saw playing at Aylesbury backed by the Drifters, before they changed their name to the Shadows. His band could play, and Cliff certainly knew how to perform, but he lacked the authenticity of the Americans.

During that time, my family had moved to High Wycombe. My parents thought that I'd do better staying at the same school as I had my exams coming up, so I'd spend weeknights at the house of my friend, Richard Hill. He'd started a skiffle group and although I was a bit annoyed that I wasn't involved, I didn't really have the time. The group rehearsed at the weekend, when I was in Wycombe with my family, and with athletics meetings, training and rowing for the Maidenhead Rowing Club, which I'd got involved with, I wasn't able to fit in any more commitments. Anyway, I was still more interested in listening than in performing. Stick to what you're good at was my motto, and it stood me in good stead. I was a good-looking lad, everyone knew me as an athlete and to be honest, I had girls running after me. Forget all the stuff you hear about how they weren't interested in those days – they certainly were by then. There's at least one women from Slough, for obvious reasons I won't name her but she'd be in her mid-forties now, who could stake a claim to a share in the Watts family fortune.

It was around this time that I started to go into the Co-Op record shop in Slough, and working behind the counter was this woman who made it clear she fancied me. We'd chat and one day she told me to pick out four LPs for a pound the lot. That was a bargain – in those days they'd cost about £1 12 shillings (£1.60) each, so I was right in there. For some reason I picked four jazz albums. The Great Ray Charles was the only jazz album that awesome singer ever made, and there was also Shelly Manne & His Men at the Black Hawk, Turk Murphy & His San Francisco Jazz Band and Suite Thursday by Duke Ellington. The reason I can remember them all is because I still own them, and I still play them after all these years. That tells you something about how good they were, and also how long lasting vinyl is, as well.

On the subject of women, I used to get the bus from school and on there was a young girl from St Bernard's Convent school who I later found out was almost the same age, having been born just six days earlier than me. She was stunningly beautiful, but a true ice maiden, and showed not the slightest interest in any of us adolescent grammar school boys as she got off the bus to go to her dad's farm in Hitcham. Her name, I learned, was Jean Shrimpton and she went on to become one of the most famous models in the world. No wonder none of us stood a chance.

By the time I was 19 I was moving from jazz into blues, and the delta sound of Muddy Waters and Robert Johnson. Then came the moment that might sound corny, but it changed my life. I'd just passed my A levels and got a job at the Midland Bank in Wycombe, so I was able to really get started on expanding my record collection. I paid the usual 32 bob for a copy of Singin' the Blues by Jimmy Witherspoon, which had come out a year or so earlier, and it blew me away. Good Rocking Tonight, All That's Good, Spoon's Blues. Classic jazz arrangements over that wonderful blues voice I was to get to know and love so well. I knew then that I wanted to be in the music business. He may never have had the same commercial success as his contemporaries such as B.B. King or John Lee Hooker, but Jimmy Witherspoon was the greatest influence I was ever to know.

By coincidence, at around that time I saw a mention in either Jazz Weekly or Jazzbeat, two magazines I'd buy and study religiously, of a new club opening in Ealing that would play rhythm & blues. I'd seen r&b acts before, but I was curious as to how they would work in a club setting. I turned up one Saturday night in the summer of 1962 and didn't know it, but I played a part in a bit of musical history, because it was the opening night of the first r&b club in Britain. Situated underneath a café on Ealing Broadway, 100 yards from a railway station that had direct trains to High Wycombe so it couldn't have been easier to get there, the club featured Alexis Korner's Blues Incorporated. Four shillings and sixpence to get in, once you'd got to the front of the big queue of people who turned out with the same sense of curiosity that drove my girlfriend Pauline and I to attend. Dick Hickstall-Smith was on tenor, Cyril Davis played harmonica and sang, Charlie Watts on drums and the whole thing took place in a room not much bigger than the lounge of a semi-detached house. There were three rooms, one opening out on to a roof terrace, which was lucky as the night got a bit hot.

We all stood round not knowing what to do or what to expect. For all the audience knew six men from the moon were about to walk onstage. Were they going to play guitars, or what? Did you clap, did you dance, and if so what kind of dance was it? There weren't many women in attendance, and I wasn't about to share Pauline with anyone. Being British we were all a bit reserved, but soon got into the music. The band weren't just churning it out, they were having fun, and the audience followed suit. I talked to Cyril Davis during the interval. He was a great musician, although sadly, he died of leukaemia a couple of years later. And I won a raffle prize, an EP by the American boogie-woogie pianist Meade Lux Lewis.

The club continued for a couple of years, until it got so popular that it had to move to the Marquee. If a bomb had gone off on any night the British music scene of the sixties would have hardly existed, as so many future star musicians regularly attended. Eric Clapton was a regular, Jeff Beck, most of the Rolling Stones and the Yardbirds. Mick Jagger used to do the door; he looked so cool and bohemian in what would become known as a Beatle jacket, and the price of admission used to go up as the night went on. I don't know what happened to the extra money, but I've got a feeling it was used to get one of the biggest bands in the world started. If you're reading this Mick, I reckon you owe me about three quid.

Blues Incorporated had been just about the only blues band in the country, but they were quickly followed by the Yardbirds, then the Paramounts, who later evolved into Procul Harum, and suddenly the floodgates opened. The Stones started performing, John Mayall came down from Manchester and was playing regularly, Long John Baldry emerged from the shadows, talents such as Rod Stewart and Elton John began their careers in what was becoming not so much a boom period for the blues as a fully-fledged explosion.

Being from the terminally uncool High Wycombe and a former pupil of Langley Grammar School, I was in total awe of these art school bohemians. Everything they did, everything they wore, was just right, and standing at the back wearing a suit and open necked shirt, I felt exactly what I was – a bank clerk from the sticks.

I was still going to jazz dances, usually at High Wycombe Town Hall or the Court Gardens, but by now the trad boom was starting to run out of steam. George Melly, Acker Bilk, Humphrey Lyttleton, they were still putting on good shows but their audiences were declining week by week. On the other hand, I was buying the Jazz Journal magazine which helped me on a voyage of discovery into the blues. Every issue featured a list of new releases by the likes of Howling Wolf and Muddy Waters, as well as the lesser names such as Harold Burrage, a pianist from Chicago who was to die at the tragically early age of 35. I made it my duty to track down as many of these releases as I could, regardless of how obscure they may be, or how much they cost.

By now, another event had taken place that was to help shape the course of my life. An r&b club opened nearby in West Wycombe and John Mayall's Bluesbreakers were performing on the first night. It was packed, but as had happened in London at first, the audience wasn't responding. Because I was into the blues scene by now I was feeling a bit braver than usual, so midway through the band's second set I walked up to John and said to him, "You need to mix things up a bit here, mate." To my horror, and to probably the crowd's delight, John announced to the band, "This guy's gonna sing." I'd never, ever done anything like this in public before, I didn't even know I could sing, but we went through the Little Richard rocker Jenny, Jenny and it went down a storm. A couple of days later I bumped into a mate of mine, Jim MacIntyre, and he said how well I'd done. "I got there when you were up on stage, and I thought you were with the band," he said. That encouraged me and I knew then that I fancied a life of being there on stage, singing in front of an audience. Unfortunately I had an impending marriage to a woman who had an impending date with a maternity ward, but these were things I reckoned I could work round.

Chapter 3

Boom Boom

Pauline also lived in High Wycombe. She was a year or two younger than me, but attended Wycombe High School, so we didn't see each other until we met one night in a local youth club. I think I was 18, so she would have been 17.

Surprisingly for that time, we stuck together after leaving school. I went to work in the bank while she became a hairdresser, the first of a few hairdressers I've known over the years. They're a breed I've always got on with, maybe it's because they're more outgoing than most. We found out Pauline was expecting, so we 'decided' to get married. It was obviously a rush job; we were married in August 1962 at the church in Terriers, near Wycombe, and Terri Ginnette Watts came along in the following February, by which time Pauline and I had moved into a flat above a newsagents' shop in Farnham Rd, Slough. Looking back, we never had a chance of staying together. We were both too young and I didn't know what I wanted at the time, but in the beginning we were determined to make a go of it. I wasn't earning much, so I packed in the bank and got a job with Mars, the sweet manufacturers, at Slough. I started off in their sugar factory, making Opal Fruits and Spangles, and either I had a natural aptitude for working in a great big sweet shop or a lot of people started leaving as soon as I arrived, because I seemed to get a promotion every couple of weeks. I moved up through quality control and ended up as a dispenser, making the flavours for the sweets, which was a very responsible job for a young person.

I was still keeping up with the music scene, buying all the records and magazines I could afford, and attended plenty of gigs locally as blues started to work its way out of London and into the Home Counties. The Ex-Servicemans Club in Windsor had started putting on trad, then moved to blues, and the Thames Hotel also had weekly blues nights. Most of the gigs were well-attended, but there were always some surprises. I saw the Animals in 1965, right at the height of their popularity, at the Drill Hall in Maidenhead. The venue held 800, but there were less then thirty people in the audience, despite the band being one of the biggest names in the country. When they sang Don't Let Me Be Misunderstood, I reckoned that there wasn't much chance of that happening. They could have gone round the audience and explained themselves to everyone, in person.

The Beatles were, as you can imagine, a different story. I saw them at the Adelphi in Slough, around 1963, when they were just starting to make it big. Unlike the Rolling Stones, who were still performing to crowds of 200 at the local r&b clubs, the Beatles were already selling out larger venues. Their stage presence showed that here was a band who were going to be enormous, even though I could hardly hear the music for the screaming girls everywhere. They set the town on fire, and although their music was much too poppy to inspire me, I was interested in the night as an event.

With my love of music growing stronger, it was no surprise when I started thinking about becoming more than just a member of the audience. The first club I was involved with was the Ricky Tick, held at the Star & Garter in Windsor. Until then, the pub had been more famous for its boxing links, particularly the fact that the legendary American middleweight Sugar Ray Robinson had trained there before his fight with Randolph Turpin, who had beaten Robinson on points in one of the greatest nights British boxing has ever known.

The club was run by John Mansfield and Phillip Hayward, with the help of Les Watts, who I think was a distant relation of mine, although we never worked out how, and they used to use me and my reputation to help sort out any problems that might occur whenever the customers got a bit boisterous. It was a small venue. Looking at it when the room was empty you'd think it couldn't hold more than about 50 people, but, as is always the

Boom Boom

case, they found a way of cramming up to 200 customers in. We had some well-known American acts, such as Jesse Fuller and Jimmy Reed, as well as Georgie Fame, who was just coming to prominence with his Blue Flames and gaining a name as a top-class organist and singer.

Jesse Fuller was a one-man band, born in Georgia in 1896, and amongst other things he played guitar in a rough and ready Chicago style. He also invented an instrument called the fotdella, a six string bass viol that he played with his foot via a complicated system of pedals and levers. It might have worked in a waterside San Franciscan bar, and it sounded good enough on this side of the Atlantic as well, but it didn't have much chance of catching on amongst other musicians because it was too awkward to hump around. I was told about one of Jesse's less-charming habits by his roadie, who said that he had never got out of the ideas he developed living in a one-room shack, so when he was in a hotel he'd shit in the washbasin rather than use the toilet.

Jimmy Reed was a younger man, in his thirties when he played at the Ricky Tick. He was a Mississippi-born guitarist and harmonica player whose work was a big influence on the Rolling Stones for one, even though his twin battles with epilepsy and alcoholism meant his live work wasn't always as good as it could have been. Jimmy was touring Europe because his reputation in America had diminished due to his habit of appearing on stage drunk, and it was great to see one of the authentic blues legends appearing on my doorstep.

A band who were more local and who became a big influence in my life, even though I only knew them for a few months, were the curiously-named Hogsnort Rupert and the Good Good Band. They were the first British band to perform New Orleans type r&b, together with what would now be called soul, and I played trumpet for them at a few gigs – well, after a fashion. Rupert (who was rumoured to be a student from Farnham Art College named Bob McGrath, but never confirmed that to me or anyone else) asked me to join them, but I think he was more interested in coming round to the flat and leafing through my record collection than he was in my limited musical ability. I was doing a lot of shift work at Mars in any case, so I was hardly much of a help to the band.

As you can imagine, Rupert was a strange figure. He lived on a barge with John Renbourn, who later went on to great things as guitarist with folk band Pentangle. Rupert was a very authoritarian figure, drilling the band in the same way that James Brown did with his Famous Flames, although the Godfather of Soul got away with it more easily than could a 24 year-old from Berkshire. Then, just as he was on the verge of breaking into the big time, Rupert emigrated to Canada, and as far as I'm aware nobody from the music scene ever heard from him again. I still get journalists asking about him.

Pauline and I split up for the final time in early 1966. We'd given it a go, but we were just too different in our ways. She wanted domesticity, I was getting more and more determined that a life in music was for me. We still get on, but my only real regret was that I didn't see Terri very much for the next couple of years. Whatever else I was up to, she was my daughter and I missed her. Pauline went off recapturing her lost youth, working with Paul Raven in his pre-Gary Glitter days when he fronted a club in Corporation St, High Wycombe. I went in a different direction.

This was the time when blues was starting to take off. I'd been to the first festival to take place in Britain, at the Manchester Free Trade Hall in 1962. It had been an effort to get there, but John Lee Hooker, Willie Dixon and Memphis Slim raised the roof, playing for 6/6 (32 1/2p) a ticket in front of a full house, who were all going mad for their authentic sound. It was little wonder that I'd decided I wanted to get involved.

By the time I was single again, the Ricky Tick club had moved to a permanent base in an old mansion in Windsor. It had once been the home of a rich landowner, but had seen better days and been unused since being requisitioned for military purposes during the second world war. It was bigger than the Star and

Boom Boom

held maybe 300, although the entrance was down a long winding passage, made that way deliberately to stop gatecrashers from sneaking in without paying. This caused a few problems on the night pianist Billy Stewart performed; he got his twenty-stone frame stuck, but three big lads helped shoehorn him along the passage and he played another storming set, as befitted a man who had performed with Marvin Gaye and Bo Diddley.

By now British bands were beginning to get their acts together and we had some great talent playing the Ricky Tick. The Yardbirds were there, as was their former guitarist Eric Clapton, who by now was one of John Mayall's Bluesbreakers. I kept my mouth shut that night. The Graham Bond Organisation did a great set, as did Chris Farlowe, who many think of as the best British blues singer of the period. There was another memorable night when Brian Auger and Julie Driscoll came along with the band Steampacket, featuring guitarist Peter Green, later to form Fleetwood Mac, and a promising young singer named Rod Stewart. Rod was great and the audience loved him, as they did whenever I saw him prior to his making a name in the pop world with the Faces. I know Rod's had decades of success since then, he's enjoyed fabulous wealth and had his pick of just about any woman he wanted, but if you were to ask him I'm sure he'd tell you that he'd have been a lot happier if he'd stuck to singing in blues clubs around the Thames Valley.

The Ricky Tick was a great venue, even though it would never have been allowed to open these days because of the primitive electrics and lack of proper exits. They extended their chain into holding Ricky Tick club nights at several venues around the Thames Valley area, but John, Peter and Les never got the recognition they deserved for giving the blues such a helping hand in the early days. Les was a printer and he helped me do my posters when I started promoting, while John went on to restore Windsor railway station to its former splendour. Sadly, Peter died in 1993.

Apart from the blues acts, the Ricky Tick also hosted nights by chart bands such as the Kinks and Small Faces. I wasn't too interested in them, in fact I looked down on that sort of music as I thought it was watered-down and commercialised. It says a lot for the ability of the promoters that I felt spoilt enough to be unconcerned about chart acts playing on my doorstep. I doubt very much if today's big names have ever heard of Windsor, let alone played there.

I was doing a bit of singing at the club, getting up with a few of the bands when they asked me. By now I was getting a bit of a gang following me around, and most of them were musical. Spike Jones was a good blues guitarist, his brother Gary was my best mate, there were Steve Darrington and Big Mac, a pianist and guitar respectively. We used to meet up at the Antelope, a pub in the middle of High Wycombe, but because it didn't have a music licence and the police were very strict in the town centre, we'd go out to one of the country pubs in the Chilterns and take the place over. It was all good, harmless fun and the landlords would love it. They'd have 50 or 60 young kids suddenly turn up, playing the pub piano and a harmonica or two, and have a couple of hours singing along to blues standards, swelling the pub's takings before going home peacefully. One song summed up what we were doing – Big Joe Turner's Switchin' In The Kitchen (Ready For The Party Tonight) and that's what I was doing. This was all a rehearsal for what I'd go on to spend much of my life doing. As a postscript, some twenty years later I went back into one of those pubs we used to use. The same landlord was there and as soon as I walked through the door he said "Switching in the kitchen." It's nice to be remembered.

Chapter 4

Blowing In The Wind

It was about time I started promoting for myself, and eventually took the plunge in the summer of 1967, a time of peace, love and Swinging London. Farnham Common Village Hall might lack the street cred of the Rainbow or the Fillmore West, but as far I was concerned, for one night only it was the music capital of the world. Pink Sam and the Shakers, featuring my mate Steve Darrington, were booked, along with the Action from North London, a mod band who played decent blues and had a bit of a following. I'd saved enough money to be able to afford some local advertising and in the end enough people paid their five bob admission money for me to break even. The pub over the road were happy because they'd been packed before the gig and again during the interval, the audience had a good night and I'd even got up and sung towards the end.

I also learnt a lesson that night about bouncers. Because I didn't know what to expect, I'd hired a big Scottish bloke who lived, worked and drank locally, to work on the door. It was obvious from early on there'd be no problems and this guy kept looking like he'd rather be anywhere else than standing around doing nothing, so I had a word and we came to an agreement. I gave him half his pay, he went off to spend what was left of his Saturday night drinking, and everybody was happy. From then on I resolved to have as little to do with security staff as I could, unless I knew them personally. It's all changed these days, they have to be licensed and the bad element is kept out, but back then bouncers were more trouble than they were worth. A lot of the time they were thugs who wanted a Saturday night punch-up, and if one didn't start in the venue they'd go and look for it.

So there I was, looking for a way to carry on promoting, when a further opportunity presented itself. Joe Farquarson was a lovely Jamaican guy who put on some of the black music gigs in Wycombe. He knew a trio of West Indian girls who needed a backing group, and I was friendly with Wind of Change, a local soul band. It didn't take much to get the two pieces together, we rehearsed them in Slough and I put the gig on at High Wycombe Town Hall. People still talk about that night now; it was another one of the best gigs I've ever seen and again I got up and did a couple of numbers with the band while they were playing the support slot. I still think I could have really cleaned up with this act. Motown was beginning to take off and a British answer to the Supremes could have done well. Unfortunately, Wind of Change split up just afterwards and the girls vanished from the scene. Ah well, one door closes...

I'd taken the night off work to do the gig, and there had been a few people from Mars there. One of them must have reported it to my superiors, because on the Monday I was called into my boss's office and given a warning about my conduct, together with an ultimatum: "Stop this music malarkey, or else." As I was doing well at Mars, I don't think they expected me to take the "else" option, but I was getting ready to leave anyway, so I walked out and at the end of that month, January 1968, I became a full-time music promoter.

I needed a regular venue, and knew the Wycombe area, so after doing a quick tour round, decided that the upstairs room of the White Hart, a pub in the town centre, would fit the bill for what I christened the Blues Loft. Of course, there was a lot more at stake now than at my first couple of promotions. For a start, it was my only income. For another thing, well, having no other source of income was quite enough to have me panicking every day from the time I picked up my final wage packet from Mars until the night of the first gig.

I'd gained some experience from the acts I'd been involved with before, and I knew a bit about who would pull a decent crowd without asking an extortionate fee. In the end I went for Champion Jack Dupree and Shakey Vick's Big City Blues Band, from London. They charged £25 and £15 respectively, so with tickets priced at six shillings I'd need to fill the room to make anything. The big day was 31st January 1968 and I spent the days leading up to it fly-posting, begging people I knew to attend, pulling in favours, anything to get a crowd.

To my relief, the place was packed out. My local reputation as someone who knew a bit about the blues helped word to spread. We squeezed 150(ish) in, and turned as many away. After paying the band, and with a few quid taken into account for posters and other expenses, I'd covered my costs and a bit on top. Knowing this, I could settle down and watch Champion Jack. He got the name Champion because he was a highly-rated boxer back home, but was a lovely man – a pianist and singer from New Orleans who'd been a big influence on Fats Domino and had moved to Europe in 1958, later recording with Eric Clapton and several other notables of the British blues scene. Luckily he went down a storm, loved the place and afterwards came over to me and said, "You got a goldmine here, son." With so many people wanting to come to the club, and almost all of them asking who was on next week, I knew I'd done the right thing. I was a music promoter now, and that's what I remained for many years to come.

The following week we had Dr Kay's Blues Band from Wood Green, plus the 32-20s from Brighton. Another full house, although there weren't as many people turned away. Shakey Vick came back to headline after that, with a different band to the one that had opened the club, and he was supported by the Nighthawks. Both bands were good value bluesmen who put on a good show, and I used them at different venues for many years.

Of course, something had to go wrong, and it came in the form of something you can't really argue with – the ball of a demolition crane. I knew when I started that the White Hart was going to be demolished, but I thought we might have a bit of time to work out a replacement. Things would have been different now, there would have been all sorts of appeals and judgements and protests, but back then it was a case of "We're knocking it down next week. Get your things out."

I did a couple of gigs at the Exchange, which wasn't far away, but it didn't have the right atmosphere so I carried on looking round and came across the Nag's Head, just a little way outside High Wycombe town centre. I went to have a look at the upstairs room, and it was perfect. The bar was at one end of the long, narrow room, which had windows along one side and when we started there were two open fireplaces that came in handy during the winter, when the place could be freezing cold until the customers started to arrive. There were proper dressing rooms, at first to the side of the stage and later, when we had to install a fire escape in the area they took up, we used a small room behind the stage, with direct access onstage. With a capacity of 200 the room was bigger than the ones I'd used before, but I never had any doubts that I could fill the place. And for almost 25 years, I did.

I introduced myself to the landlord, Ron Saunders, and explained the situation by saying "I got a club with no home." It could have been the opening line of a country & western song, but Ron agreed to let me use his pub, and I began promoting at the Nag's Head in March 1968. The opening acts were, once again, Champion Jack Dupree and Shakey Vick, who had yet another new band with him, and it was as much a success as the first time. So many people turned up that the bar staff got caught on the hop, working flat out from opening time until last orders. I realised all the other stuff I'd been involved with had been a dress rehearsal. The Nag's was where I became a real promoter.

It didn't take long for the new Blues Loft to get a reputation. Jazz Journal and Blues Unlimited, the two biggest specialist magazines of the time, both did glowing write-ups and we started to attract audiences from some distance away. Savoy Brown played our second week, and that was another sell-out. Chicken Shack came along soon after, although they gave me a few problems. Their singer, Christine Perfect, was lovely, but guitarist Stan Webb was a pain. I don't know what he's like now, but at that time he'd get to the venue, find the nearest bar with a dartboard and if he was enjoying himself he'd forget all about the gig. We had to hide the Nags' dartboard every time they played there otherwise the band would be short of a guitarist. Travelling round the country drinking lager, throwing darts and playing the blues. Not a bad life, is it? And Stan's still touring with Chicken Shack to this day. Maybe he's given up drinking, or possibly playing darts.

Over the next couple of years, the acts who played the Nag's Head reads like a Who's Who of blues. Freddie King, my great idol Jimmy Witherspoon, but above all, men who still remain two of the biggest names the scene has ever known. John Lee Hooker was the biggest gamble I'd put on. He cost me £125, and I booked him through the now-defunct London & City Artists agency. I'd hardly been able to sleep in the nights leading up to the gig, not only because of the financial outlay, but also because I was going to be meeting one of the all-time blues legends.

I arrived on the evening of the gig to the sight of this world-famous musician asleep in his car outside, and nothing could wake him up. The John Dummer Blues Band, who were backing him, did their warm-up set, and luckily the great man woke, went straight on stage, blew the place apart, then left without saying hardly a word to anyone all night.

John Lee was a strange man. White fans over here loved his music, but the black audiences in the States never took to him. That was weird because Europeans normally preferred more accessible blues, the stuff Eric Clapton and then Gary Moore did successfully, but John Lee Hooker was the most African-influenced amongst the big names of the period. He used unusual rhythms and drawn out guitar phrasing, and I'm sure that musicians in Mali would have recognised his style, even if they'd never heard of him. Like most of his contemporaries, John Lee's style came from folk memory, handed down the generations. He was from Clarksdale, Mississippi, so maybe he was influenced by Raymond Paine, a guitarist from nearby Rossville, Tennessee, who Fred McDowell described as his mentor.

John Lee Hooker always put on a good show, and he was responsible for some of the best blues ever recorded, but I still believe the main reason that he became a big name in Europe was that he was one of the few American acts who would tour over here. Lightning Hopkins, for example, wouldn't get on a plane no matter how hard I, and all the other blues promoters on this side of the Atlantic, tried to persuade him. He'd agree to tour, someone would even send the flight tickets over, but the plane would always take off without him. Champion Jack Dupree, on the other hand, came to Europe, but the thought of flying home scared him so much that he stayed in England, marrying an English girl, before moving to Sweden and then Germany. "I'm not going back until they build a bridge," was his final word on the matter. Jack did eventually return home, playing and recording in New Orleans during 1990-1, although he soon returned to Europe and died in Germany, in 1992.

But John Lee was happy to tour all over the world, and that's how he made his reputation during the years of the blues boom. The other thing that cemented his legendary status amongst blues audiences was that he outlived most of his contemporaries, and he was still around when the big rock stars started paying homage to their influences, recording with such names as Keith Richards, Carlos Santana and Van Morrison.

Howlin' Wolf was a completely different character, and never was a musician more aptly named. A primeval animal is the best way to describe him. When I got there the bar was empty except for Wolf, but this enormous six foot three inch frame almost filled the place on its own. I introduced myself as the promoter, bought him a drink and was knocked out by the courteous nature of the man, which was in complete contrast to his reputation. John Dummer was once more leading the backing group, a guy who in Wolf's immortal words was "A little bitty guy about the size of my dick." Wolf was, indeed, rumoured to be well-endowed. Dummer, meanwhile, went on to have quite a bit of chart success at the end of the seventies, playing drums with the rock'n'roll revival band Darts.

Wolf went on stage in shirtsleeves, and showed not only was he an awesome singer, he was also a consummate performer. He used a massive old-fashioned microphone, swinging it between his legs like it was John Dummer or something similar, and he'd lie on the floor screaming. And all the time these wonderful blues songs kept coming; Smokestack Lightnin', Spoonful, Back Door Man and more. The audience lapped it up, and as he left the stage, Wolf turned to me and said, "Man, that was the hottest place I ever played." I don't know if he meant temperature-wise or the reception he'd received. Both would have caused a thermometer to blow. Another great night, which for me was made even better by the fact that the critics who'd been reviewing the gig paid as much attention to the venue as they did to the performance. There were few places that concentrated 100% on the blues, and I was the only promoter outside London doing it on such a scale. I lost about £8 on the gig, but I'd brought Howlin' Wolf to High Wycombe and it had helped my name get known as a promoter of top-line acts.

With John Lee Hooker costing as much as he did, and Howling Wolf not much cheaper at £120, I had plenty of work to do if I wanted to show a profit, even with the Nag's famous elastic walls, as ticket prices were usually fixed at 7/6 (37 1/2p). Luckily, I had a few people who helped me. Paul Wright did the door, advising potential miscreants of the error of their ways. Paul had been to university to read Oriental Studies, and later lived in Chepstow Rd, Notting Hill, six doors away from me, with Al Jones, a folk singer from Bristol. He'd been in the Cadet Corps at school and later became a police marksman, photographed on the front page of the Sun during the Balcombe Street siege of 1975, when IRA gunmen were captured in London. Les Watts did my posters and Nick Pring, a big bearded guy, drove a van round with his mate Ivan, that we covered with Blues Loft advertising. I arranged to have posters plastered over the hot dog van that worked the town centre at night when the pubs closed and one day, in an act that I still haven't decided showed initiative or stupidity, I climbed up a tree in Marlow Park to nail a board up there. From then on I'd go up every week to put the new posters up, and to my surprise nobody ever stopped me or took the board down. Maybe the park keeper was a fan of the blues, or maybe they couldn't get anyone as daft as I was to get my advert down.

We'd go fly-posting around Wycombe, Marlow, Slough, anywhere that there were potential customers who might want to know what attractions were coming up at the Blues Loft. Then, as now, Bill Stickers was liable for prosecution, and the routine was the same whenever I got caught. Arrest, charge, plead guilty by letter, £2 fine with a pound costs. I could never work out why I had to pay the costs of them prosecuting me. After all, I hadn't asked them to. But the odd fine was a minor inconvenience and for the privilege of being able to cover an entire county with posters every week, or so it seemed, it was cheap at the price.

I put into practice at the Nag's something that I'd learned from the Ricky Tick, when I insisted that the acts I promoted signed exclusion clauses forbidding them from playing within eight miles of the venue for a certain time before and after they appeared for me. After all, I didn't want to take the risk of booking an act, only for them to play a couple of miles away the week before and halve my audience. And if I'd gambled on an unknown who turned out to be a crowd-pleaser, I didn't see why anyone else should be able to book them once they were a guaranteed big draw. Naturally, this aroused the hostility of other promoters in the area, who thought I was trying to keep all the money that could be made from the blues for myself. They didn't understand that the potential audience was only so big, and if it was spread too thinly, nobody would be able to pull a crowd. I didn't mind bands promoting their own gigs, but I wasn't going to have anyone coming along and copying me, putting us both out of business.

Then there were some who were just jealous that I was earning money out of something they'd have liked to do. One night I was at a party in Amersham, a town near High Wycombe, when, within ten minutes of arriving, some bloke came up to me and said, "You're Ron Watts from the Nag's Head. We don't like you here." My reply was "And?" My place was packed every week, so I wasn't much bothered about what some drunk from the next town thought of me.

Of course, because I was doing so well, other people wanted to share my success. I lost count of the number who asked me to help them co-promote festivals. In the end I used to just say, "Fine, we'll do it," knowing that would be the last I heard of them. To this day they're probably still talking about the big festival they're putting on with Ron Watts 'next summer'. You get them in every walk of life; they never have the initiative to find their own niche, they wait until someone else is doing well then try to get a piece of the existing action without realising that the way to make money is to be in and out before everyone else knows what's going on.

Luckily, I developed a useful bullshit filter early in my promoting career. Most people go through a stage of wanting to be a rock star, and I suppose that when some of them grow out of it, they develop into wanting to be a promoter.

Chapter 5

Hey Joe

As the sixties drifted to a close I could see that the blues boom was beginning to fade. It had been around for most of the decade and like all good things, it had to end sometime. I was enjoying being a promoter, so I had to start looking around for ways of keeping the Nag's going, while at the same time trying to stay true to my ethos that I wanted performers who had a bit of originality and weren't just churning out whatever was the latest trend, or watered-down copies of something that had been exciting five years earlier.

One of the first acts I booked who weren't strictly blues was Jethro Tull, in May 1968, and I learnt something with this particular promotion that stood me in good stead later on. The normal price of admission was six shillings, but rather than reduce the price for an unknown band as Tull were then, I charged 6/6 (32 1/2p). I gambled that people would think that the higher price meant Tull were well-known, and potential customers would be too embarrassed to admit to their friends that they'd never heard of the night's star attraction. The gamble worked, the place was full and Tull did a great set, with their charismatic singer Ian Anderson showing that he'd make it as one of the most enduring stars of his era. Then again, a six-foot tall guy with a beard playing a flute while standing on one leg is always going to make an impression, wherever he is.

Six months later Tull's first album, This Was, had made the top ten album charts and the band had been the hit of that summer's festival circuit. People were coming up to me in awe, saying, "You booked them, and they became stars." It was nothing to do with me, I'd hardly heard of Jethro Tull when they played the Nag's, but they helped me to get a reputation for being able to spot up and coming acts. That meant people were happy to see bands they didn't know, because they thought that a few weeks later they'd be watching Top of the Pops and telling everyone that they'd seen all those performers playing at the Nag's.

Blodwyn Pig were one of the best bands around at the time, although they never got the success they deserved. Their leader, Mick Abrahams, who ironically had left Jethro Tull shortly after their first album came out, is still one of the best guitarists in the country, although my opinion of him lessened one night when he took an air pistol on stage and started shooting the lights out all around the room.

Status Quo were another band who performed at the Nag's at the end of the sixties. They'd started off as a pop group at the time flower power was the big thing and had a couple of hits, then changed their image to become a blues rock band. They'd lost one audience and were trying to find another, which is why they were playing smaller venues again, although there were still some of the crowd who'd come along to hear the old stuff. One punter, Gus Cannon, who was more a drinker in the pub than an upstairs regular, kept shouting out for them to play Pictures of Matchstick Men, which had been Quo's biggest hit until then. Rick Parfitt, their guitarist, must have been influenced by John Mayall because he replied down the microphone, "If you want it, you can sing it." I think he was a bit surprised when Gus came up onstage, but to the band's credit they played along as Gus sang the words, after a fashion, although I doubt if Rick ever challenged the audience like that again. Another claim to fame – the last time Status Quo played any of their pop hits was at the Nag's Head. They were another band who packed the venue out, but we didn't get the chance to bring them back because they went on to massive success and are still touring the world almost forty years later. Quo might have become a bit of a joke amongst cool and trendy youngsters, but I doubt if what's on the front pages of the NME now will still be going in four years time, never mind four decades, so good luck to them.

We carried on booking whatever blues acts would pull in a crowd, as the demand was still there for the right names. Alexis

Hey Joe

Korner, for example, hadn't played in Britain for ages, as he'd been touring Europe where the crowds were still into blues. When I announced that he was appearing at the Nag's, I got the same response as when John Lee Hooker and Howling Wolf had been billed. People were coming up to me in the street and saying, "Is it true? Have you really got Alexis Korner playing?" Because he'd been off the local scene for some time they thought he'd vanished, even though he only lived thirty miles away in London.

Whenever I was offered an act, I usually used the proviso "Would I pay to see them?" in deciding whether or not to put them on. It didn't always work this way and there were a few times when so many people told me that a band was good, I'd put them on even if I had my doubts. Roger Chapman was one such singer. The first time I saw him I thought he had something stuck in his throat, his was such an unusual voice. I was never too keen on Roger's music, but he was a decent bloke and people enjoyed his act, so I was happy to promote him. He's another performer who has had chart success, mainly with his seventies band, Family, and still tours to a loyal following.

Still the crowds came. I was once described as never moving out of a ten-foot radius of a crate of pale ale all night, except for when it was time to introduce the band, which I have to say was fair comment. Then when the show was over and it was Time Gentleman Please we'd all troop down the road into the town centre to carry on our night out at the hot dog van that formed High Wycombe's sole after-hours entertainment spot. My customers could see that I was enjoying myself as much as they were, and that helped the atmosphere of the club.

The whole town seemed to get caught up in what was going on at the Nag's, and there were plenty of spin-offs for other business people. That hot dog seller in the town centre would have a queue a hundred yards long at midnight, the record shops did good business selling blues stuff, other pubs would do better trade than they might expect as my customers met elsewhere before moving onto the Nag's. Taxi drivers, bus companies and petrol stations did well out of the people who travelled from miles around to spend a night at the Nag's Head.

Ron the landlord was especially proud of his pub. Draymen would say to him, "You've only got a small place here, but we deliver more to you than to anywhere else. How do you do it?" His reply was always the same; "Because I've got the finest blues club in the south of England." And not only did the audience use it when there was a band playing, for a lot of them it became their regular haunt seven days a week. They liked the pub and they knew the clientele, so they were happy to drink there.

The biggest surprise of all my years at the Nag's was how it avoided being raided by the police. Ron and I tried to keep drugs out, but with so many people in the audience and bands attracting the drug scene we could never hope to keep entirely clean. I'd say that the biggest problem came when drugs had been taken elsewhere and the effects were seen at the Nag's, but as usual, the worst affected casualty came from drink. On the opening night one young lad got so drunk, or maybe he was affected by the music, that he ran out into the middle of the road, got hit by a car, and fell into the river with a broken arm.

Detectives would be in the pub, and they were easy enough to spot, but they'd always enjoy themselves and couldn't have seen anything worth reporting, because other establishments were raided but we never were. In fact, the only effect the police had on the Nag's was to stop our customers parking outside because it led to traffic congestion. That was another improvement the Nag's made to life in High Wycombe; we were the reason for the double yellow lines on London Road.

Apart from that there were one or two fights, but nothing that really sticks out. Gus Cannon, of Status Quo fame, was prone to get involved in a dust-up, although he was tolerated by all concerned because he spent plenty of money in the pub and would help out if we had a problem. But he was hardly ever called upon; my reputation (which I encouraged) discouraged troublemakers, even if I was too out of shape by then to do much about

Hey Joe

them. Gyms weren't much in evidence then and my idea of a good night was to have a few beers, go for a curry, then go home. If I made a few bob in the process then so much the better.

I might have had a (sometimes undeserved) reputation for being able to spot up and coming talent, but I was also able to make some mistakes. I've been told that David Bowie played at the Nag's, but for the life of me I can't remember a thing about him, so he couldn't have been all that memorable. Of course, he became one of the biggest-selling artists in the world, so the experience didn't do him much harm.

Tyrannosaurus Rex, I do remember. Marc Bolan was a strange little bloke, a nice lad, but very hippyfied and not my scene, all acoustic guitars and songs about wizards and unicorns. Four years later he was the biggest name in the country. As with Bowie, I could say that I'd been knocked out and knew right away that he was going to be a star, but in truth, he didn't impress me very much. It wasn't my type of music and I don't suppose he or Bowie were going to change their act to please one minor promoter in High Wycombe.

On another occasion I booked a band called Spice, who were okay but nothing special. However, one of the audience, a manager/producer named Gerry Bron, must have seen something in them because he signed them to his Hit Record Productions label on the strength of that one gig, changed their name to Uriah Heep, and they were set for stardom.

Thin Lizzy played for us when they were still a three-piece, in April 1969. They'd only been in Britain a month and played just half a dozen gigs outside Ireland. Unlike Bowie and Bolan, I could see Phil Lynott's potential from the off. He had charisma by the bucket load, and his death in 1985 is still one of the greatest wastes of talent I've known. I paid Lizzy £30 and charged 6/- (30p) admission, which turned out to be one of the best bargains, both for me and the audience, that I ever promoted.

I booked King Crimson, featuring Robert Fripp and Greg Lake. I wasn't too keen on their music but they were starting to break through and I knew that they'd pull a huge crowd. Then the day before they were due to play I received a message from their management saying that "The gig's off. One of the band's ill so they can't make it." They didn't exactly know who and they were even less sure what was wrong with him, but who was I to question them? Strangely enough, they played the Isle of Wight festival the day after so whoever was ill must have made a marvellous recovery.

Hawkwind were unknown when they played the Nag's in March 1970, but they still pulled in a good crowd and performed well enough, although they weren't outstanding. Again, not overly impressing Ron Watts was just the boost their career needed and they became a big name very quickly. Their exotic dancer Stacia wasn't in the line-up on the night they played for me, and I remember the first time I saw her performing. Martin Stone was doing some business with the band, so we both went backstage. Stacia was there, still naked; she wasn't the best-looking woman in the world, but her face wasn't the main attraction.

Principal Edwards' Magic Theatre worked on the same principle, or at least they did for me. They were a psychedelic showband with close-harmony singers and a couple of dancers. I'd get the coal fires burning before they arrived so when the girls began to limber up for the show they'd strip down to their leotards and I'd have a very pleasant view while I was waiting for the doors to open. It certainly distracted my attention from worrying about how many customers would turn up.

One thing that I was noticing about the Nag's was that, even though most live venues attracted an audience that was about 80% male, I was getting a 50/50 spilt between men and women. This was a bonus because it gave people another, obvious, reason to come to the gigs and I encouraged it by sometimes offering half-price admission to women. The Nag's was a great place to socialise, we were drawing people from the posh villages as well as the council estates, and I saw a lot of relationships blossom over the years. Two girls used to come from Stokenchurch, which was a fair hike, but they were always the first two through the door. One of them got married to Bruce Langeman, who

Hey Joe

played guitar for Shakey Vick and another local band, the Nighthawks. They made a nice couple and I hope they're still together and happy.

By now, I'd moved to London. In September 1968 I'd started renting a flat in Chepstow Rd, Notting Hill, with Ian A. Anderson, a folk blues guitarist whose name caused some confusion, especially when he was on the same label as Jethro Tull, whose singer, Ian Anderson, wasn't too happy about the situation. Ian was a lovely bloke, and not as uproarious as I was. In fact, he said that I led him astray, and on one album cover he wrote, "Who was to blame for the winter of 68/69?" Me, I suppose. There were people in High Wycombe who would find a way of blaming me if it rained.

Ian was also a great guitarist, although his singing was a bit stilted. Through him I was to meet several of the top folk blues performers in the country, and began to promote that area of the music at the Nag's Head on Wednesdays. We had the likes of Roy Bookbinder, who come over from New York. Dave Kelly, who went on to play with the Blues Band, did a night and we also put on Mike Cooper, from Reading. Mike played steel guitar, in fact he was the best white folk blues act I've ever seen, and his wife Annie was just as memorable, although that was more for her impressive frontage than for any musical ability she might have possessed. We ran the Wednesday nights for about six months; they were never as well-attended as the Friday shows, but things ticked over nicely until the summer of 1969. Attendances always take a downward turn when the weather's warm, and that's what killed us. There weren't enough people willing to turn up during the summer months for me to keep going until autumn, so we had to close the Wednesday gigs. A shame, but I couldn't afford to stand the losses.

I may have failed to keep the folk shows going, but I gained a consolation, of sorts, when I laid a claim to have been the man who invented idiot dancing. For those of you lucky enough never to have seen this particular form of entertainment, the name says it all. Move as many limbs as you're capable of, preferably all at once, and try not to fall over. I started off at the Bath Blues festival in 1969. The big names on the bill were the usual staples – Fleetwood Mac, John Mayall, Chicken Shack, bands that would have been interesting a few years earlier but were starting to sound tired. I was getting bored and decided to stand up and dance around, with my limbs waving. A bit later, I got up again and a few equally bored observers cheered. When I began my third performance, there was a massive cheer. Some of them got up and copied me, they looked stupid, and so the term 'idiot dancing' was coined.

It was round about that time that the Nag's just failed to have what would have been its greatest night. A band by the unlikely name of Heavy Jelly, with Jackie Lomax playing guitar, had signed to Island Records, and word was that they were going to be massive. I'd done the usual promotion on them, making out that the next Rolling Stones were going to be appearing at the Nag's Head for six bob, and there was already quite a decent crowd in the bar when I arrived. I went upstairs, had a few words with the band and then once they'd set up and sound-checked, we opened for business. Nobody came up for a long time, so when the music was due to start I sent one of my assistants downstairs to see what was going on. A minute or two later he came racing back up the stairs and he could hardly get his words out, he was so excited. "Ron...Ron..." he spluttered. "Hendrix is downstairs. He's sitting in the bar drinking."

I didn't know if he was just passing by or he'd come especially to hear this promising new band, but I thought that there was definitely an opportunity here. I went down, introduced myself, and invited him up for the evening. He was perfectly polite, but after I went back to the band room my mind was racing with the possibilities. Jimi Hendrix, here at my club. Hendrix maybe getting up and jamming. He sees what a great place we've got and fancies the idea of playing a small, low-key gig. Imagine that – Ron Watts presents Jimi Hendrix. The influential people from the London music scene come to watch him, they see what a great gig the Nag's is and they start hanging out here.

Hey Joe

I was shaken out of these daydreams by the sound of the support act beginning and as the music began, a steady stream of punters started to drift up the stairs and queue to get in. One of them told me that Jimi had left, which was why they were moving upstairs. He never did come back, the Nag's Head didn't become the Berkshire outpost of the Speakeasy, that famous West End hangout of off-duty rock stars, but at least I can say that I met Jimi Hendrix there. The gig wasn't bad either, although Heavy Jelly never did become as well-known as they once might have been. The same can be said for most Next Big Things.

Ian A. Anderson was also a promoter, in Bristol. We both agreed that there was a need to bring more American bluesmen over, and in particular the originals. Not just the ones who'd got lucky and had a bit of commercial success, we wanted the real originals who had influenced everything that came afterwards. Ian and I hit on the idea of forming a co-operative of some of the most knowledgeable blues brains in the country and invited Alexis Korner to get involved, as well as journalist Mike Leadbitter, Chris Trimming, who ran a record shop in South London, and Mike Raven, pirate disc-jockey turned respectable BBC presenter. Also involved was Mike Vernon, who ran the top blues record label of the time, Blue Horizon. He later sold out to CBS, and Blue Horizon records now go for anything up to £300. Mike was usually busy and sent his brother, Richard, along. We held meetings, first of all at the flat at Chepstow Rd, then at a pub in Soho, the Polar Bear. It was here that the idea for the National Blues Federation came into being.

At this time, the confusingly-titled National Blues Convention was held. Simon Napier, Mike Leadbitter and John Broven were running the Blues Unlimited magazine, and they put the show on at the Conway Hall in London. I helped out with a bit of the booking. I got them Taste, featuring Rory Gallagher, as well as Curtis Jones, a pianist from Texas who, like his friend Champion Jack Dupree, came to Europe and stayed here. I take no credit for the promotion though; it was a massive success and I can't claim anything for that. There wasn't just music, there were forums, seminars, lectures and every type of blues enthusiast was involved – writers, musicians, promoters and fans. Paul Kossoff of Free took part, playing at one of the guitar workshops even though he was only 18 years old. He cut a sad figure; so much talent but looking like a little boy lost. Even when Paul came to visit me in Wycombe, he wandered around helplessly. Free became one of the greatest blues rock bands of the period but Paul took to drugs and this was what caused his death, from a heart attack, in 1976. He was just 25. Many musicians suffered the same problems as Paul. Most survived but he, sadly, was one of the casualties. I felt really sorry for his father, the actor and writer David Kossoff, who I'm not sure was fully aware of his son's problems. It must be difficult to accept that your son possesses so much talent, yet has so many troubles.

Another tortured genus was Janis Joplin. In 1969, I was with Chris Trimming at the Albert Hall, watching Clifton Chenier play alongside Magic Slim. Chris and I were talking about establishing the National Blues Federation in the wake of the events at Conway Hall, and we got talking to Janis in the bar. She was with Christine Perfect, who was about to leave Chicken Shack following her marriage to Fleetwood Mac's John McVie. Janis was highly complimentary towards my knowledge of the American blues scene. "You sure do know about our music," was her comment, between slugs of Southern Comfort.

My final glimpse of these two great singers was of them walking back towards Knightsbridge. Janis was to die of a heroin overdose within months, while Christine later found even more fame, and a great deal of fortune, with Fleetwood Mac. I was pleased for her, as she'd always been a lovely girl and a great talent. I'd booked Chicken Shack a few times, one of them as Freddie King's backing band. She was playing some wonderful blues piano, and the great Freddie was so entranced by her performance that he kept looking over his shoulder in disbelief at this beautiful woman who was such a talented musician. Christine had a great voice as well, winning the Melody Maker

Hey Joe

Best Female Vocalist award in 1968 and 1969. She went one way, Janis the other. It's hard to think of death when you talk to someone who was so full of life, but Janis was not the first, nor the last, musician to die prematurely.

Back in the humdrum world of trying to earn a living, I was adamant in my belief that the quality American musicians were being neglected and we should be bringing them over here. They weren't getting any younger and if we didn't do something about it, blues aficionados in Europe would never get the chance to see these icons of musical heritage.

For example, B.B. King and Muddy Waters were big stars, but they were just evolving the blues tradition. Muddy in particular was greatly influenced by the Mississippi bluesman Son House, the man who first claimed that Robert Johnson had "sold his soul to the devil to play like that". One day, when Son was supporting Muddy at Carnegie Hall, the legendary venue in New York, the old man was walking across the stage with his awkward country gait and some of Muddy's band started making fun of him. Waters turned on them immediately. "Without Son House there'd be no Muddy Waters," he snapped. "And none of you would be playing Carnegie Hall. Don't you ever make fun of the man again." Muddy regularly came over to Britain, and started to get a great reception every time, but Son House was unknown on this side of the Atlantic. I figured that he deserved some of the recognition his protégés had achieved.

Mississippi Fred McDowell was another of the old, straight from the roots, blues performers I wanted to bring over. Here was probably the most unreconstituted artist left alive; pure Deep South from the streets. Johnny Shines was another – one of Robert Johnson's contemporaries, who had played with that greatest of all blues guitarists back in the thirties. These were the kind of guys we wanted to perform in Europe, because often they were being ignored in the States and we wanted to show them in what esteem they were held around the world.

We started the NBF in early 1969, originally from my flat in Chepstow Road, then later rented an office in Shaftsbury

Avenue, in the West End. You can imagine how I felt about that – running a business from one of the swankiest addresses in the entertainment world. The NBF was open to anyone, whether they were involved with the blues or were just a fan. It cost five shillings to join and members received regular newsletters, advance news about promotions and discount tickets for clubs.

Just round the corner from our office, on Charing Cross Road, were Doug Dobell's two record shops, one of them catering for jazz and the other blues. Ray Bouldon managed the blues shop, and such was the reputation of the place he would often find some of the best-known musicians in the business browsing through his stocks. Very often Doug would head them off in the direction of the Polar Bear, we'd invariably find out and work would be abandoned for the afternoon as we joined some of our great heroes. Or sometimes we'd spend an hour or so in the strip club over the road. We were getting to know the characters of Soho, and after a while we became accepted as part of the local scene and the girls who worked there became friends. This was a time when Soho was good fun, rather than the seedy area it later turned into. We never saw the gangs who were supposedly running the place, or much of the porn apart from our friends over the road, but we knew the music shops that were on every street together with the Jewish tailors, delicatessens and all the other places that made Soho so fascinating.

I got to see the blues festivals that used to come over – Magic Sam and Earl Hooker, Clifton Chenier, those packages that would tour in the late sixties. One guy who performed with them was Whistling Alex Moore, from Dallas. He was an old guy even then, born in 1899, and his barrelhouse piano style always went down well. I gave him my address and phone number, hoping that I could bring him back, and although I never got the opportunity, he would often write great, long letters telling me what he was up to. Sometimes I wouldn't hear from him for over a year, then I'd get this rambling epistle covering almost every day from the last time he'd written. He got a job demonstrating pianos in a department store in Dallas, but there was no happy ending for Alex. He died in 1989, at the age of 89, in his sleep on a bus. Legend has it that he didn't even leave enough money to be buried.

Things were going well for the NBF. We started bringing some of the American artistes over – Larry Johnson for example, an acoustic bluesman from Georgia, who although he was a great player caused us some problems with his attitude. Juke Boy Bonner was another, he played guitar and harmonica and gave us a great night. He was from rural Texas and had been brought up in poverty. His songs were more like poems set to music and he was a genuinely authentic voice of the blues.

While he was in England during 1969, Bonner recorded his album Things Ain't Right, which Blues Unlimited called "the best European blues album ever." Moving into recording had been the logical step for the NBF. I did some of the production, but credits were usually given as National Blues Federation. Son House, for example, recorded much of his Live in London album at the 100 Club, backed by Dave Kelly and Al Wilson, guitarist and harmonica player with Canned Heat.

Jimmy Witherspoon came back and played the Bull's Head in Barnes for me. The place was so full that you could hardly drive onto the car park for the crowd milling around outside once we started turning people away. That was another night when I worried about laying out so much money, but the crowd and the reaction they gave the Spoon made it worthwhile.

I was still promoting at the Nag's Head, and often I'd get up and do a song or two with the headline acts. On New Year's Eve 1969 we saw the old year out with an act called Big Ron's Porkestra, which was me and a few local musicians messing around. More and more people were telling me to take up singing seriously, and I remember a guy named Keith, whose father had been one of the many policemen to book me for fly-posting, saying, "It's not to late to make it as a singer. You give it a go." As I was only 27, I didn't appreciate him saying that it wasn't too late, as I still didn't think it was too late for me to do anything, but yet again I'd been given some encouragement.

The thing that really made my mind up was a festival held on Wycombe Rye, a big park over the road from the Nags Head. I'd sorted them a band I was using, and as the festival wound down I got up and sang a few songs, to a good reception, and that more or less made my mind up. I was going to form a band, and I had an idea of what sort of music we'd be playing.

Bobby Walker was a regular at the Nag's. He used to come in for the second half by slipping me two bob and a pint of bitter. People had told me that he was a drummer, and when I talked to him he seemed to have the right background. I saw him at a Fairport Convention gig at the London Palladium, and during the interval asked if he fancied joining my band, which I'd decided would be called Brewer's Droop. He agreed straightaway, which left me in a dilemma because I didn't have a band at that time, but it also meant that I had to get something sorted quickly.

We had a couple of false starts with some local musicians, nice lads but they didn't have what I was looking for. Eventually I got together with another local band, Mahogany, who had impressed me when I'd seen them and, more importantly, possessed a long wheelbase Transit (the van all bands aspired to owning) and had their own PA system. They'd been backing Marty Wilde, the old fifties rocker and father of Kim, but these gigs had dried up and the album they released on Epic had bombed, the record company had lost interest, so they agreed to join my fledging band. Malcolm Barrett, a bass player I knew from nearby Chesham, completed the line-up and Brewer's Droop was born.

Chapter 6

Got My Mojo Working

Once the band had got together I had little trouble finding us some dates. Lanchester Polytechnic in Coventry had asked me to bring veteran blues singer Arthur 'Big Boy' Crudup over, to headline a blues festival they were promoting, so I used that as the basis of a six-week British tour, with Brewer's Droop as support act and his backing band. I figured that it gave me a breathing space to get some extra gigs, as well as showing potential audiences what we could do. Before the tour we did a few warm-up shows to make sure everything was working well. For some reason two promoters, Andy Kilderry and Martin Cole, booked us to play a wedding reception in Ascot. It was at a run-down church hall, hardly the sort of place you associate with the royal horseracing town, but we went on and played.

I wanted Brewer's Droop to be a fusion of all the music I liked – blues, r&b, doo-wop and most of all cajun, the swinging type of jazz that came out of the bayous of Louisiana with an obvious French influence, courtesy of the settlers who had lived there from the eighteenth century onwards. Quite clearly, this wasn't going to go down too well at an English wedding, and so it proved. We weren't that bad, just knocking about, enjoying ourselves and generally treating the whole thing more like a rehearsal with beer and an audience than a proper gig, but things predictably ended in chaos. The bride was in tears, her father refused to pay us and the situation was looking ugly until guitarist John Mackay, ever the diplomat of the band, came to some arrangement and we left in one piece. We never did play another wedding, but the promoters had thought we were great and booked us for their 1832 club in Windsor.

Arthur arrived and I took him to his hotel, the Riviera in Maidenhead. The following day we went off to the Nag's Head for a rehearsal with the rest of the band. We all had a great time, but I didn't notice how much lager Arthur was drinking and, as it was all being bought for him, neither did he. Everyone was enjoying themselves and the band were doing their best to be hospitable to the guy who was paying their wages.

On the way back to the hotel, Arthur collapsed and we had to rush him to casualty. Everything was now in chaos. We were two days from starting our first British tour and the headline act had been admitted to hospital. I visited him the day after and he was comfortable, sitting up with the nurses fussing over him, but not saying much. The following day I got a call to tell me I had to get straight over there, so, fearing the worst, I went with our roadies, Steve Kane and Keith Welch. Arthur was sitting there, and when I arrived he said, "I ain't come all this way to lie in hospital. I'm outta here." With that he discharged himself and went on tour the next day as right as rain. He'd probably just been feeling the effects of the flight, and the marathon drinking session the band put him through had caused him to keel over. A couple of nights sleep, some attention from the nurses, and he was fine.

You may not have heard of Arthur, but everyone interested in rock'n'roll knows at least one of his songs. Born in Mississippi in 1905, he'd written That's Alright Mama, and My Baby Left Me, which were later recorded by Elvis Presley, not that Arthur received anything from them. In true blues style, he remained in poverty while others made fortunes from his work, and while these songs were helping change the world, Arthur was living in Virginia, scratching a living by picking up migrant workers in Florida and driving them along the east coast in an open truck, finding work for them wherever he could. He had no idea how influential his music had become, or how well respected he was around the world. He still thought that a couple of his songs had been covered by a white boy named Elvin Preston, and that they'd sold a few copies in Tennessee.

The first gig of the tour was the Lanchester Poly festival. There was a good crowd and we went down well, although there was a touch of attempted one-upmanship when Steve

Darrington, our pianist, was playing louder than the rest of us put together. He was even drowning our Arthur's guitar, which annoyed the audience. During the interval I told Steve about it, and he claimed he couldn't turn the volume down on the electric piano he was playing – which we all knew was rubbish. Steve ended the show on harmonica, and nothing like that ever happened again.

We had a lot of fun on the tour, and it certainly helped to get our act together. I'd always seen us as being a band whose visuals were as important as what we were playing. Music had become too serious by that time; gigs were often two hours of technically proficient boredom. We wanted people to enjoy themselves. I'd hold up boards with instructions for the audience written – on one said it would say "SILENCE" then when they were quiet I'd turn the board over, and on the other side would be written "BOLLOCKS". Things like that got them on our side and helped us gain a reputation from the off. Critics were coming to write about Arthur, but they found themselves devoting as much space to us as to the headline act.

We played up in Glasgow, at the Jazz Club, just off Sauchiehall Street, the main road in the city centre. It was a strange place – totally bare with no furniture and no licensed bar, just a stage and a small counter selling soft drinks. Hardly the most promising venue, but a Friday night crowd in Glasgow is unlike any other in the world. One guy was beating himself up, punching himself really hard and banging his head on the wall. He was a one-man assault team, but luckily for everyone else he was the only one to feel the force of his blows.

The promoter, a guy named Douggie, was so taken with us all that he invited us to his office, which was up about four flights of rickety stairs into a room full of filing cabinets. He opened one of them up and we found to our joy that they were filled with beer and whisky. Remembering what had happened before, we tried to discourage Arthur, but he got very pissed again, so all we could do was sit him back in to the van next to the window and hope there were no ill-effects.

We were travelling to the port of Stranraer to catch the ferry to Northern Ireland, and it was a beautifully moonlit night, although so windy that as we drove along, the sea was breaking over the coast road. Arthur woke up, looked at the sea, looked ahead, back at the sea, and said "Drop me off at Billy Brown's on 33rd Street." He was totally gone, and he thought he was back in Chicago, driving along the shore of Lake Michigan.

Belfast was a bit of an eye opener, to put it mildly. The gig itself was a stormer; we played the main hall at Queens University and filled it to capacity. As was the case every night, I fronted the band during the first half of the show, then when Arthur came onstage I left the stage as the others backed him and I became the manager again. Jim Daly, a great Irish blues pianist, sat in and he talked about the night for many years. Arthur ripped the place apart – the crowd was so wild he could have played thirty encores. With the problems in Northern Ireland starting to get serious I suppose any excuse for a good night was taken up.

After the gig the promoters had laid on a supply of beer and because of Arthur's previous form we were worried, but in the end he behaved perfectly. There were two promoters, one Catholic, one Protestant, and they took it in turns to show us around their own parts of the city. There we were, late at night driving down Jamaica Road, when one of them turned and said "That's where an English soldier was killed last week." Not what you want to hear late at night in a strange town when a bunch of you are in possession of English accents. We were also told the story of how one afternoon this old man had got out of his car carrying an old hunting rifle which he set up on a tripod, taken a few potshots down the fiercely-Catholic Ardoyne Road, then took his gear back to the car, packed up and drove off. Nobody knew who he was, and he was never heard of again.

We went down to play in Dublin, then caught the ferry back to England. Unfortunately it was delayed in docking and we were running late for our next gig, in Birmingham, so once we got to Liverpool I rang Jim Simpson, who was promoting that night's show. I explained that we'd been delayed but would get there eventually and could he hold the fort for a while. Jim moaned a bit, as all promoters do in these circumstances, but agreed. We thrashed the van down the M6 and eventually arrived at Henry's Blueshouse, a venue above the Crown pub at the back of New St station. We set up and got on stage in ten minutes and did another good show, although the venue was one of the stranger ones around at the time. The pub was used by gays and transvestites, and I'd been a bit surprised when what I thought had been a barmaid followed me into the gents and began using the urinals. But the music was fine and I was later given a tape of the show. Considering that it had been recorded on an early seventies hand-held tape recorder by someone in the audience, the sound quality was superb and I still play it now.

Jim was sweetness and light afterwards, and when we mentioned that we needed an agent to start organising our dates professionally, he volunteered his services. Jim's Big Bear agency had been in business a couple of years, and he'd been managing Black Sabbath, who had left in controversial circumstances that were to end with him successfully suing them some time later. We spent a day with Jim at his offices in Edgbaston, close to the Perrot's Folly tower that had been one of the inspirations for the Lord of the Rings, and then in the Ivy Bush, a nearby pub where I was to spend much time and money over the coming years. Jim outlined his plans, we told him what we wanted, and everybody had a great time. Whatever might have happened between us in later years, I've got nothing but praise for the way Jim treated the band back then. He got us dates and wouldn't take commission because he knew it was early days for the band and we weren't earning much.

Jim found us plenty of work once we came off the Big Boy Crudup tour. We did almost 300 gigs in 1970, and about 1,000 in the four years the band was on the road. Sometimes we'd do three shows in a day, and if we ever had a free Saturday it was by mistake – one afternoon we played at an open-air festival in Slough, then I ran off stage, straight into my car and went off for a week's pony trekking on Bodmin Moor with my girlfriend. That was the only holiday I had for about four years. We played all over the country, and, despite our initial misgivings that the music wouldn't travel well, played to hundreds of people at a time in places like Chester and Derby. We were particularly popular in Bristol; we broke the house record at the university and gave the Granary, Acker Bilk's club down by the docks, the busiest night they'd ever known.

At one gig, though, we had the definitive mixed reception. The Irish Club, Luton, on a Friday night. We were playing with the Equals, who had done well in the charts with Baby Come Back and Viva Bobby Joe. Droop went on first and the crowd liked us, but as soon as the Equals took to the stage, pandemonium broke out. It turned out that the regulars didn't like to see black guys on stage; the Foundations had had the same reaction a few weeks earlier. The band, to their credit, carried on, and seemed to regard the fights as a bit of entertainment laid on for their pleasure. No sooner had one ended than another started. The audience showed their dislike of the band by beating themselves up, something that I didn't understand and haven't spent too much time trying to work out since. At the end of the night the club owners paid up, good as gold, and offered us a return engagement. We said we'd find out when we were next available and let them know. I checked our date sheet and realised the Twelfth of Never was as good a time as any to make a triumphant return to Luton.

Almost as bad was the time I got us banned from Bolton. We played Rivington College, out on the moors just outside town, and the night before our gig the London boxer Chris Finnegan had beaten a highly-rated middleweight from Liverpool, Harry Scott. Being boxing fans the band had watched the fight and I started haranguing the audience about how Londoners would always beat anyone the north could throw up. They weren't best pleased and although we avoided having to show how five southerners would fare against five hundred Lancastrians, the band didn't hang around once the show was over. As we were leaving we were informed that we wouldn't be welcomed back, and Brewer's Droop never played Bolton again. It was no great loss and as far as I was concerned the rest of the band should have thanked me, although as they weren't very happy with my antics on stage that night I thought it best not to mention the good deed I'd done them on the way home.

We played Bracknell College, supporting Slade just as they were breaking into the big time. They were impressive and the crowd went bananas. It was one of the few gigs when I was glad we weren't headlining, because we'd have had no chance following them. Slade had worked the circuit, played all the downmarket dives, then graduated to the college and club circuit before getting hit records, and good luck to them. From early on you could tell they were going to be something special. Dave Hill, even before his dress sense took a turn for the bizarre, had great stage presence, and his image contrasted perfectly with Noddy Holder's down to earth showmanship. I'd see Noddy at the musicians' hangout the Speakeasy, situated at the back of Oxford Circus in the middle of London. He always looked badly out of place, sitting there in the small hours wearing an old ratting jacket and a flat cap, surrounded by models and showgirls. Noddy was a good bloke, and to this day there aren't many people who've got a bad word to say about him.

The food was better at the Speakeasy than at any other club in London, but it still wasn't our favourite gig. We'd never start until well into the small hours, and that's no time to be playing our sort of stuff. We played the kind of music that had to be heard properly, not the jazz and blues that's best suited for late nights. The Speakeasy had another problem, and that was the crowd it attracted. A lot of musicians and their camp followers were far too cool in those days to admit to liking any other band, particularly one as irreverent as us. They did provide us with a Melody Maker headline, though, when during one gig I got annoyed at the lack of attention we were getting and began to berate the audience. "I'd rather be in bed with my missus," was one of the less abusive insults.

But the Speakeasy was always good for star-spotting, if that was what you fancied. Alexis Korner was a regular, as was Keith Moon, who I'm told once paid the compliment of saluting me on his way out of the club on one occasion when I was asleep on a bench just inside the front door. He must have thought I was out of it on drink or drugs, but I was just knackered after a gig.

When I was fully awake I would notice that the club was very factionalised. There were all these famous names, but they'd be in small groups never talking to each other. One man was always guaranteed to cause a stir, though; Elton John. I'd always thought that his image was a bit false, but no. Late at night while he was having a quiet drink with friends he'd still be walking on foot-high platform heels and mincing around outrageously.

Which leads me onto another product of the glam era. I'd met Freddie Mercury at a party in London, and even back then he came across as sexually precocious, someone to be avoided unless you were extremely careful. A few years later I heard that he'd got a band together and they were causing a stir, but Queen didn't go down the usual route of starting out by playing pubs and working their way up to bigger venues and then a recording contract. Their first gigs were private affairs for their own social circle, and they signed to EMI almost immediately after they went public, did a tour supporting Mott the Hoople, and went straight into the charts, which meant they were out of my league for either promoting or supporting. I can just imagine what would have happened if Brewer's Droop had ever shared a bill with Queen.

By the middle of 1971 we were starting to attract record company attention. Jim Simpson told us that several companies were interested, including Vertigo, who had just signed Status Quo, and Charisma, which was Genesis's label. How we'd have got on playing with them and how their audiences would have reacted I shudder to think. Tony Stratton-Smith, the boss of Chrysalis, was a also big fan of ours and regularly attended our London gigs, invariably ending up with us in whichever curry house was still open when we had finally finished playing.

Got My Mojo Working

Eventually, Jim recommended that we sign to RCA, who had the best marketing network around the world. They agreed a £3,000 advance and we got another £2,000 from the publishers. That was a nice day's work, even after we paid Jim a few hundred to cover the back commission he had never taken from us.

We did some test recordings in a studio on Oxford St, and they sounded pretty good although they were never released. Jim's probably still got the demos and he'll release them when we're all dead. We then went into a studio on the Old Kent Road, near the Thomas A'Beckett pub where Henry Cooper and other boxers trained. It was a friendly enough area and we all felt at home there. Tom McGuinness, who had played with Manfred Mann and had just had the number one with McGuinness Flint, When I'm Dead & Gone, produced, and brought a few of his mates along to help us out. There was a female backing trio, whose names and phone numbers we never discovered, and the jazz saxophonist Dave Gelly led a horn section.

The main problem was that I wasn't too happy with my vocals. I was nervous and my singing sounded a bit strident. I don't think I really found my voice until much later, and looking back, if I'd been a better singer then the band might have been a bigger success. We could always cut it live, where the stage act obscured my shortcomings, but I'll admit that on record I was shown up.

The album Opening Time was finally released in the summer of 1972. We fancied a gatefold cover, so we gathered all our old mates from Wycombe outside the Antelope one Sunday morning for a picture of them waiting for the doors to open. One guy, Ray, was so pissed off at being made to wait for a pint that he started shouting at the staff, and the photo on the inside cover shows him being served through an open window. The front cover had a picture of the band outside the pub, with some old bloke standing next to me. His name was Harry, and he'd been walking past, seen all the people standing round and wandered up to me to ask what was going on, not knowing or caring that I was having my photo taken. When the shots came out, the best one was of all of us plus him standing to one side, and that's how Harry got on the cover of an album.

We released a single that wasn't on Opening Time, a Jay Stultz song called Sweet Thing that sold quite well. It got just outside the Top 50 in the UK, and reached number two in Holland and Denmark. We were very big in the North Sea, although there were a few headline bands who wished we were under it.

It was at this time that we briefly became known as The Droop. I figured some people thought we were a comedy band because of the name, so if we changed it we might attract more fans. Nobody took a blind bit of notice so after a few weeks we were Brewer's Droop again.

The album wasn't a big seller – I later said it had all the impact of a feather hitting concrete - but RCA stuck with us, which was more than Malcolm Barrett was able to. He was the victim of a really dirty trick. Malcolm's girlfriend moved into his house and gave him the classic rock'n'roll ultimatum, "It's the band or me." He chose her, left the band in the week the album came out, and just after that she dumped him. She later said that all the fun was in getting him out of the band, to show how much power she had over him. It was a really low trick, especially as Malcolm was never again in a band that was anywhere near as successful as we were becoming. He was a bit of a hippy, and he had a strange metabolism imbalance. As soon as he got into the van he'd fall asleep. Sometimes we'd take his glasses off and swap them for sunglasses, and he'd often wake up and not notice anything was wrong, except that the world was a lot darker.

Malcolm's replacement was a guy named Derek Timms. Derek was a well-known musician in the Wycombe area, very talented and a quick learner, but he always thought he was a bit grander than the rest of us. After he'd been with us a few months, he announced that he'd registered the name 'Brewer's Droop' to himself. Nowadays that might have serious implications for the rest of us, but back then we just laughed at him. Apart from playing bass Derek would play guitar, with John Mackay switching to bass. He did some recording with us, but eventually got tired with life on the road and quit the band, possibly in shame after he got his kit off in a sex club in Rotterdam during a Dutch tour, but failed to function. Derek's still playing now, and his greatest claim to fame is that he wrote the incidental music for the Open University.

Steve Norchi, an Anglo-Italian, was our final bassist. Steve was a happy-go-lucky character who fitted in well with the band. He played on our second album, but disappeared from view when the band split and I don't know what he's been up to since.

Throughout the band's career, Bobby Walker played drums. He was originally from Dublin, but moved to Richmond, Surrey, because he was infatuated with the Stones and the whole London blues scene. He played with all sorts of touring bands, and whenever we went over to Dublin, Bobby would always vanish for a while, never taking us to meet his family or friends. Bobby was gay, but kept the fact quiet for a long time because he wasn't sure back then of what the response would be. He eventually came out when he burst into tears on someone's shoulder, but we'd had an inkling when the van broke down on our way back from a gig in Blackpool. There was a village about a mile away, and we decided to run there. Bobby had a strange, mincing way of running, and that made me wonder. He was a great drummer, a vital component of the band, and he was so proud of his work with us. Bobby stayed with me right until the end, then went on to play with several local bands including the Blueshakers for years, but never really toured again. Sadly, Bobby died of cancer during the summer of 2005. I travelled down to Marlow to visit him in his final days, and it was tragic to see how such a man had been stricken.

John Mackay was a guitarist, singer, organiser and business head, which was just as well considering the state we used to get into. Whatever else happened, we could always rely on John to get the show on the road. John still plays now, but has never come near the same sort of success that Brewer's Droop achieved. He says he doesn't like thinking about those days, because they were so good. John was always even-tempered, which was an advantage when you had evil buggers like me and Steve Darrington wanting to argue with the world.

Steve played accordion, harmonica and organ, and was probably the most important musician we had. He was a very adaptable player, who taught himself the Cajun style amazingly quickly and could get a noise out of almost any instrument. Steve had contracted polio at the age of seven, leaving him badly crippled and with an uncertain temper, which led to him upsetting a lot of people. After he left the Droop, Steve played in a lot of country & western and blues bands, and now promotes, plays occasionally and campaigns for disabled rights.

By now we were playing just about everywhere, and going down a storm with all kinds of crowds. The Speakeasy in Crewe was a rockers bar where Judas Priest had played the week before, but we had a room full of denim and leather screaming for Brewer's Droop. At the other end of the scale was the Aquarius in Lincoln, which we played during a month when the rest of their attractions were acts such as Hot Chocolate and the northern soul legend Major Lance. Again, we blew the crowd away.

We did two contrasting gigs in one day, thanks to Jim's insistence on never wasting a minute or an opportunity. One night we were playing a college in Stoke-on-Trent, so Jim booked us to do a lunchtime gig at a school in Tipton, in the Black Country, which was on the way up there. The kids were into Slade or the Osmonds, we'd had to be up at the crack of dawn to get to the gig on time, and neither us nor them wanted to bother about Brewer's Droop playing in a school hall at lunchtime. We played for an hour, shot straight off afterwards, then went up to Stoke and performed a stormer, getting home almost 24 hours after waking up. It was twice the money though, which helped.

Sunderland and Durham were regular haunts, bit of a homage to my roots. Going up there was such a shock to us soft Southerners – driving past a bit of Hadrian's Wall one day made me realise how the Romans must have felt. One minute they're sunning themselves on the Mediterranean, then they see a poster for the army, think they could fancy a bit of Africa or the south of France, and before they know it they're stuck up near Scotland, freezing their togas off and finding the nearby sheep looking more alluring with every passing day. We got to know all the border roads, and in particular one afternoon we were driving along the A696, on our way from Stirling to a gig in Newcastle. It was a dark, cloudy, horrible day and we stopped at a café that was the only building for 20 miles for a very welcome hot meal.

We played a club in Liverpool that was owned by Allan Williams, who was the Beatles' first manager before, as legend has it, he passed them over to Brian Epstein because they owed him £15. We'd finished the show and were packing away when Allan came to us and asked, very nicely, if we could do another show at his other club, because the band due to play had let him down. With a two hundred mile drive home we weren't too keen, but he pleaded with us, arranged to pay us another £30 and helped us with our gear. Allan was a weightlifter, so had no trouble carrying twice as much as we did, and we got to his other club, down by the docks, played our set and started packing up for the second time that night. One of the audience came up to us and said, "You haven't by any chance been playing his other place tonight, have you?" I replied that we had, and the Scouser said "He's always doing that, booking a band for one then getting them to play the other as well." It had been a profitable night, but a tiring one as we arrived home at 7am the next morning. Of course, we'd been helped on our way by tales of how the Beatles had been big friends of everyone in both clubs. Everyone you met in Liverpool at that time had gone to school with a Beatle, given Jimmy Tarbuck his first joke and had a trial for Everton, scored a hat-trick, then got injured in the last minute and never played again. Even the women.

Life on the road can be addictive and I certainly got that way. There was always a sense of anticipation before a gig, especially at a new venue. What will the place be like? Will there be much of a crowd? How will we go down? Will there be much in the way of women and drink? Being in a band's a bit like being part of an invading army. You're a self-contained package and you have to get the logistics right, otherwise you're doomed to failure. Musicians, roadies, equipment, all reliant on each other. It's a real team effort, and no matter how well a gig has gone, travelling is always better on the way than on the return. Everything you were looking forward to has gone, you're physically and mentally drained and all that's left is the journey home.

Chapter 7

It Ain`t The Meat

Of course, life wasn't all touring, drinking and avoiding a proper job. I'd first met Maureen Tilbury when she was still at school. I was at home one Sunday and my dad said "I'm just off to see Alan, if you fancy coming with me." Alan was a friend of my dad's, an electrician who did some work at the butcher's and after we arrived at his house, just down the hill from us in Wycombe, he and dad were talking when I saw at the back door this beautiful young girl, who looked like an angel. She couldn't have been much older than eleven, but I thought to myself "I'll marry her when she grows up." And of course, I never thought any more about her.

Then in 1968 I'd been running the Nag's Head for six months when a gorgeous blonde reporter from the local Buckinghamshire Free Press turned up to interview me. Being a small town we'd bump into each other from time to time after that and always say hello, then as time went on she started drinking in the Antelope. I invited her to a party over at Beaconsfield, things went on from there and after a while we decided to get married. We arranged for our parents to meet, and when mine turned up at her house, dad was stunned when her mother and father were waiting outside. "That's Alan!" Of course, Maureen was the little girl I'd seen all those years ago and my schoolboy vow did come true. We were married in February 1973, at Priory Road Methodist chapel in High Wycombe. The minister had made us attend the Sunday morning services for six weeks beforehand, and this hulking fat singer with hair halfway down his back, trying desperately to stay awake because he'd been performing until the small hours, had looked strangely out of place amongst the prim Methodist congregation.

I'd had to teach everyone the strategy of being a successful touring band, because they hadn't done many gigs when they were with Mahogany. Once we'd got started they were always telling me how some mate of theirs wanted to put us on in a local venue. Of course they did; the mate knew we'd pull a crowd and he'd make a few bob without any worries and without doing much work. I had to remind them that we'd soon lose our audience if we played High Wycombe and the surrounding towns three times a week. If we played once a month or less, we'd be big news every time we played, and we could concentrate on getting a name everywhere else. I told them how we'd progress from pubs to the college and club circuit and play festivals, and it came true even though a couple of festivals disappeared over the horizon.

We were due to perform at the first Glastonbury, in 1970, but were pulled off the bill two weeks beforehand, with no explanation. The same happened with the 1972 Reading Festival. I still don't know why we didn't play, but the ironic thing is that because we were billed to perform, we're down in many archives as having been on both bills. There were probably some reviewers who wrote that they saw us. I hope they enjoyed the show.

There had never been anything like Brewer's Droop before, and even though we were becoming a big live draw, nobody tried to copy us. They wouldn't have been able to – we were originals, and anything else could only have been a pale imitation. I wanted to take the audiences to places they'd never discovered. Droop were described as "The only Cajun band outside Louisiana" although we were more than that. Cajun played a part in our make-up, but we were into putting on a show. We got very popular, very quickly, because we were striking a chord with a big chunk of the gig-going public who wanted a good time rather than endless guitar soloing. We sang about the things we liked – sex, drinking and music - we played pubs and with a name like ours how could we be mistaken for serious musicians? You might have turned up at one of our gigs and not liked what

It Ain't The Meat

we played, but nobody was ever bored when Brewer's Droop were performing.

Some people didn't appreciate what we were doing. We played a college in Manchester with Shaking Stevens & the Sunsets, when he was with a serious rockabilly outfit before becoming a pop star. They thought we were a progressive rock band who would make them look better, but were unhappy when we put on a better show than they could. We used to annoy a lot of bands because the serious musicians thought we were too flippant and the rock'n'rollers didn't like us showing them up.

There was one time when a band didn't have to worry about headlining over Brewer's Droop, and it had to be one of our biggest gigs. We supported the J. Geils Band at the Lyceum in London, a prestigious venue and a good chance to show what we could do. John Mackay turned up pissed after falling out with his girlfriend, uttering the immortal words "We've had the knives out. It's over." I didn't have time to walk him round the block to try to sober him up, so he went on stage and, like his playing, he was all over the place. We were awful, the crowd didn't like us and, perhaps luckily, we got no press coverage.

Brewer's Droop also incurred the wrath of the more puritanical elements of society. There were complaints after some of our gigs and we ended up being banned from, amongst others, Bolton, Hemel Hempstead (although they let us play there after we promised to behave), Ipswich and Penzance. I was reported to the CID in Birmingham after a show at Digbeth Civic Hall. They asked me what I'd said on stage, so when I repeated my act they roared with laughter before issuing a caution for obscenity, which sums up the hypocritical nature of our legal system. We also had the honour of being the only band mentioned in Lord Longford's report on pornography, which came out in 1972.

And what were they up in arms about? Well, the typical Droop gig would feature songs such as "I Can See Your Pubic Hair," complete with audience participation, and "It Ain't the Meat it's the Motion," which wasn't one of our own, but was written by fifties r&b band the Swallows. I'd parade around on stage with a four-foot foam phallus, as well as using a drumstick and the two differing ends of a funnel to describe girls I had known. It wasn't exactly sophisticated, but it was harmless enough, and anybody who might be offended didn't have to be there.

We weren't all that worried about being banned. There were plenty of places that did want us, and anyway, it was all good publicity. The early seventies was a golden era for music magazines. There were the specialist jazz and blues publications as well as the big nationals Sounds, New Musical Express, Record Mirror and Melody Maker. All of them featured us heavily, although sometimes not in flattering terms. "Childish sensationalism" and "unadulterated filth" were two of the descriptions of Brewer's Droop, and I couldn't really argue with either.

But however we behaved, we could still be upstaged by bigger names. During 1972 we played a gig at the university in Salford, arriving to be met by the sight of three girls running down a corridor being chased by Tony McPhee, of the Groundhogs, waving his dick at them. Years earlier I'd seen Eric Clapton, in his days with John Mayall, playing at the Royal Grammar School, High Wycombe. There was a hole in the backdrop, and during the set Clapton went round the back and exposed himself to around 800 people. Nowadays both he and Tony would have been arrested and probably jailed. Back then, nobody said a word.

Brewer's Droop were starting to earn big money. When we started out we'd been getting a tenner a gig, but within a year this had risen to £120 and more, at a time when a new band would be lucky to pick up a quarter of that and, as our reputation grew, so did the fees. Right from the start we were sensible about money and used to bank everything we earned, paying ourselves no more than enough to live on each week. Every Wednesday we'd troop off to Lloyd's bank in High Wycombe and take our wages out. We'd save up for bigger items such as new gear or repairs to the van, and three or four times a year we'd have a shareout of the money we had left over.

The saddest thing that happened to us during Brewer's Droop was when our roadie, Keith Welch, left to join the Marines. We

It Ain't The Meat

said goodbye to him, saw him off on the train to the Marines depot at Plymouth, and followed his career as he kept in touch by sending us photos of his training. Keith had married a lovely girl, then suddenly we heard that he'd collapsed and died of a mystery illness that no-one could ever diagnose. It shook us all; here was this supremely fit young man, in his mid-twenties, Royal Marine, black belt in judo, and he'd died. What did that say about a bunch of fat drinkers who spent all their waking hours in pubs?

Much as we missed Keith, we carried on having the time of our lives. Life was just too hectic, and I know that if I tried to live that lifestyle now I'd be unconscious within a week. Gigs were rolling in and every one was the opportunity to have a party and get paid for it.

We first toured Belgium and Germany in the summer of 1971. Then the following year was the Bilzean festival near the German/Belgian/Dutch border. There was an eclectic mix of acts, with Rod Stewart & the Faces and jazz greats such as Ornette Coleman, but we stole the show. The 1972 festival went down in history as the year of Brewer's Droop. There must have been 40,000 people watching us in this natural amphitheatre just outside a small town, which completely devoted itself to music while the festival was on. You'd be walking down the street and hear the Rolling Stones playing from speakers tied to the lamp-post. We'd got there via Zeebrugge, which was an experience in itself. Once off the ferry I'd gone into a small café and it seemed like walking into a timewarp. The place was full of old people wearing forties clothing and the jukebox was playing Vera Lynn, while to add to the surreal nature of the occasion, we could see the Atlantic Wall fortifications from the second world war through the window. I half-expected the Gestapo to come bursting through the door at any moment and arrest me as an escaped prisoner.

Chapter 8

Good Times, Bad Times

Scotland was always good for a tale. We were playing a few dates up there, and stayed overnight in a B&B at Cambuslang, on the outskirts of Glasgow. Breakfast was served by a real stunner, who quite sensibly didn't want anything to do with us, then we left at 9am to drive into Glasgow city centre. Even at that time of the morning there were drunks staggering around, banging on the van windows when we were stuck in traffic and asking for money. One guy was shouting at us particularly loudly, so I opened the window and bopped him on the nose. He fell over and as we drove off I could see him sitting in the middle of the road, wondering how he'd come to be there with the traffic going past. We spent that afternoon in a bar that even had bouncers fully occupied during the day. The inevitable fight broke out, which they dealt with by throwing the miscreants out, opening the doors with their faces. It passed the time for us.

We were always wary about gigs in Scotland, and especially Glasgow. How would a Cajun-influenced, south-west-tinged band cope five hundred miles from home, in a strange land with a different language and customs? We always did alright, and some of our best gigs were in places such as Edinburgh and Aberdeen. Glasgow, though, still held unimaginable horrors.

We'd got a gig booked for Stratchclyde University on Friday, and we were in Stirling on Sunday. True to his ethos Jim Simpson got us a date for the Saturday, a pub at Maryhill, a suburb of Glasgow. The old hippy Donovan was born there, but he must have left at an early age because as we drove to the venue we could see every Glaswegian cliché coming to life. Arriving at 5pm we looked round the venue, working out where to set up, the quickest way to the exit and the safest place to barricade ourselves in were retreat to prove impossible.

The friendly barman's opening words were "I hope you're insured. They won't like you, being English." John Mackay said to him, "Can you guarantee that our equipment will be safe here?" and got the reply, "No. And hurry up. They'll be getting back from the match soon and they won't want you making a noise while they're drinking."

That did it. We held a quick band meeting and decided that we weren't going to play. Nobody likes to pull a gig, and it remains the only one I've ever refused to do, but nothing was worth the threat to life, limb and equipment. We rang Jim to tell him what had happened and drove off. We later found out that the Saturday night sport in the flats surrounding this pub was to stand on your balcony and watch the fights when the pub chucked out.

Our other trips north of the border were usually a lot more fun. We drove through Montrose once, and wondered what we were looking at when we saw a strange-looking building in the middle of a field. I stopped the van, got out, and found it was the main stand of the local football ground. A few miles later we were driving through the village of St Cyrus and because it was a quiet road Steve, our roadie, had his foot down. Suddenly from nowhere a huge policeman stood in the middle of the road, waving at Steve to pull over. He walked over to the van, Steve wound down the window, and this big, bearded guy bellowed "What are you doing, Jimmy?"

I thought it only happened in cartoons, but he really did call Steve 'Jimmy', and to his credit, Steve decided that for once, discretion was the order of the day. He agreed that he'd been naughty, promised to pay more attention to speed limits, and such was the imposing strength of the policeman's personality that Steve drove at 30 miles an hour all the way to Aberdeen.

Mike Patton was in the band Timebox, and was a real singer's singer. He was very talented and I put him on regularly at the Nag's. We'd often come across Mike on the circuit, and one night when we were playing Aberdeen University, he and Duster Bennett turned up with their band to see if there was any chance of getting a gig. They were in Scotland as part of their 'Autumn Tour to Buy the Kids Winter Clothes' week, but a few dates had fallen through so they were hoping to play with us.

Unfortunately we couldn't sort anything out, so Mike did a cabaret in the students' common room after our show. It was similar to the stage act Puppetry of the Penis, but thirty years earlier. One guy worked the lights, another held cardboard over the microphone as Mike went through such routines as 'Last Sausage on a Plate' and 'Nudes in Flight.' You can use your imagination as to what he was doing and what he was doing it with. I can still recall the oak-panelled room and a load of very posh Scottish kids loving this blatant obscenity.

Both the performers that night had tragic ends. Mike contracted throat cancer and although he still performed for a while, he died at an early age. Duster, a devout Christian who had a large family, had worked with Peter Green and John Mayall, then dropped out of the music business for a while. He began playing again with Memphis Slim and was living in Tamworth when he was involved in a car accident on his way home from a gig and was killed. Such incidents were an occupational hazard of the business, as musicians are driving late at night, tired and often under the influence of some substance or another. Promoters were even more at risk, because we were usually the last ones to leave the building after a gig. I always tried to have either someone to drive me or I took a taxi. I might have lost a few women that way, but at least I always got home safely.

Brewer's Droop enjoyed playing festivals. This was back in the days when anyone could hire a field and put on an event that went on non-stop, for days. The Great Western Festival in Lincoln took place in May 1972 and attracted an amazing range of acts, from Slade and the Faces through to Genesis, Don McLean and even the Monty Python team did a set. For once the weather was okay for us and we went down well. The actor Stanley Baker organised the festival through his company, Great Western Productions, and as we were coming off stage he banged me on the head and said, "Here, you're quite a character, aren't you?" Stanley was great, and he was really keen to be involved, willingly getting his hands dirty shifting equipment and sorting out problems when he could have been swanning around backstage.

In the same year we played a festival at Kendal, in the Lake District. I took a tent up and camped with Maureen, then we played in the afternoon. During the set Steve motioned to me that when I stood on a certain plank on the stage, he jumped up. I told John Mackay about it, and we started jumping on this plank, which would send Steve six inches in the air. He was delighted to be part of the show and proud that all the times he went into the air he didn't miss a note. Maureen, for her part, didn't get much reflected glory. She got used to turning up to festivals in a van and hanging around backstage while we played and then got drunk.

Far less enjoyable was Buxton the following summer, which summed up everything that could be bad, dangerous and downright disgraceful about the festivals of the early seventies. Whoever had the bright idea to stage an open-air event on an exposed moor in a place that has the highest annual rainfall in England should have been forced to endure the conditions their paying customers went through. Chuck Berry topped the bill, and a host of other acts played, including the Sensational Alex Harvey Band, Nazareth and Wizzard. It rained, the field turned into a quagmire and the Hell's Angels who had been hired as security drank until their money ran out, then went though the crowd soliciting 'donations' for more beer. Chuck was pissed off with the situation, as we all were. The dressing rooms were an old RAF bomb shelter and the people running the event completely amateurish.

Mr Berry came on, did twenty minutes and then went into his famous duckwalk. He started at one end of the stage, carried on into the wings and, as rumour had it, duckwalked straight into a waiting car and away. We were due on stage next and the atmosphere was evil. Right from the first number the air was filled

Good Times, Bad Times

with flying bottles, cans, anything that could be thrown was coming at us, and I was the main target of anyone who wanted to vent their frustration at being ripped off and treated badly. I stopped in mid-song and launched into a rant with all the venom I could muster. "I know you're pissed off, but it isn't your fault, it isn't our fault. It's the promoter's fault." That got some of the crowd on my side, and then, with miraculous timing, a helicopter flew overhead. "Look, " I shouted, pointing up at the vanishing craft. "There he is. There's the bastard flying off now. And he's got all the money with him." That got a cheer, and we finished the set without any major incident, although it wasn't one of our best. Next time we were playing in the area, some very serious-looking men came into the dressing room, introduced themselves as detectives and thanked us for our performance, which, they said, had averted a riot. Steve Darrington claims that we got a mention in the Police Gazette, but that might just be wishful thinking.

Some of the festivals that were being put on at the time were potential deathtraps. An unscrupulous promoter would rent a field in the middle of nowhere, stick a couple of portable toilets in one corner and let some of his mates charge whatever they liked for hot dogs and cans of pop. Backstage facilities were almost as bad, PA equipment the bare minimum and medical facilities consisted of a St John's Ambulance tent staffed by a handful of overwhelmed volunteers. Bands who were billed to appear often didn't show up, sometimes because they'd never been approached, or else they'd take one look at the stage or the weather and claim it was too dangerous to play. The crowd – and at some of these events you'd be talking about hundreds of thousands - were exposed to the elements for three or four days and often had to walk miles from the nearest train station to the venue and back because the shuttle buses that had been promised never materialised. Most of the promoters were undoubtedly decent people who couldn't cope with the scale of what they were trying to put on, but others were cowboys making as much as they could for as little outlay as they could get away with.

In a similar vein was the dreariest gig we ever played, on the moors above Halifax, in Yorkshire. It was in August, and everywhere else in the country was bathed in glorious sunshine, but the Yorkshire moors were freezing cold and wet. We were playing for some jewellery business social, and had an inkling of what was in store when we got there and saw heaters inside the cow shed that was the venue for the evening. The band tried our best but it was a horrible gig to a horrible audience in horrible weather. Halifax also hosted our least favourite regular venue. Clarence's in the town was up about six flights of stairs. The only band member who didn't hate the place was Steve, because he didn't have to carry the gear.

It's reckoned that around 75% of all the men born in Wolverhampton and Walsall between 1945 and 1960 know either Robert Plant or Noddy Holder. I found out the truth of this story after a gig up in Chester at the end of July 1973. The band played at Quaintways, a beautiful 15th century building, and stayed the night, driving back on the Saturday morning when we stopped at Hilton Park services, on the edge of the Black Country. Being a main holiday weekend the place was packed and everyone was in a good mood, when suddenly people started shouting and running around. I wandered over to see what was going on, and as with such matters, it all ended as soon as it had begun so I thought no more about it.

We were at Rockfield Studios the next week and I was told the police wanted to interview me about a serious assault. I rang the station at Walsall, close to Hilton Park, and was informed that all the witnesses to the incident had identified me as being involved. I suppose it was because with my long hair and beard I'd stuck out a bit from the crowds of happy holidaymakers.

I travelled up to see the police and they were fine with me once the victim, who worked in a residential home, told them that I wasn't his attacker. I'd told the police that I was recording at the time and they were quite impressed with having a rock star in the back of their car. They were all big friends with Robert and Noddy.

Ultimately, the original line-up of Brewer's Droop were like a football club that were always at the top of the second division, but never managed to get promoted. In one way we were ready for it, but in others we wouldn't have made the step up. Our biggest problem was that we needed to get new material, but we were reluctant to introduce it into the set while the old stuff was going down so well. Writing and rehearsing would also have been a problem. When you're playing in Bradford one night and Bath the next, there isn't much time for rehearsals. It was the age-old dilemma of having to go one step back to go two steps forward, but we were happy where we were and didn't want to take the backward step. We played in enough different places to get away with it for a few years, but performing the same set every night was bound to catch up with us eventually.

With Brewer's Droop playing so many dates, my promotion work had become a struggle. Chris Trimming had carried on with the National Blues Federation (more about that later) but the offices were virtually uninhabited. Mail went unopened, the phones were hardly ever answered. Chris left to work for a property developer and I let John Curd, who managed Heavy Jelly and Quiver, and ran Head Records, promote at the Nag's for me. One of the attractions for him was Jay's, one of the first pizza restaurants in the country. It was run by an ex-US army cook, who had been stationed at the base nearby and seen a gap in the market. Things were doing okay at the Nag's until I had a phone call from Chris Trimming telling me that John was temporarily out of circulation for reasons that aren't clear even now, more than thirty years later.

To their credit, RCA persevered with Brewer's Droop, even though they must have known that we were primarily a live attraction who would never shift massive amounts of records. They released "Hearts of Stone", a Cajun-influenced song we'd written, as a single, and again we did reasonably well with it. They also paid for us to record a second album, at Rockfield Studios in South Wales. This was a beautiful place near Monmouth, surrounded by fields, rolling hills and with a river running alongside, which formed the border between England and Wales. Kids on either side kept throwing stones at each other, which I suppose was a continuation of the border disputes that had been going on for hundreds of years. It certainly kept them amused.

Dave Edmunds produced us and we had a different line-up to the original Brewer's Droop. Martin had been replaced by Derrick Timms, who was more experienced and fitted into the studio better. We also had a new guitarist on some of the tracks.

Mark Knopfler first came to my attention during the early days of the NBF. He was from the north-east and would write us letters, phone and send demo tapes. These were certainly good quality, and I wish I'd kept them. One day he turned up at the office, hoping for some gigs, but I told him there was no real market for an unknown guitarist who was doing the folk stuff that Bob Dylan was playing. "Start turning up at venues unannounced and sit in with a few of the well-known names. If you can cut it you'll get yourself a reputation, then we can start talking about getting you some gigs on your own." That was what I said to him, and I like to think that he took some notice. I could afford to be magnanimous. I mean, what future was there for a folk guitarist from Newcastle?

The next time I saw Mark was when we played at Leeds and he came along to meet the band as he was a student at the university there. Mark was a nice lad and a great guitarist, but I'd forgotten all about him until Derrick left the band midway through recording the second album and I advertised in the Melody Maker for a new bassist.

We'd arranged auditions for a day at the Nag's Head, and had about thirty applicants lined up. Mark was there, and when I pointed out it was a bass player we wanted he said, "No problem. Stick your guitarist on bass and I'll do lead." By now his playing was light years away from the tapes he'd sent the NBF so we hired Mark on the spot and brought in Steve Norchi to play bass. This was the line-up that completed the second album and played together for about six months, from late 1973 onwards.

Good Times, Bad Times

RCA also had an act on their books called Drupi, an Italian pop singer who they were trying to promote in Britain. Steve Darrington thought that they shouldn't be involved with someone who had a similar name to us, and Jim Simpson set up a meeting between us and the company to sort out the problem. I wasn't that bothered about it. We were hardly likely to be confused with some pretty boy Europop star, and when I found out he was a keen angler we spent more time talking about fishing in our respective countries than discussing musical problems. He was a nice guy, good-looking and probably got more than his fair share of women on tour. Drupi never did much over here although he did graze the top twenty in 1974 with a ballad called Vado Via, and the matter was quietly dropped, in much the same way that he was from RCA. He's probably still performing in Italy to this day, playing at those massive festivals they have that seem to feature every different type of music under the sun and draw enormous crowds to watch acts nobody's ever heard of outside Italy.

We carried on touring the country, and were going down particularly well in the north. Barrow-in-Furness and the area around there was a particular favourite. The gigs were good and the audiences always friendly. Maybe it was because they were so remote everyone up appreciated any band who would visit. On one occasion, we were driven up there by one of our mates from Wycombe, the quaintly-named Nimrod Ping. Nimrod was a nice young lad who desperately wanted to be involved with us. He owned a Daimler limousine and we kept explaining to him that we couldn't afford to pay his petrol, let alone wages. But on one occasion he drove us three hundred miles to a gig in Workington. We felt very pop starish, being chauffeured up the motorway in this limo while our gear followed on in the van with the regular roadies.

The gig went off well and because we'd had such a long drive, we all stayed the night in a hotel. Unfortunately, we'd followed a good time at the gig with an even better time after the gig, and in the morning none of the band could remember where the roadies and our van were staying. Nimrod drove me around Workington looking for them, and we stopped for directions outside a bank. Now, two big lads with southern accents, in a fast car, parked outside a bank. Did it really look that suspicious? Was there really any need for anyone to phone the police, or for two squad cars to come screeching to a halt in front and behind us? Luckily we were able to convince them that we were just looking for our gear and they went away muttering to themselves about long-haired, drug-taking flash Cockneys, probably with a bit thrown in about us going up there, taking their jobs and stealing their women.

We regularly played at Whitehaven Civic Hall, which was so close to the Irish Sea that it was almost a pier, then did a gig at Windermere Teachers' Training College. It was here that I realised what a massive talent Mark Knopfler possessed. He was doing a warm-up instrumental at the beginning of our set, and the audience reaction was uncomfortably good. Whose band was it anyway?

Mark was a nice bloke, but he had his own ideas and once we got back on the road after the album recording was completed, I could tell that he was trying to take the rest of the band away from me, promising them bigger gigs and better record deals. Of course, nothing was being said publicly but I heard whispers, I could see the signs so I started getting together another bunch of younger lads who would take over when the time came. I'd been in the business long enough to know that the only way to survive was to be prepared for any eventuality.

The inevitable happened, Knopfler left, and the rest of the band quit with him. I started up straightaway with Brewer's Droop mark II, and hit the ground running. Knopfler went back to London and the rest of his supposed new band heard nothing of him until a few years later, when he emerged with Dire Straits, featuring Pick Withers, who had played drums for us for a while. The ex-members of Brewer's Droop who thought they were on to a good thing were left high and dry, without a band and without work. I had a certain sense of satisfaction at the

Good Times, Bad Times

time about the way Knopfler treated them, but it's all water under the bridge now and those of us who survive are the best of friends.

With the musicians who'd been involved now gone, RCA naturally enough pulled out and the album didn't see the light of day until 1989, when someone finally realised that an early Mark Knopfler recording would be a decent seller. It came out under the title The Booze Brothers, with a cover that was a pastiche of Dire Straits' multi-platinum Brothers In Arms, and I understand that to date it's sold something like 250,000 copies. However much money it's earned, I've never seen any. That's one authentic element of the blues lifestyle I could have lived without.

The new line-up soldiered on and for six months we did as many gigs as before, but things weren't the same. There were some good overseas tours, and one memorable occasion when we played Oslo, which was a nice city but had very strict laws, then as we crossed over the border into Sweden we saw a big tent pitched in a field with a neon sign saying "SEX SHOW!" Naturally we had a look, purely out of curiosity, but it was nothing out of the ordinary for someone who was a regular visitor to Amsterdam and Hamburg and I left the rest of the band to it.

That brief interlude apart, they were naïve young lads who couldn't get into the philosophy of Brewer's Droop and couldn't handle life on the road. I'd got a Dutch tour lined up, but they wanted to bring all their families along and have mates roadieing for them. I knew that such a situation would have been a recipe for disaster so I got rid of everyone except the musicians, roped in Derrick Timms and our old roadie Steve Kane to work for us, did the dates and that was it. We finished the tour without any problems, but without any enjoyment on my part either, went home and I disbanded the group. Brewer's Droop were no more.

Chapter 9

3 O`Clock In The Morning

Even though I'm from the Wycombe area and promoted at the Nag's Head for many years, I will always be best remembered for my time at the 100 Club in London.

My association with the venue began in 1969, when Chris Trimming and I were running the National Blues Federation from our offices in Shaftsbury Avenue. The tours we were putting together had been going well, but we needed a London outlet to promote the acts ourselves. One day Chris came into the office and said, "Wattsy, I've been talking to Roger Horton at the 100 Club. He says he might have Tuesdays free for us." We arranged a meeting with Roger, who was the club's manager, and he explained the score. Tuesday was their quiet night and Roger was willing to let us have the place for a one-off trial to see how we went. We booked Brice Portius, who had been with the original line-up of Savoy Brown and was a good quality, if overlooked, singer, and he drew a decent crowd. Roger enjoyed himself, it was agreed that Chris and I would have Tuesdays from then on, and we'd got ourselves a prestigious West End venue.

Millions of tourists, shoppers and office workers must have walked past the 100 Club's inconspicuous entrance on Oxford Street without realising its significance in the history of British music. The club began promoting live jazz in 1942, when it was a restaurant called Mack's and was known as a safe haven during the German bombing raids due to its underground location. After a couple of name changes it became known as the 100 Club in the sixties, by which time blues and beat acts were regularly appearing alongside the biggest jazz names.

Once past the front door, access to the club was down three flights of stairs, with the box office halfway down. There were two bars, one at each end of the room, and the stage occupied the middle of the wall between them. There were no dressing rooms as such, bands using either the cloakroom or the manager's office, and with a capacity of 400 and no air conditioning, temperatures would regularly top 100 degrees in the summer. As a venue the Nag's was better in almost every way, but the 100 Club was, and still is, a wonderful place.

One characteristic they shared was good acoustics. Many venues, especially pubs where the upstairs room was often built for a reason far removed from rock music, have high ceilings that can cause a problem, but the only acts that complained about my two rooms couldn't have got a good sound anywhere.

The time spent at the Nag's had shown me the ropes as a promoter, and as a result of the lessons I'd already learnt I was able to put together decent bills. Far from being the 100 Club's quietest night of the week, Tuesday was now often the liveliest. We started putting some good quality British acts on. The Nighthawks were a solid band who played for me early on, as did Dr K's Blues Band, who had formed in the late sixties and were still going twenty years later. Sam Apple Pie, as you can imagine, weren't the most serious of blues artistes but their early-influenced r&b was good enough to go down well on the seventies festival circuit as well as at the 100 Club. Audiences appreciated the quality of the acts I was booking and I began to build a reputation that would last for many years.

The big problem with the NBF was that it was always underfunded. It was being run on a non-profit making basis, and as a result we weren't able to bring over some of the big names we'd have liked. In an attempt to get round this, Chris and I approached leading members of the British blues community and asked them to perform at a benefit gig for us. With the proceeds we hoped to bring over Otis Rush, who at that time was probably the top blues guitarist in Chicago. Plenty of top quality musicians agreed to play, including the legendary Peter Green, who was then still with Fleetwood Mac, Tony McPhee and Jo-Anne Kelly. On drums all night was Bobby Walker, who

3 O'Clock In The Morning

played for hours and regarded it as one of the highlights of his life. We raised a lot of money, and although plans to bring Otis to Britain fell through, we were able to safeguard the future of the NBF and attract many other top US acts.

Far and away the biggest name in the blues at this time was B.B. King. He toured the country to sell-out audiences and when I saw his Albert Hall show I was knocked out by the quality of the performance. Then one night at the 100 Club we had Lowell Fulson (or Fulsom – he changed his name regularly) performing with a band led by Steve Miller, a pianist from close to my neighbourhood, in Sawbridge. To US audiences Lowell was one of the main men. Sam Phillips, for example, had always credited him as a big influence on Elvis. I was in the club early that evening when in walked a smartly-dressed black guy who was instantly recognisable as B.B. Despite being one of the greatest and best-known musicians in the world he sought me out and politely introduced himself, "Hello, I'm B.B. King. It's nice to meet you and a pleasure to be here." For my part I almost fell over, recovered, regained the power of speech and took him over to meet Lowell.

I didn't know it at the time, but there's a protocol amongst bluesmen; when a big name drops in to see another musician he's expected to jam onstage. I was unaware of this tradition, but I did wonder if B.B would get up and play, although remembering the time Jimi Hendrix paid a fleeting visit to the Nag's I wasn't too hopeful. Lowell began his set, and as he did, the great man took me to one side, bought me a drink and we chatted for maybe half an hour. He asked about the club and I explained that it was the only authentic US blues venue in the country. I told him that we'd have any blues act that was good enough and he replied, "Tonight, you got me." With a guitar he borrowed from Fleetwood Mac's Bob Weston, B.B took to the stage and performed his song 3 O'Clock in the Morning, which Lowell had recorded. It seemed to go on forever, he and Lowell swapping solos, saxophonist Lol Coxhill joining in, the crowd giving them a tumultuous ovation in appreciation of this wonderful bonus they were enjoying. Lowell was good, but B.B was good on top of good. As the night ended I was so happy and proud to have played my part in such an occasion.

As the reputation of the 100 Club continued to grow, so did our ability to put on the biggest names. The great Texas-born guitarist Freddie King played for us, at a time when he was enjoying a renaissance thanks to British musicians such as Peter Green and Eric Clapton recording his tunes, and we did a return promotion of Howling Wolf, although the night was nowhere near as hot as that time he'd played the Nag's. Both men were present at a reception to which Chris and I were invited, at the home of rock'n'roll singer turned music promoter Roy Tempest. Roy had become notorious for a festival he'd staged at the Sophia Gardens, Cardiff, featuring acts with dubious names such as the Fabulous Drifters, the Magnificent Supremes and other such examples of what would now at best be called tribute bands, and was then described in blunter terms. The only genuine article was Ben E. King, formerly of the proper Drifters, and the event caused such a scandal that it made the Sunday tabloids. Roy wasn't overly bothered – he ended up making so much money that when he'd paid off the bands he was still carrying a satchel full of banknotes home.

Roy lived in a penthouse in Portland Place, opposite the BBC, his wife was young and beautiful and the champagne was flowing. Freddie, Wolf, Chris and I stood in the kitchen, three of us trying to avoid the fusillade of nuts fired by Wolf as he scooped up handfuls and they shot out of his mouth as he talked. The musicians chatted, Chris and I listened, enthralled, to the tales of life in the Chicago blues scene – the clubs, the characters, the late-night diners, the women. "You supposed to be a one-woman man so who was that girl I seen you with that night? You don't kiss your sister like that," was just one of the many gems.

Roy had obviously done well out of the promotions game, but he still wasn't the wisest man in the business. We offered him a Robert Johnson tour once and he called back a few days later to say that he'd booked Johnson into some venues, but most were a bit sceptical, and how could we persuade them that the tour was genuine? Their scepticism was hardly surprising – Robert Johnson died in 1938. We had to let Roy in on the joke after that, although I was tempted to ask him if he fancied booking some studio time for Mozart.

While Brewer's Droop were on the road I was able to continue with the 100 Club. Tuesdays was usually a quiet night for gigs with the band, so I could usually make the club, but if I wasn't there I had a few trusted assistants who would run things for me. There was also a bit of mutual co-operation in that I must have booked my own band at least a couple of dozen times. We could always fill in when there was a blank Tuesday, the exposure to a London audience was good for us and the band would pull a solid crowd. Someone interesting would invariably drop by and the night would often end at whichever Indian restaurant was still open.

As I'd found at the Nag's, the audience for blues in the West End was dropping as the seventies got properly underway, and we had to diversify. I put on a Danish band called Burnin' Red Ivanhoe, and despite a name that probably sounded better if you were a Dane in the early seventies they were very good. They weren't afraid to mix jazz into their sound and featured a brass section very reminiscent of Charlie Mingus. They drew a good crowd and in their way, were forerunners of what was to come.

Brett Marvin & the Thunderbirds were regulars almost from the beginning. Despite sounding like a rock'n'roll band they were very similar to Brewer's Droop, and drew similar audiences. The Americans were still the biggest draws, though. Duane Eddy came over with a ten-piece band featuring the best white blues singer I've ever heard. I didn't find out his name then and I've never found it since, but he deserved to have been a major star in his own right.

Another great act that I was proud to promote was the Johnny Otis Show, featuring such names as Gene 'Mighty Flea' Connors on trombone, the great vocalist Esther Phillips and Johnny's son, guitar prodigy Shuggie. On the day they were due to play I arrived at the club early to be interviewed for a radio programme, and I was glad that I was there so promptly. Customers started arriving at four in the afternoon, and the queue was soon stretching down Oxford Street. Johnny was rehearsing a new drummer and I spent two hours trying to do some work, but in reality just listening as the band went through their paces.

I never stopped realising what a privilege it was to work how I did. Johnny and his band did five shows for us on that tour; they loved the place and whenever they had a free date the promoter would ring and ask if we wanted them back. They almost had a residency. I was happy to help Johnny and his band in ways that I wouldn't have done for other acts, bringing them in extra drink for after the show and letting them use the club to rehearse on their days off. It was never anything but a pleasure to watch the band go through their paces, and Johnny was such a nice guy that I felt it was him doing me the favour. Not only was Johnny dubbed the Godfather of rhythm and blues, he also possessed a strong social conscience. Born the son of Greek immigrants, he decided as a boy that, "If I had to make the choice between being black and white, I'd be black" and was heavily involved in political issues, as well as starting up a chicken farm in Los Angeles so that the ghetto children could eat fresh eggs.

Of course, in with all the successes there were some disappointments. One strange incident occurred when I got to the NBF offices on a Monday morning and opened up a desk drawer to find a .358 Magnum revolver and bullets that certainly hadn't been in there when I'd left the previous Friday afternoon. I was used to shotguns, having seen them on my relatives' farms in Wiltshire, but as far as I was aware nobody ever went hunting their Sunday dinner with a Magnum. I didn't want a gun around the place even as a gift, so I got an acquaintance to take it away and never mentioned the incident to anyone. Nobody asked where it had gone and to this day I don't know who owned the gun or why they put it in my drawer. I look back on the incident sometimes and wonder if I dreamt it.

Another setback came during the summer of 1969. Chris and I found what seemed a perfect venue, in Walthamstow, east London. It was the upstairs room of a pub, a huge place the size of a ballroom, and the landlady was happy for us to promote there on Mondays. We booked bands in for three weeks, got decent crowds, and things were looking good when Chris told me that we had to stop. It turned out that the landlady had a regular promoter and unbeknownst to us we'd been covering while he was on holiday. Not wanting to get mixed up with any potential East End gangsters, we retired to the 100 Club.

Speaking of which, there was a lot of corruption and racketeering in Soho and the West End during the time the NBF operated, but luckily enough we were never involved. The criminals – both in and out of uniform – preyed on those who couldn't go to the law. After all, a pornographer wouldn't be able to make a complaint about having to pay bribes to a police officer if his own business was illegal, any more than a clip joint could complain about paying protection money to gangsters. But the 100 Club and the NBF were totally above board. It helped us that the club was a regular haunt of many members of the Establishment. Politicians would turn up, and we would even find ourselves playing host to minor royalty on occasion. There were no fiddles, no lawbreaking, nothing for criminals to prey on. In fact, we very rarely saw a policeman. Uniformed officers came into the club only once, and if any detectives were present they never made themselves noticed.

To earn an extra crust, Chris and I were involved in a couple of diversions. Mike Westbrook was a jazz composer who wanted to do a multi-media show in the manner of Sun Ra and we helped him out. We also promoted a folk group, the Humblebums, featuring a young singer named Billy Connolly. After watching them do a showcase at one of the rooms in the Royal Festival Hall complex we could tell that Billy was going to be a star, but not as a singer. His voice wasn't too hot but his song introductions had us on the floor with laughter and his stage presence was immense.

I also gave an unwitting helping hand to another duo, although not a directly musical one. The West Indian Social Club was situated in Reading, which in those days was like the Wild West. There were fights in the town centre every night, and twice at weekends, but the club was a good venue with a decent-sized room and stage. I promoted a few bands there, none of which were a great success, and paid a pound each night to have a couple of guys, who called themselves Alpha Centauri, put on a light show with home projectors and the like. They're now A.C. Lighting, one of the world's biggest distributors of lighting rigs to the entertainment industry.

The NBF offices were becoming a focal point for many Soho characters, who would wander round once the pubs had chucked out, this being in the days when they had to close during the afternoon. Promoters would be hanging around, probably snooping to see how business was doing, record company bosses turned up, and we soon learned to do all the important work during the morning, because after lunch it would be impossible. We were close to the drum shops on Shaftsbury Avenue, and Ginger Baker was a regular passer-by. I was getting recognized as a Soho character; one or two of its longer-established figures began to take umbrage, as they thought I was on the rise and they tended to guard their own notoriety jealously. There were plenty of famous names around. Michael Caine, Rod Stewart or one of the stars of programmes such as Z Cars would regularly be popping into the French House or the Coach & Horses for half an hour. I loved Soho and, with my bohemian tendencies, I felt right at home there.

I've always had the knack of being able to entertain people, and when I was with Brewer's Droop I found that I was doing things on stage that I'd been doing in the outside world for years. No wonder I felt at home in Soho; one more eccentric was never going to be recognised amongst the thousands who patrolled its streets. One guy spent a very pleasant lunch hour with a daffodil on his head, directing the traffic. So when I saw him, I naturally shinned up a lamppost and began pointing, saying, "He's over there." He'd pulled a crowd of 500 by the time the police arrived, which was more than most of the gigs I was putting on. If I'd got down the lamppost quick enough I could have taken up a collection.

With there being so many watering holes around, Soho was the natural habitat of journalists. I'd talk to them, they'd feature me in their stories and I got even better-known. Many a time I'd be walking along the street and have someone come up to me and say, "Hello Ron." Very often I'd reply, "Fine, thanks, and who are you?" I loved Soho but I wasn't daft enough not to realise I couldn't live there. If I'd been around the place all day and night I'd be long dead by now. You can't pretend you're 21 forever.

Bill Ferris, a musicologist from Mississippi, came to visit. He'd been sent by Simon Napier, the editor of Blues Unlimited magazine, and had a pile of tapes which he'd recorded in juke joints back home for his university thesis. We listened, and sent the tapes off to the Transatlantic record label, who we would regularly supply with quality material. Chris Strachwitz, of the Arhoolie label in California, dropped by one day. He took us out to lunch and told us some unprintable stories about West Coast music legends. He said that he wanted to get into Mexican music, but the bars where it was played were too dangerous for an American to enter, which reminded us that things were still different on the other side of the Atlantic.

Chris and I were feeling content with life by now. The average day would consist of two or three promoters coming round to the office to see what was happening, musicians and fans hanging around and talking, broadcaster Charlie Gillett would usually pop in to get the latest news. We'd founded an informal blues social club and I was only too aware that people were undertaking what was virtually a pilgrimage to take part in our work.

I made the acquaintance of Roger Eagle, one of the great unsung heroes of the British music scene. Roger had started out as a DJ in the early sixties, playing r&b records to a mod audience, and later went into the northern soul scene before running Eric's, a punk club in Liverpool which influenced the scene on

Merseyside that produced Frankie Goes To Hollywood, Echo & the Bunnymen and others – another example of how decent music transcends all labels. Sadly, Roger died after a long illness in 1999. He was typical of a number of us around the country who worked hard keeping music alive at the grass-roots, only too often having ideas stolen by the bigger fish in the ocean.

Someone who rarely got noticed by any size of fish was Larry Roddy, the most bohemian man in Ireland. He'd put on gigs featuring acts we sent over, although he was always hard to get hold of. Eventually we found out why. He lived in a cave in the Wicklow mountains. Larry never had a penny to his name, but somehow managed to be a successful promoter, and one Friday afternoon in the summer he turned up at the NBF offices with his girlfriend. The first thing she said was, "I've been looking at the people. You can tell they're rich." Chris and I looked at her open-mouthed but for once I kept quiet. We thought she might have been on something, but she was just taken aback by the city, as enthralled by London as any cave dweller ever has been. For his part, Larry was a legend in Irish music circles. One musician should be forever grateful, after getting himself arrested for the sort of serious offence that could have seen him sent to prison, yet Larry got things sorted out within minutes. How he survived, I don't know. Larry's still in Wicklow, still promoting, but I understand that he's moved into the vaguely modern era now and has both a proper house and a phone. I hope he's doing well and enjoying himself. He deserves it.

Johnny Shines, a slide guitarist from Tennessee, had mixed feelings about Ireland. Johnny must have seen just about everything in his career, but wasn't prepared for the night he played in a pub close to Dublin docks and a rat ran across the stage and into the crowd. There was pandemonium, and when I asked him later why he hadn't trod on the rat and killed it, Johnny explained. "Man, that was such a strange place I was afraid they was part of some weird religion where rats is sacred."

Rodents apart, I always enjoyed going to Ireland. I travelled the Irish Sea regularly, whether it was on holiday, with Brewers'

Droop while they were touring and also when I took bands over. There was such a different way of life back then, although I never enjoyed myself as much as Keith the Brewer's Droop roadie. We arrived in Dublin for a tour and Keith was greeted by a woman holding up a six-month old baby. Yes, we'd last played Ireland 15 months earlier. Keith kept quiet about it, didn't set foot anywhere outside the gig venues and hotels, and we heard no more about the incident.

Chris Trimming didn't always have such a pleasant time as I did. One day he was walking down Shaftsbury Avenue when some little bloke reached up and knocked his hat off. Chris, naturally, gave his mystery assailant a bit of a shake, then the police arrived. Chris told them what had happened and they asked if he wanted to press charges. "There's no point," Chris replied, "Look at the state of him." Another time, Chris was at a tube station after a 100 Club gig when he was set upon by some skinheads. He picked up a milk crate and set about them, escaping uninjured. It's a pity Chris hadn't been in the company of some of the people whose acquaintance we made around Soho. Henry Cooper and his manager, Jim Wicks, were familiar sights, while I would regularly see Henry's contemporary, the heavyweight Billy Walker, on the train into Paddington.

Life was sweet but Chris was obviously not earning enough. I had my other enterprises to keep me going, but the NBF wasn't so profitable that we could pay Chris a decent wage. He was regularly being offered good money by people in the music business and eventually moved on. Incidentally, I never found out what happened to the publishing advances that we'd been getting for NBF recordings, but I didn't get them and I'm sure the musicians didn't, either.

Brewer's Droop were getting busier by the month and with Chris gone the NBF was too much for one man to cope with, so something had to go. I wound down our arrangements, gave up the office and the National Blues Federation was no more. It had provided an enjoyable couple of years but was never a great money-spinner. Brewer's Droop was an exciting project that I wanted to devote my time to, and, as I was later to discover, it's always better to do one new thing properly than go at it half-cocked because you're clinging on to the past.

Chapter 10

All The Young Dudes

Now that I wasn't spending so much time involved with blues, I was able to cast my net wider in the hunt for quality acts. One of the best bands I promoted during this period was Mott the Hoople, who had just recruited a new singer named Ian Hunter. They played a fantastic gig at the Nag's and had star quality written all over them. I knew they'd be big and although it took a few years and a bit of help from David Bowie, they got there in the end. Back in those days a band could afford the time to build up a live following by word of mouth and, if they were lucky, that would translate into record sales. It might have taken longer, but they learned their trade playing places such as the Nag's all around the country and that helped them sustain their success. These days a band will be formed, get into the charts, make a lot of money for all concerned, and split within a year.

Some bands, of course, never wanted to be stars. Brewer's Droop had that attitude. We enjoyed ourselves, but we never had the determination to be famous. When you get stopped walking down the street by people who you've never met but who talk as though they know you because they saw you on stage a few months previous, well, that's not for me. It would have taken away my freedom and made me feel as though I was under scrutiny every time I left the house. If I didn't have the time to do what I wanted when I wasn't working then, as far as I was concerned, life wasn't worth living. Some of the minor notoriety and press attention my band got was fine, but on the whole I preferred to stay anonymous.

Brett Marvin & the Thunderbolts were another band who chose to stay away from the big time. Formed in 1968, they'd missed out on the blues boom, but were happy to continue playing the club circuit afterwards. For a time they promoted at Ken

Colyer's Studio 51 club in Great Newport Street, Soho, on Sunday afternoons. The usual suspects of the British blues scene were invariably there, such luminaries as Tony McPhee and Dave Kelly, and there was often so many of them jamming that the distinction between band and audience was difficult to see. The venue was run by two old ladies named Pat and Vi who only sold soft drinks as the club was open outside licensing hours. Then, once they knew you and provided you asked nicely, they'd sell you a slug of whisky to go with your Coke. I'd nip along to see who was playing, maybe join in, and we'd all go off to the Star of India restaurant near Leicester Square for dinner.

I'd seen the Doors at the Middle Earth club in Covent Garden in 1968. They were brilliant then, but two years later at the Isle of Wight festival they were just sad. They'd turned into a second-rate blues band, the sort of thing I could watch any week in High Wycombe, doing Backdoor Man and other long, boring blues covers. Jimi Hendrix headlined the festival, but I missed him. I'd seen Jimi at the Klooks Kleek club in Hampstead when he first arrived in the country and been knocked out by his talent. Later on, when I was promoting the 100 Club, I asked him to perform for us, but he'd outgrown such a venue by then and even a secret gig would have been seen as a step backwards for him. There can't be many promoters who were turned down by Jimi Hendrix for so many different venues.

The Crown at Pishill, near Henley, often saw top musicians playing in secret, mainly because it was the only pub in the area with a late licence, meaning you could drink there until after midnight. It's a lovely place, right in the middle of the Chilterns, and you could always tell a local's background by how they pronounced the name. If they made it sound like it had two s's, they were working-class. If their pronunciation was 'Pieshill' they either lived in the big houses or else aspired to them. George Harrison lived in one of the biggest houses of the lot, and he was a regular in the Crown, often accompanied by his drunken mate Ringo. I never promoted there, but I'd go and watch bands, and the two of them were sometimes in attendance. They were both approachable, even though Ringo drank so much in those days he rarely made sense. I'd occasionally talk to someone who'd say "I was in the Crown the other night watching a band and George got up to play with them, with Ringo singing," but I never witnessed it, although if I had, I'd have probably tried to book them for the Nag's. On second thoughts, maybe the Town Hall would have been better. Ringo never played the drums at the Crown, which was a pity; playing in a pub band was about his standard. Sorry, that's an easy jibe to make and I should really be ashamed of it.

It was becoming impossible for me to promote at the Nag's Head, as it was a weekend gig and Brewer's Droop were almost constantly booked to play elsewhere. I tried to hand over to some others but none of them could make a go of it. Their big problem was that they weren't autocratic enough. Most successful promoters work on their own – look at Bill Graham and Harvey Goldsmith. The less people involved, the more purpose there is. Music isn't like an ordinary industry, where you have to bother about buying in materials, designing products and marketing the finished article. In our industry you book bands and sell tickets, that's all. I've been in partnership a few times but it's always ended in tears.

One venue I booked on my own ended up in more than tears. I'd started putting on bands at a hotel in Maidenhead every Saturday night. It all started when I used to rehearse there with a blues band from Windsor. They didn't play any gigs, in fact they hadn't got a name, but it was fun, and I, with my promoter's eye, thought that this decent-sized room right next to the Thames would do good business during the summer months. I had a word with the landlord and he agreed to let me rent it from him.

My instincts were right. I'd found a perfect venue, just outside the town centre, yet in nice surroundings and with a large car park. I put on Judy Driscoll, Brian Auger & the Trinity, who were all one band and attracted a good crowd as their hit single This Wheel's On Fire had not long been in the charts. The charmingly-named Scottish act White Trash played, as did a few local acts. We went on like this for eight weeks, until one Thursday I got a message from the landlord. I was living with my parents, and my mother, bless her, wasn't the best at passing messages, so when she told me that someone had rung and said there was a problem with Saturday night, I didn't take much notice. With my mum a bit unaware of the vagaries of the music business and dad's stock answer to every enquiry when he answered the phone being "He's not here" due to his deafness, I often wonder how many acts I missed out on during these years.

Saturday came and I went to the venue as usual, to meet the band. Steve Miller and his band were a good local draw, and featured Lol Coxhill, who went on to become a saxophonist of renown. I pulled into the car park, and there was, indeed, a problem. The hotel was no longer standing. It had been demolished, and all that was left were a few piles of rubble and the remnants of one of those fires you see on building sites, that smoulder for days and always have a charred door on the top. The band arrived and, with the flair for saying the wrong thing that musicians invariably acquire, asked "Where do we set up?" I pointed out that there wasn't a venue anymore and sent them on their way with £10 petrol money.

I eventually found out that the hotel had been closed for months, pending demolition, and the 'landlord' was a squatter. I had to admire him; he'd been so convincing that I'd never thought to ask his name, or the name of the hotel. I hadn't even bothered to wonder why this four-storey Thameside hotel never had any guests, nor staff other than a couple who ran the bar.

He'd taken it right to the wire as well. The previous Saturday we'd cleared up as normal, sweeping the floor and stacking away the chairs in preparation for his next customers and he hadn't said a word to us. There hadn't even been any locals who knew what was going on; in fact, some of them turned up on the night as I watched from over the road. They hadn't noticed anything untoward over the previous week, despite the hotel being demolished.

That venue could have been the best of the lot. It held 400, had a perfect location and a great atmosphere. I could still be promoting there now, and if I ever ran into the landlord/con man again, I honestly don't know whether I'd strangle him or buy him a drink.

This setback made me more determined to find a suitable venue for the bands who had outgrown the Nag's. I hated turning people away when the place was full, especially if they'd travelled a long way, so I looked towards the biggest nearby venue, the town hall. Broome & Wade were a large engineering firm in the area and their apprentices association asked me to put on a gig for them. I booked Savoy Brown, backed by the rock'n'roll band Wild Angels. Ron Saunders from the Nag's ran the bar, a couple of girls did the lights and we pulled in a big crowd.

The night was made more memorable by the sight of the two lighting techs kissing after the gig. This was an eye-opener to me, as I was still surprisingly naïve about many things. Drugs, for example. A member of Savoy Brown and I took a couple of young ladies over to Wycombe Rye, and when he started smoking dope all I could think was "I haven't done this before." I've never been interested in drugs; a few beers have always sorted me out.

Drugs, whether illegal or otherwise, have caused so many problems in music. I'd seen that right back in my early days of promoting. When I was living in Bayswater I used to see Clyde McPhatter hanging around the big agency nearby. They couldn't have got him much work, because he was always walking the streets and he was always skint, hassling me for coffee and burgers in the local Wimpy bar where we'd talk for hours on end. I'd have loved to promote Clyde, but I only had the Nag's at that time, and he wouldn't have played there. Anyway, I'd heard that he was unreliable. He had a marvellous voice, he'd been with the Drifters in their early days and then gone solo, having a few hits including A Lover's Question, which has been covered by many soul greats. Unfortunately, Clyde's talent had been eroded by alcohol, and he cut a sad figure, down at heel and often rambling. Some times, though, he'd start to sing on the street corner and crowds would gather to listen to this marvellous voice. Clyde moved back to America and died of a heart attack in 1972, at the tragically early age of 39.

I also got involved with the Wycombe Arts Festival, with a show called The Evolution of the Blues. I had to appear before a committee at the Guild Hall to assess my suitability to be involved in the festival so I went along, gave a presentation, and then left the room while they mulled over my application. I was informed that everything was fine, so I got on with the show. I was working alongside the manager of the local branch of the local-defunct Martin's Bank, which made a change from my usual co-workers. The show was headlined by Mississippi Fred McDowell and featured home-grown talent such as Jo-Ann Kelly, folk-rock guitarist Mike Cooper and Black Cat Bones, a local band who in a previous incarnation had boasted Paul Kossoff and Simon Kirke in their ranks before they left to join Free. It was a great night, but I almost got locked up at the end. Radio One presenter Mike Raven was compere, and at the end everyone who had appeared was on the stage, jamming. One country blues purist who thought Mississippi Fred should have been playing on his own climbed on stage and began trying to drag the other musicians away. I picked him up, threw him out and he threatened to report me to the police for assault. He must have thought better of it next day and I heard no more.

There was, inevitably, a postscript to the show. The town hall caretaker was less than pleased when, on cleaning the balcony, he found several condoms strewn around. I could have explained that they were filled with red, blue, gold or silver colouring, as they'd been used by the lighting girls (yes, the same ones as the Savoy Brown show) for effects. I don't know if my explanation would have been believed, and I harboured the suspicion that every time I booked the Town Hall from then on, the council were convinced it was for an orgy. I didn't have the heart to point out that the two girls responsible were probably

All The Young Dudes

the only people in the venue who wouldn't need condoms to enjoy themselves, but I decided that this particular fact was too much for the local worthies to comprehend.

By now my only connection with the Nag's was when Droop used it to rehearse or when we were off-duty, as an alternative to the Antelope. John Curd had come along and straightened the place out, and he put us on a few times. It was strange to be working there for someone else, but it was a lot less hassle. I kept my High Wycombe connections for a time by helping out Joe Farquarson in a venture he started up called the Twynight Club. It was just a concrete bunker underneath the main flyover in the town centre and didn't have much in the way of atmosphere. Joe put an eclectic mix of acts on, everything from Genesis to Arthur Conley, but it wasn't a great success and didn't last long. That was typical of Joe; he'd look everywhere for venues. He'd have promoted an open-air festival at the council rubbish tip if he thought it would make money.

The 100 Club was hosting rock and soul bands as well as being the home of the biggest blues club in Europe. Rock was becoming discredited due to its overblown nature and we had to get people enjoying themselves if we wanted them to continue supporting live music. I started to promote a lot of rock'n'roll and rockabilly. In addition to Duane Eddy, Shaking Stevens & the Sunsets did a residency, we brought over Charlie Feathers and Warren Storm, two old Southern rockers who had recorded for Sun, and Buddy Knox also played. I was trying to get away from the heavy, boring rock scene that many other venues were plugging. I could see that music fans were being conned into accepting a lack of excitement in the guise of musicianship, and others began to think the same. Charlie Gillett was behind me all the way on his Honky Tonk show on Radio London, and we were getting a reputation as THE place to listen to authentic music.

Muddy Waters played the only UK date of a European tour at the club in May 1972. It was another wonderful occasion, and if there's a blues heaven it will have to go some to be better than that night. Here was the man who had almost single-handedly helped create the Chicago sound, playing like he'd brought the whole of the American blues tradition with him. One review described the night as "The nearest a UK audience would get to listening to Muddy in a Chicago juke joint." I was so proud – for a fan of the blues, who had graduated from listening, to buying records and then promoting, this was the justification of everything I'd ever done. I tried so hard to get the club exactly right, and here I was being told I'd succeeded.

Muddy had enjoyed a strange relationship with British audiences. He'd first been brought over by Chris Barber in 1958, but his band were amplified and the blues purists booed him, just like the folkies would with the electric Bob Dylan six years later. On his return Muddy decided to give the people what they wanted, so he played acoustic, which didn't go down at all well with an audience who by then had got used to electric blues and expected it from him. But you can't keep a genius down, and by the time I booked Muddy, he and his band were at full throttle, with the audiences lapping them up.

Freddie King came over some time afterwards, and gave me another great impromptu night. He arrived at the club when Kokomo, a British r&b/funk band, were playing, but he didn't have a guitar with him. The band's guitarist Jim Mullen, a doyen of the British jazz scene, lent him one and Freddie sat in for two numbers. When he gave back the guitar, Jim said, "I don't want to play that again," such was the respect in which he held Freddie. Kokomo were a great band, although they never made the big time, despite having some great musicians and a unique three-man singing line-up.

Freddie, for his part, would often badger me to put on two houses at the 100 Club, as he would always sell out. I had to explain that licensing laws meant the first house would have to start at 6.30 and it would be impossible to get audiences to attend so early. He also asked me, "How'd you like me to play at that Blues Loft you got? I'd love to go back there." Sadly, he died before we could arrange what would have been one of my greatest promotions.

Sunnyland Slim, born in 1907, in Vance, Mississippi, was in his late sixties when we brought him over, but he was still a wonderful pianist. He should have been one of the big names of the blues scene, but like many other great musicians, he'd never received his due recognition. I got him to autograph an album, and it must have taken him fifteen minutes just to write his name. My wife Maureen, her sister Titch and I took Sunnyland to Windsor Safari Park on a day off from his tour. He looked at the lions and tigers with concern, which is only natural as neither animal is exactly common in the Deep South, but what really caught his eye were the monkeys, doing whatever it is that monkeys do in spring. Later on we sat in the safari park café and he said, "This would be a great venue, with all those animals out there." I did enquire, but the park's owners wanted to charge too much.

I asked Sunnyland how he managed to keep such a great band together and his answer was simple, "I go home every autumn and recruit them." The area in which he was brought up, and in particular the Mississippi town of Clarksdale, must be the world capital of blues. Whenever one of the greats needed a new sideman, they'd travel down and ask around about which new musicians were getting a reputation. That's how the great singer and harmonica player Jimmy Cotton apparently got his first break. He was walking along the street when Muddy Waters came up and asked Jimmy to join his band that night. Muddy had arrived looking for a singer and when he'd asked about the best young talent, Jimmy's name was mentioned so Muddy tracked him down. It's always been my great ambition to tour the area. I'd love to visit some of the last juke joints, miles from civilisation.

I was still as much a member of the audience as I was a promoter, and I'd go to gigs for the enjoyment of the music. Fats Domino came over round about 1971. He played one of the big West End theatres on a Sunday night when they would normally be closed. Fats brought his full band over from New Orleans and treated an enraptured audience to a great old-fashioned show. Almost every song he performed had been a hit for him.

As the seventies moved onwards, so the 100 Club grew in importance. It was rocking, the number one blues venue in Europe. We were also doing well with other types of music; it was a time when more and more people wanted a reaction to the tedious, introspective stuff they were told was the fashion. If you wanted authentic good-time music, whether it be blues, rock & roll, soul or whatever label you wanted to put on it, the 100 Club was the place. I realised, though, that I had a responsibility to put on British bands whenever possible. They'd been big influences on me, they'd helped me when I was getting started and I believed I had to repay the favour. We'd have a British Blues Festival every couple of months, with the usual names who could pull a crowd – Tony McPhee, Jo-Ann Kelly, Brett Marvin and the like. Things were ticking along nicely.

Chapter 11

Higher & Higher

Even though I wasn't promoting at the Nag's anymore, I was still associated with the place and trying to help them. They used my name and reputation to get people in, and sometimes to throw them out again. Mick Fitzgibbons was the landlord and I told him that he should put bands on for free in the downstairs lounge on Saturday evenings. This was another bit of trailblazing for the Nag's: I didn't know of any other venue where bands played in the main room of a pub. Word soon got round and the place was packed. The free Saturday nights were a way of breaking bands that I knew were good, but weren't well known at the time. Some promising local acts picked up a local following this way.

Pub rock was at its height and the Nag's was part of the circuit. Brinsley Schwartz used it as a base, which caused Brewer's Droop a few problems as both bands would use the pub for rehearsals and book the whole day, so we had to reserve the place well in advance. The Brinsleys had a history that's well worth a book in its own right, and are still best-known for one of the biggest publicity fiascos in the history of the music business. They'd started out by hiring a jumbo jet to take a load of media types to see them playing in New York, but the trip had been a disaster from start to finish and the resultant bad press had almost destroyed them. Now they were going back to their roots in an attempt to start all over again.

They still had an eye for the main chance, though. The band were living in a farmhouse out at Beaconsfield which they'd persuaded the estate agents to let them rent by turning up at their office in a Rolls-Royce. The estate agent thought he was dealing with a big-shot rock star. He wasn't to know the limo had been hired for the day. Nick Lowe, who went on to be a producer and have a few hits himself, was their guitarist and I'd often see him cycling around the surrounding countryside, keeping fit. The other good thing about the band was that they, like their pub rock contemporaries Ducks Deluxe and Bees Make Honey, could be replied upon to fill decent-sized venues.

Taking about pub rock, what exactly was it? Bands such as Dr Feelgood, Kilburn & the High Roads and Brinsley Schwartz played entirely different types of music. Some of its leading lights were dismissive of the phrase, and with good reason. "It was in the pub, and it rocked," was the oft-quoted comment on the scene from promoter and record label owner Dave Robinson. It was handy to go along to watch a band in a pub, but the music was never going to cause a revolution, and in any case, it had all been done before. I'd seen pub rock at the Plough at Shalbourne in 1957, when a rock'n'roll band played in a pub.

Once Brewer's Droop had finally split, I had more time to promote other bands. By 1974 I'd started putting on gigs at the Crown, in Marlow. The function room was bigger than upstairs at the Nag's, and I could get bigger bands than John Curd could attract. When I first moved there, a few of the locals who knew my reputation must have thought, "Aye aye, what's he up to here?" but there was never a real problem. Marlow was a much less wealthy area than it is now, the local population was very close-knit and rural. There were a lot of farm labourers around, and if they wanted to cause trouble they could be worse than any city gang, but despite my worries that they might resent me moving in on their turf, things worked out fine.

The Crown was a lovely venue, right on the High Street and close to the historic suspension bridge which goes over the Thames, with the rowing club not far away. I put on my usual roster of American blues acts, together with a more general mixture of what was happening in Britain. Sassafras, who were a folk-blues band, played there, as did Back Door, a jazz rock band featuring bassist Colin Hodgkinson, who had played with Alexis Korner and went on to join Whitesnake. Back Door should have been a lot bigger than they were, but they had the attitude that pub gigs were beneath them, so they lost a lot of goodwill. Audiences can tell when they're being looked down upon, and many's the band who have thought themselves too good to play certain venues, gone through the motions for a few gigs and soon found their date sheet emptying because word's got round that they weren't worth watching.

We'd also put some good local acts on, and typical of them were the Tequila Brown Blues Band. These were a ten-piece with a singer who was a complete nutter. He didn't make a lot of sense but he enjoyed himself. As musicians the whole band weren't too good, but they were enthusiastic and the crowd always liked them. They were ideal for Friday night, when the Crown was full of people wanting to wash away the dirt and dust of a working week and have a good time.

Unfortunately, the landlord wasn't really interested in running a live music venue. I gave him some of his best-ever nights but he was never enthusiastic. His attitude was typical of many publicans; they liked the good times but would complain when things were quiet. A good pub venue has to have a landlord who's into music and who appreciates that there will be bad nights as well as good. There's always something to do even on days when bands aren't playing – musicians will drop by, leave tapes, phone on the off-chance of a gig. I'd paid out of my own money to improve the stage and got Steve Kane, who by then was working for Rick Wakeman, to help me install it in the upstairs room where the bands played, but in the end I walked away. Maureen and I were going through one of our 'separation' phases, and the Crown was losing me money so I ditched it.

My commitments at the 100 Club now stretched to two or three nights a week, often more. Roger Horton would let me have the club whenever I wanted provided the customers turned up, which they usually did. We had regulars that I knew of from Devon, Wales and a couple who would catch the ferry over regularly from Belgium. People would travel massive distances for a night at the 100 Club. Kevin Coyne did a week-long residency that saw me undertaking a massive publicity campaign, but it paid off as the audiences were good, which he deserved as he had a lot of talent in his band. At the other end of the scale I became the first promoter to put on Northern Soul nights in the south, if that isn't a contradiction, and I was the great soul singer J.J. Barnes' first promoter in the UK.

We started to attract the main faces of the London soul scene, particularly record shop owners and writers. I did a column for Blues & Soul magazine for a while, which I enjoyed, and got involved with helping the magazine's owner, John Abbey, with the tours he was organizing. I let him use the 100 Club as a rehearsal room for the American acts and their British backing bands, and often found that the big names were very knowledgeable about the blues scene back home. Soul had a bad name amongst 'serious' music fans in seventies Britain due to its connotations with disco and pop, but in its heartland it was closely allied to blues, and rightly so. After all, was Otis Redding, to name the most obvious, a soul singer, or did he sing the blues? The answer, of course, was both. I'd counter the prejudice by putting on blues act to support a soul singer. Ann Peebles, a genuine soul diva, and my old harp-playing standby Dr Ross did one such Memphis Night and both were well-received by an appreciative audience.

Singing live, Jackie Wilson had probably the best soul voice I've ever heard. He'd perform one amazing song, then when you thought he'd reached the climax of his act he'd top it with another. I promoted him at the 100 Club on his birthday and managed to smuggle his wife (they'd divorced, although they never got round to breaking up), baby and a cake, all of whom had flown in from America that day as a surprise, into the dressing room while he was onstage. Although it wasn't a massive audience, Jackie performed superbly and everything went swimmingly. He came off stage pouring with sweat, then his eyes lit up as he saw his family waiting. I discreetly slipped away, and another special moment had entered 100 Club folklore.

Jackie had a great stage presence, built like a middleweight boxer, but he never really found his own niche. If he'd stuck to one style of singing he could have been up there with the biggest soul names, but as it was, the hits stopped coming and Jackie had found himself relegated to the cabaret nostalgia circuit by the time he suffered a heart attack in 1975. He never recovered, but stayed in a vegetative state until dying in January 1984, by which time his talent was beginning to gain its full recognition. Dexy's Midnight Runners had a top ten hit with the Van Morrison song Jackie Wilson Says and after his death the man himself scored his biggest UK hits. Jackie had never had a great deal of luck – by the time I promoted him he'd already been divorced, shot by a jealous lover, convicted on morality charges, filed for bankruptcy and seen his 16 year-old son shot dead. After his heart attack the Black Panthers put on a fund-raising show, although little of the money filtered through for Jackie's benefit. I wish I could have helped him more. He'd given me a lot of pleasure and helped me earn a few bob as well.

Not everything I was involved with became a big success. Robert Knight, for example, had a number one hit with Love on a Mountain Top when he played the club, but didn't pull in a big crowd, because the people who bought his records weren't the sort who would travel to Oxford Street to watch him in a small club. They'd rather stay at home and listen to records or watch Top of the Pops to see what they had to buy next week. Still, everyone enjoyed themselves and my soul shows gained a few more regular customers, so things didn't turn out as badly as they could have done.

The ultimate embarrassment for a promoter is to put on a gig where those on stage outnumber the audience. Luckily it never happened to me, although I did worry sometimes. For example, the forgettable night when Sunnyland Slim and Mickey Baker, a guitarist from Kentucky, played at St Pancras Town Hall. I don't know why I used that particular venue. Everywhere else must have been booked, because it was in the wrong part of town, away from the tourist areas and with nowhere to drink or eat nearby. The building itself was a lovely old place, and Son House had sold it out previously, but it seemed hardly-used and

Sunnyland and Mickey, even with the members of Brewer's Droop backing them, scarcely pulled in a hundred punters when I needed five times that many to break even. I had a gig on at the 100 Club the same evening and I reckon I could have put both audiences in there, with room to spare. I've had better days, but to survive in the music business you have to accept that you won't always go home at night with pockets stuffed with fivers.

At the other end of the scale were the pub rockers, who never sold many records but could always pull in fans that wanted a good time. The bands used to love playing the 100 Club. It was a prestigious venue with good facilities and didn't mean having to hump gear upstairs. One of the bands who performed regularly for us were Kilburn & the High Roads, with Ian Dury singing. I'd known Ian for many years, as he'd been a pupil at the Royal Grammar School in High Wycombe. Ian was a short guy, crippled from a bout of polio when he was younger, and he seemed to have a complex about his stature. It was the classic little man thing, always trying to be aggressive to make up for his lack of inches. He'd mess around with knives on stage and hire real psychos as roadies. Ian tried so hard to look like Gene Vincent, his big hero, and in a way he succeeded. Despite his persona, though, I liked him well enough. He could be a very genial man, even though there were deep undercurrents there.

The Kilburns were a real freak show. Apart from Ian they had cripples, an albino, and Humphrey Ocean, their bass player, was about eight feet tall. No-one had seen anything like them – it was a real human zoo. To round things off their guitarist was a very good-looking lad, and in that band he seemed the freak. They always gave us a memorable performance and Ian always looked as though he had something going for him. So it eventually proved, when for a time he was one of the biggest acts in the country, with number ones and New Boots And Panties becoming one of the biggest-selling albums of the decade.

It was a fun time to be in the music business, although none of the bands were putting on the sort of show Brewer's Droop used to do. In fact, Brinsley Schwartz took things to another extreme.

After one 100 Club gig we found that they'd left a notebook in the office, with different set lists for whatever type of venue they were playing – a 'school dance', a 'smooth cocktail club', whatever that was, a 'rough East End pub' and so on. I couldn't have done that. Droop's attitude was to just go on and play, regardless of the type of audience, and there weren't many others versatile enough to get away with it, but Brinsley Schwartz were a very clever band, whose members were multi-talented.

By now a lot of acts were coming out of the Southend area. This had always been a hotbed of rock'n'roll, and, as often happens, if one good band comes from a place, it inspires a lot more. Dr Feelgood went on to be the best-known band from there. I got to know them when John Curd promoted them at the Nag's, and they soon progressed to the 100 Club. Within months they had a chart-topping album and were playing the Hammersmith Odeon, but not before giving us some great hot, sweaty nights; most of the mid-sized venues in London did amazing business with the Feelgoods in the couple of years before they hit the big time. They played basic blues, but in a very powerful style. Lee Brilleaux could, as the saying goes, do a bit. He was a great singer with a real stage presence and his premature death in 1993 was a great loss to the British music scene.

Lew Lewis was another Southend musician, a harmonica player and a very strange character. I was giving him a lift through Walthamstow when he started thinking the police car behind was following him. I turned a corner and he dived out of the car. I carried on – it was easier than going back and explaining to Lew that the police weren't interested in him, at least not on that occasion. He'd had his brushes with the law; one day he was due in court for non-payment of yet another fine and when the magistrate asked him how he intended to put this right, Lew took out his harmonica and said "Let me go and I'll start playing to get the money." The magistrate didn't know how to deal with him so the case was adjourned.

Lew played for a while with Eddie & the Hot Rods, another band who gave us a good time. They'd been associated with the

Marquee, where they ended up vying with AC/DC for the house attendance record, and we arranged a swap so that they could play for us and we gave the Marquee another band. We definitely got the better part of the deal, as the Rods were fantastic and thoroughly deserved the chart success they were soon enjoying.

Unfortunately, things didn't go so well for Lew. He formed Lew Lewis' Reformer, who had a bit of success on Dave Robinson's Stiff label, but after the band's demise Lew had problems with drink and drugs and ended up in prison after a farcical attempt to rob his local post office with a replica pistol.

As a promoter you have to observe everything, you have to be ahead of fashion and think about what's going to happen rather that what's already happening. It's easy to be wise after the event, but to be successful you have to create the event. That's not to say that I always managed to get it right. After all, if success in the music business was just a matter of the best talent becoming the biggest stars, everyone could be a promoter, and then where would I have been? There are some big names whose appeal I could never work out and many more artistes who should have been huge but to this day I can't understand why they didn't enjoy the success their talent deserved.

I asked such a question about Mickey Jupp to one artiste, and got the reply, "Because he's a miserable bastard." Mickey was singer and guitarist with Legend, who came out of the Southend Area Finishing School for Rock Musicians before most of its other graduates. Their 1971 recording, which became known as the Red Shoe Album because of the cover, was great, emotive stuff and remains one of the lost masterpieces of the era. But Mickey failed to capitalise and although he put on a decent show whenever I booked him, he never built a live following so could never do great business. He rode the post-punk wave after a fashion, alongside his contemporaries Nick Lowe and Dave Edmunds, then pretty much disappeared off the scene. The last I heard of Mickey, he was running a shop in the Lake District.

Duffy Power had been one of the early rock'n'rollers, signed to Larry Parnes' stable that included Billy Fury and Marty Wilde.

Despite appearing on television regularly and making some highly-acclaimed records, he had failed to make the big time and disappeared from the scene. In 1965 Duffy recorded some demos featuring John McLaughlin and Jack Bruce, but which had never been released until he brought us the tapes to the NBF office. We knew the material was good and got Transatlantic to bring out the album, called Impressions, and a single, Mary, Open The Door.

Despite their obvious quality, neither sold well and although I put him on at the 100 Club and attempted to launch him on the pub circuit, Duffy's career fizzled out. The last time I saw him was when he appeared with the Mean Red Spiders at the Nag's many years later. He sang a few numbers with them and still showed what a great voice he possessed.

I thought Duffy was capable of being another Georgie Fame. He was a good-looking lad who could sing, write his own material and play harmonica, and he had a few of us in his corner, but it never happened for him. He did, though, provide me with an abiding memory. One day we were driving around Bayswater, his birthplace, and Duffy was pointing out places and people of interest. Old dancehalls, coffee bars and pubs, women he knew and other scenes from London in the fifties, the early days of British rock'n'roll and a magical time which has gone forever.

Errol Dixon used to turn up at the office so often I thought he was haunting us. He hailed from Jamaica and moved to South London, from where he would travel every day to chew the fat and drink our coffee. Errol was a nice guy with a deep knowledge of the blues, and when he told us he'd made some records in Jamaica and had some other material he'd recorded, we were keen to listen to it. The songs were brilliant and we got Transatlantic to put out the album That's How You Got Killed Before, featuring a cover shot of Errol at the 100 Club piano. It sold about as many copies as Duffy's album, but at least I got Errol some gigs and sent him on tour. My last sighting of him was in a very upmarket pub in London, round about 1997. He was playing with a trio and although the place was packed, I couldn't but think how he could have done so much more. Another one had fallen through the cracks, although Errol's work, particularly the ska singles he recorded early in his career, is now highly collectable.

Not all the failures were down to bad luck. One guy I first came across when he was in a few bands around Wycombe. He was a heavy drinker and a druggie, who disappeared without trace, as drug users do, and I later met up with him when Brewer's Droop played in Lincoln. I found out that after we played there he'd booked a gig featuring some top names. He'd done all the right things, booking acts that would draw a crowd and publicising the event well, so there was a big audience on the night. Then midway through the first half, when everyone who was going to attend had arrived and paid, he collected all the money and vanished. He probably thought he was a smart operator, ripping people off like that, but he was so blinded by the lure of easy pickings that he hadn't realised he could probably have run similar nights every month, rather than one quick theft that meant he had to leave town for good.

What I promoted often wasn't what I was listening to, and I came to realise that public tastes weren't always on the same wavelength as mine. Avant garde for example, I quite liked but I knew that there wouldn't be enough of a live audience for it to be worth my while promoting. It was at times like this that I realised I was running a business rather than a crusade. If you compare my situation with, say, that of Riverside Records in New York, they recorded jazz pianist Tadd Dameron's album The Magic Touch and it took them thirty years to recoup their expenses even though the album was regarded as a masterpiece. I didn't have anywhere near that length of time. I had one night, one chance to sell. You can't promote a gig and hope someone will like the band and pay you the cost of a ticket years later.

I'd have loved to put on jazz regularly, but the audiences were never big enough to make it pay. If Ronnie Scott's could struggle in Central London with the reputation they had, nobody else had much chance, although I enjoyed Stephane Grappelli playing

Higher & Higher

the 100 Club, on one of Roger Horton's own promotions. The great violinist was well into his sixties then, and still playing beautifully although he struggled to make himself heard above the noise of a packed-out Friday night crowd. "I'm used to it," was his only post-gig comment on the noise that had meant my father-in-law, Alan, who I'd taken along as he was becoming a jazz fan, and I straining to hear.

Stephane could have done ten encores, even though he had to compete with those who wanted to talk throughout his set. I can never understand why anyone would want to pay good money and then ignore the main attraction, annoying everyone else in the room in the process. It's like the smartarses who shout obscure titles at the end of every song a band plays. They might think they're clever knowing every b-side and album track ever released, but it's just a pain for everyone else and the band are never going to change their set to accommodate one bloke with a big mouth.

A promoter has to listen to the beat of the streets, even if sometimes he doesn't want to be there. Pub rock was a great thing to listen to, but it wasn't making an iota of difference in the world outside the venues and a few mentions in the music press. On the other hand heavy metal was the music of the moment and I didn't like it one bit. To me, it was for 14 year-old kids to act tough in their bedroom. I was still looking for that edge, and although I had a few more experiences to go through, I would soon find it with a vengeance.

Chapter 12

Hail To The Chief

I'd known Martin Stone for a long time, through his work with Savoy Brown and Chilli Willy. I was living with Maureen at Lane End, a village just outside High Wycombe, and Martin lived up in the Chilterns with his girlfriend. They were in a gypsy caravan, a beautiful old thing, but basic, with no electricity or running water and a hole in the ground outside for a toilet.

Martin was a wry character and we shared similar tastes in literature and music. He'd often come over to our house to hear the latest blues records I'd picked up, and one day I said to him that as neither of us had bands, we should think about forming one. He agreed, and we set about putting the plan into action.

We wanted a pianist. Martin's former colleague in Savoy Brown, Bob Hall, was as good as anyone and as a bonus he'd bring along their bass-playing mate Bob Brunning, who had also been with Fleetwood Mac in their early days. Shakey Vick wanted to join on harmonica, but instead Martin roped in his friend Will Stallibrassy, and we finished the line-up with Pete Miles, a New Zealander living in South London, on drums. The name Jive Bombers reflected what we were a straightforward blues band with no real connection to my previous singing incarnation. Nobody came to see us expecting Brewer's Droop part II, which was just as well because we were a completely different entity. We were never a full-time band, as all the members had other things going on. The Jive Bombers were more of a hobby, enjoyable and a diversion from the real task of earning a living.

We played much the same pub and college circuit that I was used to, although we had a few interesting additions. Early on in the band's life we did a gig at a very posh house in Hambledon, so big it had its own entertainment suite. It belonged to the owner of W.H. Smith and we'd been booked by his son, Steve

Coleridge. Steve was a massive blues fan, who later went to work in the business in America. We went down well, even though we had to jam a lot of our set as we'd only just got together and didn't have much of a repertoire.

A similar gig was the May Ball at Cambridge University. Even though the rain was pouring down when we arrived, the students were in evening dress and ball gowns, punting along the River Cam. Someone had seen fit to book the notorious American anarchist band MC5 with us, and their singer Wayne Kramer, later to be jailed for drug dealing, started the show by screaming "This is an opportunity to get r-e-e-e-a-l-l-l-l-y gross!!!!" but he was no worse than usual, although that wasn't saying much.

As you can imagine the food was amazing – salmon and lobster everywhere and we thought we were in for a treat when we were offered a meal, but what they gave us was no better than the standard of school dinners. Never mind, we got a bit of our own back when towards the end of the set Bob Brunning saw a huge fish kettle, about four feet long and used to hold a whole salmon or something similar, and decided that it would be better holding beer than salmon. He got our roadie to help him fill it and drag it into the van. We put it on the dashboard, and of course as soon as the driver had to brake, the beer came gushing out and covered everyone who was sitting at the front. We stank of beer all the way home. Bob Brunning was dropped off at about eight in the morning and later claimed he went straight to work, although as he was a headmaster he must have got changed somewhere.

The Jive Bombers went down well everywhere we played. Critics liked us, often commenting on the authenticity of our sound, and audiences knew they'd always be in for a good night. My one regret from the time is we never recorded any of our material. We were influenced by Southern blues emerging from Texas; Freddie King and Albert Collins had made their mark on us. It was great to be in a band where everyone could contribute. My voice was improving as I learnt to relax on stage and I can't remember any reviewers complaining about my input.

My father, George Watts, in his shop

Me, aged seven, in that period between the war ending and music beginning

Where my sporting heritage came from. Hetton le Hole FC, managed by my grandfather Ted Whitfield (front row right)

Me, Pauline, mum, dad
and Lieutenant Commander A.G. Watts RN

Pauline and I
with me trying
to escape in the
second shot

Best man John Mackay and I on my first
wedding day. I thought the suit looked
rather dashing

Brewers drooping

You wouldn't have thought a line-up like the one below would end in a stage invasion

By 1972, I was doing a couple of nights a week at the 100 Club

WYCOMBE ARTS FESTIVAL
"Evolution of The Blues"
(TOWN HALL)

SATURDAY, 1st MARCH, 1969
Doors Open 6.45 p.m. — Start 7.30 p.m.

PROGRAMME

JO-ANN KELLY
with BOB HALL
JEROME ARNOLD BAND

INTERVAL

MIKE COOPER
DUSTER BENNETT
MISSISSIPPI FRED McDOWELL

Master of Ceremonies — RON WATTS

Presented in Conjunction with the Blues Loft and the National Blues Federation

— BLUES —

---

100 CLUB
100 OXFORD ST. W.1
7.30 till late
Membership not required

Thurs., 20th, 7.30 to Midnight
Soul Nite with
CAPITAL RADIO'S SOUL D.J.
GREG EDWARDS plus
RONNIE'S SOUL SOUND

Fri., 21st, 7.30 to Midnight
KEN COLYER'S ALL STAR JAZZMEN

Sat., 22nd, 7.30 to 1 a.m.
THE AVON CITIES JAZZ BAND
THE PARAGON JAZZ BAND

Sun. 23rd:
GEORGE MELLY & THE FEETWARMERS

Mon., 24th, 7.30 to Midnight
BLUE MONDAY
JOHNNY MARS
+ THE SUNFLOWER BOOGIE BAND
BREWERS DROOP
NIGHTHAWKS

Tues. 25th
JO ANN KELLY
+ THE BLUE DIAMONDS

Wed., 26th
KEN COLYER'S ALL STAR JAZZMEN

The Droop at Rockfield Studios. That's producer Dave Edmonds whose head is sticking up bottom right

Messrs Timms, Darrington, Watts and Mackay; backing vocalists extraordinaire

The Antelope, scene of many a session both musical and alcoholic (*photo - Dave Woodhall*)

Cyril Shire's
Trendsetter
INTERNATIONAL
Hairdressing Salon
104 WARDOUR STREET, LONDON, W.1.
Telephone: 01-437 3862 or 01-437 8191
Your Personnal Stylist CYRIL

My own personal Soho stylist.
Things were looking up

The late Bobby Walker and I.
A great drummer, sadly missed

A bit of self-help never hurt

THE NAGS HEAD — Thursday, March 20 — 60p — LONDON ROAD, HIGH WYCOMBE
BREWERS DROOP
N/W BRETT MARVIN & THE THUNDERBOLTS

The gateway to many an adventure
(*Photo - Dave Woodhall*)

Chris Trimming and I in the 100 Club office/dressing room

Nostalgia with the Brewers Droop!

Rockin' the blues at Swerford village hall on Saturday were the celebrated

I wouldn't say we were a nostalgia act, but it's all publicity

A self-explanatory title. I've been called worse

Lonnie Brookes, a 'happy' promoter and Lonnie's son, Chris

The "primeval animal" that was Howlin' Wolf
(*Photo - Sylvia Pitcher Photo Library*)

Errol Dixon
the one that got away

Arthur 'Big Boy' Crudup
occasionally drank too much
and often wrote great songs

The dynamic duo of Sonny Terry and Brownie McGhee

(*photos - Sylvia Pitcher Photo Library*)

A later shot of Shuggie Otis, when he was touring with his own band

Christmas at the 100 Club was always more about enjoyment than serious music

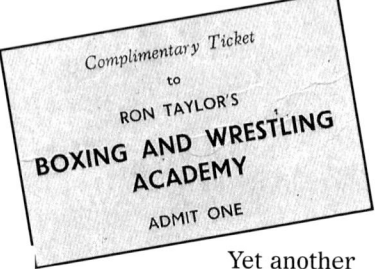

(Photos - Sylvia Pitcher Photo Library)

Johnnie Otis -
A great man in every way

Yet another part of the Soho scene

(Clockwise from top left)
The legendary Muddy Waters
at the 100 Club; Johnny Mars,
one of my regular draws
across four decades; Freddie
King, hot in every sense of
the word; and one of the great
nights as B.B. King jams with
Lowell Fulson

(Photos - Sylvia Pitcher Photo Library)

Johnny Rotten -
once seen never forgotten

Glen Matlock
at the 100 Club Festival

An early Pistols poster.
They were, inded, coming

**SEX PISTOLS
NAG'S HEAD**

LONDON RD. HIGH WYCOMBE

MUSICAL EXPRESS   **TH**URSDAY
                 2ⁿᵈ SEPT

Don't look over your   7 30 /
shoulder, but the Sex   LATE
Pistols are coming   70p IN.

ALSO THE LEGENDARY CBGB BAND

SUBURBAN. STUDS

THURSDAY 9ᵗʰ SEPT - COUNT BISHOPS/
                   60p TEQUILA BROWN
                        Party

(Photos - Michelle Brigandage)

Another of the earliest Pistols promos. The originals are now worth a fortune

Roger Horton and Rosemary, an ex-flame of mine

A modern-day shot of Oxford Street, with the 100 Club sign and the bus stop where Johnny Rotten was dragged away from the number 73

(Photo - Dave Woodhall)

Chris Spedding from the Vibrators (above) at the 100 Club Festival...

...while Siouxsie (left) leads her Banshees in a selection of easy-listening tunes

(*Photos - Michelle Brigandage*)

Mick Jones and Joe Strummer in full flight. Note the slight variations on the 100 Club poster as the week progressed
(*Photo - Michelle Brigandage*)

Where it all began

Damned drummer Rat Scabies...

...and his Transylvanian mate Dave Vanian

(Photos - Michelle Brigandage)

Hail To The Chief

We toured the pub rock circuit, the Hope & Anchor in Islington, the Nashville in Kensington and the 100 Club, although we never played at the Nag's Head. We did lots of college gigs, and had a memorable night in the unlikely surroundings of Swerford, a tiny village just outside Banbury, in Oxfordshire. Dave Gardner was the local promoter and he put us on in the village hall. It was a lovely July evening, the venue was virtually in the shadow of a twelfth century motte and bailey castle and when we arrived I noticed that Dave had several barrels of beers lined up in the kitchen. It turned out that the admission price included free beer; Bob Brunning was in heaven and I wasn't too far away. We all had a good drink that night.

Our roadie for the evening was my wife, Maureen, but she wasn't able to do much lifting because she was pregnant with Stuart, our son. The night turned into one of those magical events that are all the better for being unexpected and unplanned. Dave Kelly was supporting and also sat in with us, a good, appreciative crowd turned up, and with free beer they drank well into the night, helped by the fact that the old lady who lived in the next-door cottage was stone deaf. Blues, boogie and beer in the wilds of deepest Oxfordshire. It was the sort of gig that only Dave would dare to put on, and I was pleased for him that it had been a success.

On another occasion we were playing the 100 Club when a friend of Martin's named Phil Lithman sat in on steel guitar, and stole the show. Phil was a member of the American band the Residents, who defy description, but if I was to say that they attract fans of bands such as Television and Pere Ubu, you might have some idea of where they were coming from. By coincidence, Phil's wife gave birth on the same day as Maureen.

Stuart Watts was born on 5th March 1976. Maureen and I were fine at that point but the marriage had its ups and downs. We were okay when we were okay, but she found it difficult to fit in with my lifestyle. I'd be getting back from a gig at four in the morning and she was having to be up at eight to go to work. It wasn't easy for her.

One night we were due to be playing at the Newlands Tavern, in Peckham. Maureen knew about it, but still arranged for us to go to the wedding of a friend of hers, who was marrying a Tory councillor from Birmingham. I was in the bath when she shouted "You've got ten minutes to get out of there and get dressed. I'm off." It was the great musical ultimatum again – the band or her. She went to the wedding, I went to the gig and had a good night in the wilds of South London, helped by two unexpected arrivals in Chris Trimming and Tom McGuinness. I got back home, which by then was in Stokenchurch, another place close to Wycombe, and the place was deserted. Maureen had returned, taken all her clothes, and gone again. I was on my own for a few weeks, then she came back.

We continued this on-off existence for another couple of years, and found time to conceive our daughter, Marie, who was born in October 1977, but we finally split in 1979. We kept in touch through the children for a while, and some years later Maureen got married to a swimming teacher. I think I saw her the last time I visited Wycombe, but if it was her, she didn't seem in a hurry to say anything.

The Jive Bombers never really finished, they finally fizzled out around the end of 1975, although Martin Stone kept the name going for a few more months with a band featuring Jona Lewie, later of Stop The Cavalry fame. I gave them a few gigs at the 100 Club, including one spot supporting Roogalator, who did their set and then drove over to Camden to headline a late show at Dingwall's. We were all busy – I was promoting, the other guys were doing different projects. No-one said "That's it, we're over," we just stopped performing. There were always plenty of gigs available, but other things got in the way. The two Bobs were doing a lot of work, particularly backing Johnny Mars, while Martin went through a few confusing romantic entanglements. He played with various bands including psychedelic legends the Pink Fairies, then decamped to Paris, where I believe he now runs an antiquarian bookshop and tours the world searching out rare books for clients.

Bob Brunning was a headmaster, Bob Hall a patent agent and the others all had full-time jobs, so we were kept busy. Another problem was that we were spread throughout London and the Home Counties, which added a couple of hours travelling time to gigs. Eventually the band drifted apart. The two Bobs carried on playing together; Bob Hall later joined the Blues Band and Rocket 88, Charlie Watts' part-time blues supergroup that featured at various times the likes of Jack Bruce, Alexis Korner and Ian Stewart, while Bob Brunning is now a promoter, writer and record label owner. The others vanished from sight. I believe Pete went back to New Zealand.

Round about the end of 1975, I decided it was time I brought a bit of stability into the Watts household so I got a job as quality controller with a division of G.D. Searle, the pharmaceutical company who made, amongst other things, contraceptive pills. With this job and promoting the 100 Club, there was no time left for the Jive Bombers, even though the Crown at Marlow had now fallen by the wayside.

For a while I concentrated on the 100 Club, plus the odd gig at High Wycombe Town Hall. As 1975 wound to a close the club was carrying on much as before. I was putting on blues acts, big names such as Freddie King and the one-off Muddy Waters show, plus the British Blues Festivals, and Jim Simpson's American Blues Legends tours. I also inadvertently started working with the Krays.

Sonny Terry and Brownie McGhee were a good draw, two veteran US bluesmen who knew their stuff. Their agent was an East Ender named Harry, who let me have them cheaply. I don't know if he didn't realise how much they were really worth, or if he was doing me a favour, but he gave me some profitable nights. One night after a gig, I was outside the club talking to Harry and he said, "The Krays are behind this." It turned out that although they were doing life for murder and a few other things, they still kept active in the outside world via some of their gang members who had either avoided prison or been released. He also told me a few stories about Ronnie and Reggie, which showed that while they were undoubtedly bad men they also had a charitable side to their natures.

Sonny Terry was blind, but he could always sense when a woman walked into the dressing room. The first thing he'd say to them was, "You got your man with you?" and if they said no, he became very interested. He'd also ask who else was in the room, and I'd pipe up, "Me, you little bugger." You could never leave Sonny alone with a woman, although they could always escape if they wanted to.

Brownie was completely the opposite. Polite, urbane and witty, it was no wonder that the two of them didn't get on, despite making wonderful music together for almost forty years. Beryl Bryden, who was well known on the trad jazz and skiffle scene, would usually come along when the duo played and sit in on washboard. She was a lovely lady, and always welcome.

I fixed a deal with a Swiss promoter whereby he would book American acts for European tours and bring them in through Heathrow, with a day free on arrival and departure for me to use them. James Booker came to us in this way. He was a pianist from New Orleans in the classic tradition of the city and had played with many of the blues and soul greats, such as B.B. King, Aretha Franklin and Little Richard, as well as the Doobie Brothers and Ringo Starr. Good a musician as he was, though, Booker was to prove a real handful. He was very openly gay, which wasn't much of a problem in seventies London, but he'd been in prison for drug possession and often seemed as though he wanted to go back for the same reason.

Piano Red was from Atlanta and played a raggy style of blues that worked well. Tommy Tucker came over regularly with his brother Walt; he was also a pianist. The club had a grand piano installed and that was a big attraction for the piano players. It must have been frustrating for them, as unlike guitarists or horn players they couldn't take their instrument on tour and so had to rely on whatever the venue they were playing could provide. They'd have so much talent and often have to play on some old instrument that was out of tune.

Hail To The Chief

By now the 100 Club was probably the best-known blues venue outside the USA. Some Americans said that they wouldn't dare to visit the clubs in their home town, such as the south side of Chicago, because it was too dangerous, yet thousands of miles from home they were happy to come to the 100 Club. One young man who had visited us and appreciated the music on offer was an American student by the name of Bill Clinton. He told me that he'd felt at home there. I wish I could say that meeting him gave me a sense that here was a man of destiny, but the truth is that he was one of a number of overseas visitors who enjoyed themselves at the club and then went home with some good memories. If I'd known that he would one day be the most powerful man in the world I might have put him on the guest list.

Chapter 13

A Day In The Life

So, what was it like to promote a gig at the world-famous 100 Club? As a bad old joke would say, first catch your band. This wasn't as easy as it sounded; I was always being told about the next big thing by eager management or buttonholed while I was walking around Wycombe by somebody who wanted to tell me about this great band he'd seen in his local, and he usually turned out to be the boyfriend of the guitarist's sister. Usually I stuck to a tried and tested formula for new acts; either I'd rely on word of mouth from people I respected, or else look at reviews in the music press, both at home and in the States. Once I'd decided on a band I'd contact their management to arrange a date. It may sound incredible, but after I'd been promoting at the 100 Club for a couple of years I hardly ever worked with a contract. I was seen as reliable, so it was enough to arrange a date and fee over the phone.

The gig would be agreed and I'd set about advertising it. This was always my weakest spot, as I didn't have the budget to spend a lot on expensive advertisements in the music press and hire prime locations. I'd tour the record shops in central London getting them to display some posters for me, and there'd be a bit of flyposting, although not as much as other promoters did. I'd have a monthly diary advert in the NME and Melody Maker, and for the big gigs I'd put a separate advert in, but other than that I relied on the club's own advertising. The gig was arranged and word was out that it was taking place. All that remained was the day itself.

The music business, as you'd expect, has never been an early riser. I'd get up around ten, which is when phone calls started coming in, then leave the house at about half past one, which is when they stop as that's when everyone's out at lunch. I'd aim to get to the club for around 2.30, by which time the only people who were there were the two cleaners and Mr Chan, the Chinese chef. The cleaners, whose names I never found out, were a couple of twins from Hackney, little fellas who couldn't have been much above five feet tall. They lived in a tower block that was always getting burgled, so the club was a real break from their home lives, even if they never stayed to listen to the music. I'd be sorting the mail and answering calls about that night's gig. It got so that I could always tell within a couple of dozen what the attendance would be, based on how many people rang up to enquire what time the band would be starting and how much it'd cost and what the parking was like and could they eat there and where was a good pub to meet their friends and a hundred other queries. The benchmark was 25 calls. Any more than that and I knew we were in for a good night. If there was less, I wouldn't have a very happy afternoon. I'd never see Roger Horton, who trusted me to run the club on what he regarded as his day off, which I took as a big compliment. It was his club and he was willing to give me the keys and the run of the place.

The band's road crew would begin to arrive at four-ish. They'd turn up at the alley at the back of the club, backing onto Berner's Hotel (and yes, that alley could tell a story or two, but not here, and never involving me), and begin loading the gear. In those days bands tended to travel with their own PA, unlike now, when even pub bands will hire equipment. If they had a tour manager I'd meet him and sort out any problems that might be likely to upset the evening. There rarely were; things were always a lot more relaxed and informal than audiences realised.

I'd have already sorted the furniture to suit the crowd that was expected and the type of band. If I didn't think they would be a big draw there would be plenty of tables and chairs to make the room look less empty, and an acoustic blues singer would always be more likely to want a seated audience than would a rocking r&b band.

With that sorted, I'd take an afternoon stroll around Soho and the West End. Sometimes I'd be distributing posters, other times

A Day In The Life

I'd be eyeing what the competition was up to, or just taking a look at what was going on. There's a lot of waiting around when you're a promoter. You'd wait for the PA to arrive, then the roadies, then the band themselves. You'd be waiting while they set up their equipment and soundchecked. After that you'd wait until the doors opened, and then there was the interminable, nervous, waits while the customers started to arrive - would they turn up? - and before the band started to play – would they be any good? Then at the end of the night, if you were in charge of the venue as I usually was at the 100 Club, you hung around waiting for everyone to clear their gear away so you could finally lock up and go home. I was lucky; at least I could always go off and do something else in the afternoon instead of getting in everyone else's way

The evening's act tended to arrive at about six, maybe earlier if they were performing with a pick-up band and needed time to rehearse. I'd always make sure I was there to welcome them and have everything they wanted, within reason. Some bands would have contract riders calling for bottles of brandy, fine wines, gourmet food and the like. I'd always cross this sort of nonsense out of any contract I signed and tell them that there was beer in the dressing room and, if they were lucky, I'd sort them a Chinese courtesy of the ever-willing Mr Chan, who by now would have his kitchen cooking away and be driving me mad with the wonderful smells coming from there. If I wasn't too busy I'd pop in and watch him as he prepared the meals. Sometimes I'd lay on a spread for a band if they were going to pull in a big crowd and they'd had a long distance to travel, but I wasn't going to comb the West End for beluga caviar and vegan canapés just because some wannabes were trying it on.

The band would usually be ready to soundcheck within half an hour, and this was when I started to enjoy myself. Nobody ever complained about the club's acoustics, unlike some of the supposedly great venues of the country, where the sound was appalling. Occasionally you'd get a roadie coming up with some technical explanation to explain away why his band were getting feedback and echoes, but the amount of drapes the bands were facing meant that if such a problem cropped up, it wasn't our fault. It may have been a sweatbox, it may not have had luxurious dressing rooms, but the 100 Club's sound was as good as you'd get anywhere. In fact, the only venue that came close was some pub in High Wycombe that I'd heard about.

The bar staff would arrive as late as they could, ready for when the doors opened at 7.30. They were the only people I never really got to know, because they were at the club when it was too busy to talk, and as with all bar workers there was a high staff turnover. Once we were ready for business I'd sometimes do the door myself, working in the box office halfway down the stairs. On other nights Maureen would work there, else Shakey Vick or my Wycombe-based helper Bruv, of whom more later, would be on duty. If we were expecting a big crowd one of us, usually me, would stand on the front door to keep an eye out for who was around or to see how the queue was going but we rarely used any security staff until the back end of 1976, when something turned up that meant we had to become more vigilant.

Once the customers started to arrive I'd put some music on. I never bothered with a dj, a record player wired up to the PA from the manager's office was always good enough, provided I remembered to get back every twenty minutes to change it over.

By now I'd be pretty sure of how many people would be in the audience, even if sometimes I wasn't entirely certain that they would have a band to watch. Acts would react in different ways to being in the big city. The Americans would often love being in our "wunnerful city" and go off wandering around London to see Buckingham Palace or the Houses of Parliament, and lose all track of the time. They didn't do it out of malice, they just loved being in London and would inevitably find their way back to Oxford Street without much trouble. Others, though, were a bit more of a problem. You'd often get a band from out in the sticks travelling to the 100 Club, doing their soundcheck and then being let loose for a few hours. With Soho just round the corner they would be like kids in a sweet ship and many's the time I've

A Day In The Life

had to send a road crew to search the bars and strip clubs to find their band and drag them back. Again, though, they weren't being deliberately awkward, they were just doing what young lads invariably do when temptation's placed in their way.

8.30, and the support band begin their set. They'd often be a bunch of unknowns who had impressed me with a demo tape but didn't yet have the following to make it worth my while giving them a headline spot. By now I'd be in the main room, in my usual place against the bar. Yes, it was convenient, but it was also the best spot to watch goings-on all around the club. I could see who was coming down the stairs, who was drinking and what was going on amongst the audience. I also had the best view of the band. In those days I used to drink bottles of Brewmaster, which was quite strong and brewed by Whitbread. I'd have a couple to settle my nerves and then another few to make sure I was enjoying myself as the evening wore on.

The support would do an hour, which was longer than they'd get in most venues, and by now the night was well underway. One night I was watching Caddyshack playing a support slot for Nappy Brown, when Roger turned to me and said, "The future can't be too bad. Just look at these kids, they're great." I looked around and I could see what he meant. The club was full with youngsters enjoying the music, and it was like that most nights.

We were lucky in that we rarely suffered from the sort of problems that Ronnie Scott's, in particular, had to put up with, when tourists and business people turn up because it's the place to be seen in, aren't bothered about the music and talk throughout the gig, spoiling everyone's enjoyment. We'd have regulars, people from the Home Counties coming to London for their big night out, French students, Camden street kids, Japanese tourists, American blues aficionados, all sorts of customers, but the one thing they had in common was that they were there for the music. We helped take people out of their everyday existence and gave them something to remember.

If there were any problems, they tended to be funny rather than violent. One night a tall woman seemingly in her thirties came in. Single women in the club were a rarity, but we didn't take much notice until she walked right into the middle of the dancefloor, took down her dress and knickers, then pissed on the floor. There was obviously something wrong with her, so I rang the police and after giving a description the officer at the other end of the phone said, "That's Julie. Thanks for finding her, we'll send someone round." An ambulance arrived and she was gently led away. While I was cleaning up with a mop and bucket I wasn't very happy, but on reflection you can only feel sorry for someone like that, and thank God that it isn't you.

The headline act would usually finish their set around 11.30, or a bit later if they were going down a storm and doing a few more encores. In the early days the club was licensed to serve drinks until 11.00 but nobody paid much attention, and drinking would carry on until the band finished. After that, the lights would go up and the music stopped. I was never too heavy about clearing the customers out. I wanted them to return and there'd be less chance if they thought they were being pushed around once we'd taken their money.

The band would wind down in the dressing room and eventually leave, as their crew were packing the equipment away. One of the hardest parts of the job was getting roadies out of the club, especially if there was beer and women around. If they were local I'd let them keep the gear in there overnight if it meant getting them away earlier. The bar staff would have cleared up by now and gone off home.

And finally, everyone else who had contributed to the night would have left and I'd be there on my own. The place would look like a bombsite, with rubbish on the floor and drinks spilled everywhere, but I could look around and survey my kingdom. I'd helped hundreds of people to enjoy themselves and had a good night myself. I never got blasé about the fact that I'd been responsible for a night that some of the audience would remember for the rest of their lives. It had taken weeks to pull together, but it had worked and at times like this I realised that I had the best job in the world.

Sometimes Vick and I would go for a Chinese and I'd stay at his place. If Maureen or someone else from Wycombe was with me I could get a lift home. On fewer occasions than you might expect I ended up staying the night with a strange woman. And that was it, another successful night at the 100 Club, courtesy of Ron Watts, that "jovial tub of muscle and lard," as Zigzag magazine once dubbed me.

The live scene for most of 1974 and 1975 was pathetic. Rock'n'roll had started out as a bit of fun, but from roughly the time of the Beatles' Sergeant Pepper album rock music had begun to take itself far too seriously and was now reaching its overblown conclusion in a welter of dry ice and concept triple albums. Jazz rock and bands such as Van der Graaf Generator, a progressive rock band that symbolised the era, were taking up far too much room on the circuit, boring audiences senseless. A band called Frupp, who described themselves as "classically-tinged progressive rock," came over from Ireland and played the Town Hall. I managed to stay awake throughout their set and still regard this as one of the greatest achievements of my career.

Pub rock was fading out, although there were a few r&b bands with a harder edge taking its place. Dr Feelgood had moved onto the concert hall circuit and in their wake were Eddie & the Hot Rods and the Count Bishops, a good band who were always reliable. They shared the same management as Thin Lizzy, but unfortunately only enjoyed a fraction of the success.

I was having to look long and hard to find acts that I liked and getting very disillusioned with the British rock scene. Agents were forever trying to feed me with so much bullshit. Bands demanded massive PAs, light shows, brandy and champagne in the dressing room. They'd want an enormous guest list and then charge exorbitant fees. It would take all day to get their gear into the club and then all night to get it out again after the show. I felt it was going against everything music should be about, although I never thought about packing it in. It was still in my blood and I was going to find a way out of this morass.

The best you could get that was true to the spirit of rock'n'roll were some of the originals themselves. I was bringing over the likes of Charlie Feathers, who had recorded for Sun in the fifties and was the ultimate in authentic rockabilly to the British teds of two decades later. Charlie was a genuine southern redneck from Hollow Springs, Mississippi, and some of the things he and his band said and did were more appropriate for the Deep South than for London. These guys had lived-in faces: I could just imagine them playing a roadhouse in Tennessee on a Saturday night then brawling with the customers.

The whole rock'n'roll thing, though, was still a long way short of what I was looking for. Buddy Knox showed its shortcomings; he'd been performing right from the start – the first rock'n'roller to get a self-penned American number one hit, Paper Doll, which earned him a gold disc, but he wasn't up to much on stage. For all his recording success Buddy sounded like he was fronting a rock'n'roll band in a working mens' club, and that was just the problem. It's a mystery to me why those musicians who'd written the great songs from the early days in the fifties couldn't carry on. Great blues songs have been written for over a century, but all the rock'n'roll classics came from a three or four year period. So the music they played was about youth and vitality, and to hear men who were now in their forties singing about teenage crushes and high school hops was a bit sad, even if the audiences did love it.

Lots of promoters wouldn't touch rock'n'roll because of the reputation of its followers, original teds from Bermondsey or Clapham coming Up West for a night out and a punch-up, or so they thought. In reality, just like every other group with a bad reputation, the teddy boys were perfectly well-behaved and such exotically-named fans as Dixie Fried Dan and Wildcat Pete, who's still going strong as a dj now, remained friends of mine for a long time.

There were others who turned up to the club and weren't so welcome. Liggers were a pain in the arse. We had plenty of famous names – Mick Jagger, Keith Moon, that sort of crowd –

A Day In The Life

who would turn up unannounced, pay their money without complaint and watch the band, but I also had to put up with every kind of demand for preferential treatment and excuse to get in without paying that God ever created. The old cliché of "Don't you know who I am?" must have been invented for the 100 Club, and some of the reasons that punters came up with for trying to avoid parting with the price of admission were worth a novel in their own right. Probably the best was the time Freddie King played during the summer, in the middle of a heatwave, and we were soon full up and turning people away. London was sweltering, it hadn't rained for weeks, and with the club a sweatbox at the best of times I was glad to be at the top of the stairs where the temperature was a bit cooler than it was in the packed main room. This guy came along and said to me, perfectly politely, "Excuse me, I have to go downstairs. I left my umbrella in there last Saturday." I was tempted to let him in for his cheek.

Reggae nights were always the worst for customers trying to get in without paying. Every other punter was the bass player's cousin's boyfriend, or the guitarist's hairdresser's neighbour, or some other such convoluted reason for avoiding having to part with a couple of quid. I think it was probably because the reggae fanbase was such a tight-knit community that the fans thought they were a part of the band, so they should get into every gig for nothing.

We were trying speciality nights – rockabilly, soul, anything that would pull a crowd and entertain the customers. Agencies would give me the first crack at any new blues or soul acts that came along, and that's how I booked Anne Peebles and Betty Wright, a couple of great soul singers.

Betty was a lovely young girl in her mid-twenties, from Florida. I was surprised when she brought her father on tour with her, but Mr Wright soon proved his worth. Not only did he look after his daughter, he made sure her band behaved themselves. They were allowed two drinks each before they played and as much as they wanted afterwards. That way they enjoyed themselves but kept their discipline, enabling them to put on a proper American soul show in all its glory. Not so glorious were East Side Cruisers, made up of members of the former sixties band Love Affair, who pulled in a crowd that could have fitted comfortably onto the stage.

Pete Wingfield was a member of Jellybread, a band of students from Sussex University who released an album on their own Liphook label in 1968 and ran a blues club on the campus in Brighton. Pete also did solo gigs at our British Blues Festivals. He had a similar voice to Otis Span and played piano in an early Chicago style. Pete spent a lot of time at the NBF offices and he would always have a pile of soul albums with him, which he called 'uptown music.' In 1975 he had a hit, 18 With a Bullet, which was mainly bought by black Americans and that was his problem. His style was too black for a white audience and he was too white for a black one. Pete had originally intended to be a diplomat, and although he never sustained his solo success, he stayed in the music business, working with Paul McCartney, Dave Gilmour and Jimmy Page, amongst others. Incidentally, 18 With A Bullet was full of music business in-joke double entendres. I'm sure the only reason it wasn't banned was because nobody except musicians knew what Pete was singing about.

I was getting a reputation for putting on good stuff like this but there was still nothing happening in the rock scene, or at least not on this side of the Atlantic. Then, round about Christmas 1975, I bought my usual copy of Rolling Stone, the American music magazine, and it featured an article on a new phenomenon taking place in New York called 'punk.' In one way it looked horrific, but these bands – Television, the Ramones, Wayne County & the Electric Chairs and others – grabbed my attention and I thought that it wouldn't be too long before they crossed the Atlantic. The article gave a vivid description of the music they were playing and I made a point of listening to any record they'd released that I could get hold of.

Coincidentally, Martin Stone was working with a couple of bands, the London SS and the 101ers. He told me about them and said, "All they want to talk about is clothes." Putting the two

A Day In The Life

strands together I realised that something was going on, and so did a few other promoters. I had a discussion with Dave Robinson at the Hope & Anchor, one of the homes of pub rock, and we both wondered where the kids who used to attend gigs had gone. They weren't coming out anymore, because there was nothing for them. The average audience at a pub gig looked like their dads, so naturally they didn't want to be there. They had to be somewhere, and they had to be attracted back to gigs.

It was while I was puzzling this over that I went to High Wycombe Technical College one night in late February 1976. I had to see the social secretary about a stripper I was getting them for a show and Screaming Lord Sutch was playing, so I popped in to see him. I thought I might watch a decent gig. I didn't think that the evening would change my life.

Chapter 14

New Guitar In Town

What could best be described as a bunch of London scruffs were on the stage. There seemed to be a lot of distraction amongst the audience, which I later found out was some of their friends fighting with the PA guys, but I enjoyed what they were playing. They didn't bowl me over with obvious star potential but I did like their attitude and I found out that they were called the Sex Pistols. I thought that I might find a use for them in the future, although I couldn't imagine at that point how they could pull a decent crowd.

I kept hearing about the Sex Pistols over the next few weeks, as they played a few more pub venues such as the Nashville, and I began to think that these lads were going to cause a stir. Then one day Malcolm McLaren walked into the 100 Club. He was dressed like an Edwardian gent; drainpipe trousers, an ornate waistcoat, long brocade jacket. He certainly made an impression on me, and I like that. I didn't know then that he was in the fashion business, so he had to be seen to dress well. His first words were, "I'm Malcolm McLaren. I manage the Sex Pistols and I want you to put them on here." I shot back, "I'm Ron Watts. I promote at this club and I'll give them a go." I gave the Pistols a residency on Tuesdays, beginning at the end of March. I knew that they'd been banned from almost every other venue in London, but that didn't bother me. I hadn't seen anything at the High Wycombe gig that I didn't think I could handle and I figured that we all have to take risks to get anywhere.

I was looking forward to seeing the first show. The band had improved no end in the few weeks since I'd seen them for the first time and I was knocked out even before they started playing. Rotten had been up to his tricks before he got on stage. He arrived wearing a heavy overcoat, even though it was a boiling hot day, and he still looked cold even then. His first words to me were "Don't you find it a bit frightening having us here?" My reply was "Is there anything that me and my two bouncers can't cope with?"

Johnny was taken aback, and replied, "All right, no need to be like that." That was Rotten all over – he was a bit of a bully. He liked to trade on his scary reputation, but if you stood up to him he backed off. He'd probably only been dealing with college social secretaries and the odd pub promoter whereas I'd been around long enough to know the score and wasn't going to be intimidated by a snotty young lad.

On March 30th there were a few gigs going on in London. John Denver was playing the Palladium and Neil Young was at the Hammersmith Odeon. Elsewhere, Thin Lizzy, Dutch band Focus and prog rockers Camel were touring. At the 100 Club, the Sex Pistols were playing such a low-key gig that most of the music magazines couldn't be bothered to mention it in their listings. The Bromley Contingent were there – Sue Catwoman, Helen the dwarf, Siouxsie, Billy Idol. The rest of the audience was made up of a few hippies, straights, passers-by who wanted to catch whatever was on at the 100 Club and some curious gig-goers wondering what the Sex Pistols were all about. The artist who was to be known as Sid Vicious was there as well. More about him later.

It wasn't a punk crowd as we came to know it and there was no hint of trouble, just a short, blistering set from the Sex Pistols that knocked me out immediately. They were only on for half an hour, and this at a time when some guitar solos went on almost as long, but not a second was wasted. At one point Rotten and Glen Matlock started arguing and Rotten ran off the stage. The story goes that he ended up on Oxford Street and was about to get on a number 73 bus, when McLaren dragged him out of the queue and back into the club. Or was he hailing a taxi, or maybe on his way to Tottenham Court Road tube station? Myths and legends abound about every show the Pistols ever played. McLaren apologised to me after they'd finished for not drawing

New Guitar In Town

much of a crowd, but I wasn't worried. The band were on a percentage of the door money so I wasn't going to lose out, although with a support group and advertising to pay for I wasn't earning much out of them in the beginning. I knew that these things take time, and so it proved. Years later, this gig is still talked about and the BBC recently called it "the night punk began." Not bad considering there were hardly sixty people in the club, including band, PA crew and bar staff.

The Pistols played a dozen Tuesday nights over the next six months. They were getting better and better, they were writing new songs and Rotten was sharpening up his stage persona. I'd thought that this mock-aggression might become boring, but he always did something new every time he performed. I knew him well enough to know it was all an act, but for audiences who'd got used to watching frontmen standing motionless in front of a mike stand for two hours, John seemed the real thing. Some of them really did believe that the band were going to jump off stage and start fighting with the crowd.

The Pistols had to skip some nights because I was honouring existing engagements and they had some gigs already booked. To get round this I began looking for other punk bands, although at this point there was still only the Damned and the Clash, who were an off-shoot of Martin Stone's colleagues, the London SS and the 101ers, and played their first gig in July. Getting bands to support the Pistols was also a problem. I used a couple of rock bands, Krakatoa and Dogwatch, as well as the 101ers, but none of them were too keen on warming up for the ever-growing number of punks that were starting to show. So I was doubly pleased when the Damned came along, because they were at the rehearsal stage and glad of the gigs.

Tuesdays became punk night, and if I couldn't get a punk band I'd put on blues or soul. Major Lance, the great northern soul singer, played a good gig, although I'd dropped the other rock stuff by now. Punk was making it seem even more outdated and boring. Every week we'd get a bigger audience and they were made up of all types. We were getting Chelsea socialites playing at being working-class, tourists and curious music fans. I got used to seeing hippies turning up one week wearing flares and with hair down their backs then the following Tuesday they'd been to the barbers for the first time in years and were wearing leathers and torn trousers.

Amongst the audience were a few who went on to become celebrities in their own right. Shane McGowan was a regular, when he was still a lager-sipping ex-public schoolboy rather than an Irish drunk, Mark Perry, who formed the band ATV and began the Sniffing Glue fanzine, Danny Baker, the writer Robert Elms. Jonathan Ross was a regular, Marianne Faithful was also there most nights, as were the infamous duo from the NME, Tony Parsons and Julie Burchill. She was alright back then, before she cultivated her arrogant attitude. One man who wasn't there was John King, who became famous by writing novels about punk and football hooligans, but his ignorance of the scene at the 100 Club and in his home town of Slough shows him up.

Punk was starting to get noticed in the music press. First it had been ignored, then once it had been noticed, writers began to see that there was a genuine scene taking place underneath their noses and there was naturally a bit of hype as those who were interested started to exaggerate its importance. They spoke of the burgeoning punk scene at a time when there were only about half a dozen bands in existence and two of those, Eddie & the Hot Rods and the Stranglers, had been going since before punk had been thought of. Just how small the movement was in the early days can be summed up by an exchange of letters in the Melody Maker, when one correspondent claimed that he'd seen the Pistols and they'd been awful, then the following week a reply came from someone who stated that the first writer couldn't possibly have been at that particular gig as everyone in the crowd knew each other. But while the punk audience may have been small, it was growing every day.

We continued throughout what was, appropriately, the hottest summer on record. One particular highlight was in August, when a TV crew from New Zealand turned up. They'd been sent

New Guitar In Town

over to cover what was going on in London during the tourist season and had heard about punk. The crew were clever enough to realise that there was a big scene just breaking and came to the club to film what must have been the earliest story of punks in action. Some of their footage later turned up in the Filth & The Fury, Don Letts' film about the Pistols, and I hope they were paid well for their initiative.

Things were also looking up for me back in familiar territory. John Curd had started promoting again regularly at the Nag's Head, but taken the summer off and left Mick Fitzgibbons, the landlord, in the lurch. It's common to stop promoting during this time of the year, when audiences are down because the weather's hot and people are either on holiday or don't want to be indoors, but I think that if a landlord's good enough to let you use his premises you should take the rough with the smooth. I said to Mick, "I want back in. I've got some acts who will pull in bigger crowds than anyone else could get you." He let me book the Pistols in early September, supported by Suburban Studs, from Birmingham. Even though they hadn't pulled off their more notorious publicity stunts by then, the Pistols had been getting steady press throughout the summer and attracted a good crowd. As I expected, the audience was mainly ordinary music fans who were punk-curious, although there were a few punks there. For some reason High Wycombe and Princes Risborough had an element of youth that were into the new scene much earlier than elsewhere outside London and they avoided the more extreme reactions that punks were getting everywhere else.

The Pistols were great, there were no problems and no police in evidence and, after the gig, Mick asked me my intentions towards the Nag's. I told him I wanted to run it again and he agreed, so Mick got rid of John Curd. John was scathing of punk, he didn't like the fact that it had taken off during the summer while he was away, but I was back in sole control of 'my' venue. I started where I left off, booking acts such as Brett Marvin and Johnny Mars, as well as the increasing number of punk bands.

The Damned were the first of that genre to appear after the Pistols, then the Clash followed soon after. When they played the Nag's was about half-full, and most of the audience seemed to be A&R men from record companies. You could tell that they didn't understand the music because they kept asking me what I thought of the band. By the end of 1976 the Nag's had became an almost-exclusively punk venue. I put on Muscles, a funk act who would have sounded good even a few months earlier, but the punks made them sound pedestrian. Then there was Eddie & the Hot Rods, whose influences owed more to the Feelgoods than the Sex Pistols, but did a storming sell-out night at the Nag's when they were on the verge of breaking through.

By now, I was working so hard at promoting that I couldn't do my day job anymore. When I told my manager I was handing in my notice, he said, "I won't try to stop you. You've been so lethargic lately that you'll never make any money." I'd just come to work straight from a Pistols 100 Club gig, and I'd got more money in my back pocket than he earned in a month, so he was wrong there. I saw him a few months later and he said "I saw you on TV. How did you get into that?" He didn't have a clue that I'd been promoting all the time I'd been working for him. It wasn't long after that he got sacked for assaulting one of the women who worked there. I was still with Maureen at this point. Stuart had just been born, but we were never really settled.

That period was typical of one aspect of my life. Most of the time I've got up in the morning to do what I wanted rather than what I had to do. It's enjoyable, but it also distorts your outlook. I'd be in a pub in the evening, having a drink and chatting away to friends, talking about how great things were. I'd forget that next day they'd be stuck inside a factory for eight hours while I might be off to Blackpool singing, or else promoting some big name act in London.

The Pistols were getting bigger by the week. Their audiences were still growing, punk had started to make waves in the national media and it would only be a matter of time before the whole scene exploded out of the 100 Club and into the public's

New Guitar In Town

consciousness. They were getting loads of music press attention, although some magazines were studiously trying to annoy the whole thing, because they knew it would herald the end of everything they held dear. The old guard were clever enough to realise that, if nothing else.

I wanted to broaden the field for the scene so I asked Malcolm McLaren about the idea of a two-day festival. I explained that I was looking for other bands to promote when the Pistols weren't available and that an event like this would kick-start a few more into action. We sorted the date then set about putting a bill together. Malcolm brought in the Buzzcocks, a band from Manchester that had formed after watching the Pistols up there, and Vic Goddard, a regular at the club, put together a band he called Subway Sect. The three originals – the Pistols, Damned and the Clash – were booked straightway. Siouxsie approached me and I said she could play. Malcolm suggested Stinky Toys, who were from France and, in his words, "almost a punk band." Finally I got the Vibrators, a pub rock band moving towards punk, whose name if nothing else looked right and arranged for Chris Spedding to front them for the evening. I knew the festival wouldn't need any real publicity and as soon as it was announced it made the front pages of all the music papers. The phone never stopped ringing until the day it began.

Chapter 15

Helter Skelter

Monday 20th September, 1976. The opening night of the legendary, mythical, infamous 100 Club punk festival. I arrived at lunchtime, a bit earlier than usual, and even then the phones were going mad. The Pistols' regular sound engineer, Dave Goodman, arrived with a bigger PA than we'd normally hire due to the size of the crowd that was expected. The bands started to turn up early. Siouxsie was very nervous, as it was her first show and she hadn't rehearsed properly. She told me the band was called Siouxsie & the Banshees. I liked Siouxsie, she was always straightforward and I looked forward to hearing what she was going to come up with.

The Clash arrived, full of their usual attitude. They'd been around almost from the off, and even before they were formed they'd been in other bands, so they thought they were superior to the rest. They knew how to do it.

Vic and the rest of Subway Sect and Stinky Toys rolled up, from South London and Paris respectively. There were a lot of nerves in the air. For all their bravado, the early punk bands wanted to be successful just like everyone else did and they knew that this was an important day in their lives. Finally, the Pistols turned up and did their soundcheck with as little fuss as always. For all their anarchic image, they were thoroughly professional when they played.

By now there was an air of almost unrestrained excitement. Everyone knew that this was the big one, and everyone involved was buzzing. The press were going mad to get the inside track on the festival, the phone kept ringing and the crowds had been building up from four in the afternoon. Queues were always a problem for us on big nights, as when customers got there early and began to queue outside they blocked the doors of shops in

Oxford Street and the shop owners, who paid a fortune in rent and rates, were unsurprisingly angry. We tried to get out and break the queues up so that the shop doorways were clear, but we weren't always successful. As the Melody Maker put it a week later, in one of the most oft-quoted openings of a gig review ever written: "The 600-strong line that stretched across two blocks was indisputable evidence that a new decade in rock is about to begin." The feeling of outrage and attitude was there; this was what rock'n'roll should be about.

The doors opened at 7.30, and we were full to capacity an hour later. I'd better not say how many we finally let in. I know that I spent a lot of my time trying to get excitable young punks off the grand piano that was always in the club. It was Pete Shelley of the Buzzcocks who spread the story of the piano, making out that I was some old fart who wanted to keep an ancient relic away from the youngsters tearing down the citadels of the old guard. He should have known better. The instrument was worth about £4,000 even back then and had been played by much bigger names than the Buzzcocks – Count Basie and Duke Ellington, for starters. Pete should have realised that punk wasn't the be all and end all of music; it was another link in a chain that stretched back for decades, maybe centuries. The 100 Club piano was a part of that history and damaging it would have been like tearing down a medieval castle to build a football ground.

Unfortunately, a bigger problem soon arose in the familiar shape of one Sidney Vicious. I was on the door when a young girl came running up and told me that Sid was backstage, threatening Stinky Toys' female singer, Elle, with a knife. I had to go and disarm him, and, not for the first time, he promised to behave himself. Two years later, when he was charged with stabbing his girlfriend Nancy Spungsten to death, I looked back to the festival and wonder if what Sid did then wasn't a forerunner of how Nancy ended up.

Subway Sect opened proceedings and they did a decent set, despite having more or less been put together just for the festival. They impressed the Clash's manager, Bernie Rhodes, so much that he booked them to play their forthcoming White Riot tour. Mr Vicious wasn't helping matters, he was winding a few people up again, although even then he was fine with the Clash as their streetwise demeanour scared him a bit.

The Banshees came on but they didn't really play. Sid tapped the drums, which at least kept him out of harm's way for a while, they didn't have a bass player, but the guitarist, Marco Perroni, who went on to play with Adam & the Ants when they were teen superstars, did something vaguely musical. Siouxsie sang the Lord's Prayer mixed with bits of children's songs and Deutschland uber Alles, which wasn't too tactful given her fondness for Nazi imagery at the time, but there was no rhythm, tune or style. It wasn't music so much as performance theatre. Normally I'd have dragged the band off stage and done something myself, but it worked in that they were the real thing, genuine punks doing what they wanted. It was in the spirit of the event. The audience didn't mind too much, they were surprisingly polite about the performance.

The Clash were great that night. They rolled through their set competently and full of energy. The incident which has passed into legend, when Joe Strummer held up a radio to the mike and the audience were treated to a debate on Northern Ireland, came about because of a broken guitar string and showed how professional the band were. Even at that early stage of their life nothing could put the Clash off and I didn't know it at the time, but they would become one of the greatest rock'n'roll bands Britain ever produced. The crowd loved them, from the opening White Riot to the set-closer 1977, as they loved the entire night. They were getting what they wanted. This was the big one, the first day of a new era. Nothing could compare with it either before or since. We were making history, I knew the festival would be big, but I never dreamed that it would go on to become such a legendary event.

It was Siouxsie who said that an estimated 8.7 million people swear to have attended the 100 Club punk festival. The Jam certainly reckon they were there, although I can't say I recognised them. Even Paul Weller would have been just another face in the crowd back then. George Melly was another who claimed to have been in attendance, and if he had he would definitely have stood out. But again, I didn't notice him.

There was a bit of a problem when I told Stinky Toys they couldn't play until the following night because we were running late. Elle went off screaming that she was going to jump underneath a bus if they couldn't go on, but I didn't pay too much attention. It was time for the headline act.

The Pistols put on one of their best-ever performances. "What was it like to see the Pistols in 1976?" is one of those 'wish I had a pound for every time I've been asked it' questions, and the answer is that it was exactly as you'd imagine. Rotten would prowl the stage, insulting, cajoling everyone in the room, his eyes bulging dementedly as he made the audience as much a part of the show as the band. Cook and Jones would be standing behind Johnny, battering away at their instruments, while Glen Matlock always looked a bit bemused at the way punk was exploding all around.

The band had been playing to mixed crowds, and getting mixed responses, but they'd always managed to survive. A couple of weeks earlier there had been a riot in Paris when thousands were locked out of a show, but for much of the time they were playing around Britain to small audiences who had never heard of them and weren't sure how to react to this musical explosion. Now they were back on home turf and they knew they had to deliver. I'd seen them a couple of dozen times but this was the best of the lot. By now they'd written almost all of their classic songs and they ripped through them all. As ever, they played for little more than half an hour but they were in control of everyone in the club from the time they walked on stage until they left. They had a job to do, and they did it. In one night, punk went from an underground cult to a mass movement. You could almost feel the record company A&R men standing outside on Oxford Street, being drawn from all over London by some sixth sense.

Helter Skelter

After the show, when the crowd were making their shell-shocked way home, we were all happy with the way things had gone. Malcolm McLaren was pleased, Vic Goddard would get Subway Sect together permanently, although they never did much sales-wise. Siouxsie had taken her Banshees off to be a proper band, the Clash were ready to move onwards and upwards and Stinky Toys carried on threatening suicide. None of us said much about it but we knew we'd been involved in something more than just a music promotion.

I got to the club early again on the second day. The atmosphere was very similar to the previous afternoon, the bands knowing that they had to do the same as the first night's line-up. Stinky Toys rolled up still alive, much to everyone's disinterest, and Chris Spedding arrived to do his set with the Vibrators, feeling very blasé about the whole event. He'd been a good jazz guitarist and then had a pop hit with Motor Biking, but he knew he was there to get some street cred so he was happy to front one of the bands for the night.

The Damned made their usual shambolic entrance, everyone knew they were signing to Dave Robinson's Stiff Records, which was seen as a home for old pub rockers although they soon began to put out punk releases. There was a bit of rivalry between the Damned and the Pistols, which I never really understood, although the Clash always seemed to be aloof from such matters.

There wasn't such a big crowd as the first night but they were still queuing to get in when we opened the doors. Stinky Toys were the first band up and they weren't particularly memorable. Then came the Damned, and they knew they had to do something special to match what had happened the night before. Always the best musicians of the early bands, they were excelling themselves when Sid Vicious managed to ruin the night by, once again, being an arsehole.

He shouldn't have been there. The Pistols were playing in Bristol and he should have been with them. If he had been, or if I'd just not let him in, it would have saved all of us a huge amount of aggravation. I'd originally banned Sid a few weeks earlier, when he'd attacked Nick Kent of the NME with a bike chain, an incident that had led to him getting the name Vicious. His mother, Anne, came round to see me and begged me to change my mind. "It's all he lives for," she'd pleaded. He'd promised to behave and I, like a fool, let him back. I smiled to myself when I thought about the big, tough Sid having his mummy come round to plead his case, but not for long. I should have realised by then that Sid Vicious was not, nor ever would be, anything to smile about.

I was upstairs on the door with Maureen, The Damned were playing the Stooges' 1970 and sounding good, when Shaky Vic came running up and told me that a girl had been hurt. I raced downstairs and got her up into the alcove of the stairway. Maureen looked at the poor girl's face, which was covered in blood. "I think a chunk of her eye's missing," she said, and I knew then that it was serious. An ambulance arrived to take the girl away and a police van carted Sid off. Caroline Coon, a sixties hippy who had embraced the punk scene eagerly and was covering the gig for the Melody Maker, probably because all their other writers were too frightened, started arguing with the police so they arrested her as well.

A barman later gave a statement saying that Sid had thrown a glass at the stage, it had hit one of the pillars and shattered. The girl had been sitting near the front of the stage and had been hit on the eye with a shard of glass. A group of punks then gave statements contradicting this evidence, but most neutral onlookers were firmly of the opinion that Sid had been the guilty party. He was charged with wounding and remanded in Ashford Detention Centre for a while, although the main charge was later dropped and he was fined for possession of a knife. Not that I was bothered about what happened to him. A girl had been blinded in one eye at one of my promotions. She'd gone out to enjoy herself one night and been seriously injured. It was the worst moment of my career, and all because Sid Vicious was an idiot who just had to pretend to be a big man.

The Damned carried on playing, they didn't realise what had happened until they finished their set, although the crowd had been affected by the incident. Then the Vibrators, who were only really there by default because there weren't enough real punk bands I could have booked. I liked them, and I'd booked them for the club before, when they were still an r&b band.

They'd been the first of the old school to see which way the wind was blowing and become punks. That they put out a single called Pogo Dancing and were the first punk band to get Radio One airplay, with a piece of forgettable pop called Baby Baby, says everything about the Vibrators. The real punks didn't really take to the band, but they had their moment in the sun and can't complain. Not only did they attend the 100 Club punk festival for real, but they played it. In fact, some of their set turned up many years later on a live album, and that remains the only part of the event to ever get a proper release. Chris Spedding, for his part, must have liked what he'd seen over the two nights because he produced some of the Pistols' early sessions and was rumoured to have played guitar on their records, although that story had no foundation.

The Buzzcocks finished the night, and the festival, off with their songs of teen angst, which were probably more relevant to the majority of the audience than the Clash's revolutionary stance the previous night had been. I hadn't seen the Buzzcocks before, and they weren't up to the standard of the London bands. They'd only been together for a few weeks so hadn't had much chance to get their act sorted, but I could tell that they were going to get better. They went down alright, but a bit of antagonism had grown between some London punks and a few of the lads who'd travelled down from Manchester with the band, and the Sid episode hadn't helped the situation between them. A couple of scuffles broke out and we had to throw some Manchester lads out, but no sooner had we put them into Oxford Street than they were back inside and starting again.

After the glassing incident I was so upset that I couldn't say a word all the way home, then the following day Roger Horton told me that he wouldn't allow any more punk bands at the club. I agreed with him; if this was going to be what punk was getting like, I didn't want any part of it so I scrapped the Pistols' residency and cancelled gigs by the Clash and the Damned which had been booked. Everything I'd been building all that summer was gone. I'd still got the Nag's, but I'd lost the 100 Club just as it was starting to take off. All my hard work had been destroyed thanks to Sid Vicious.

The mother of the girl, who we later found out was a Belgian student, came up from Cornwall to see Roger. She was beside herself with anger and grief at her beautiful daughter being hurt in such a way, and Roger was deeply upset. He tried to explain that what had happened wasn't the fault of the club, or of punk, but was just down to one idiot. The Damned later did a benefit gig, but she vanished after that and has never re-appeared since. In any case no-one knew what to say to her, although in one instance 'sorry' would have been a start.

Chapter 16

Complete Control

The festival had put paid to regular punk at the 100 Club, but there was still plenty going on elsewhere in my life and not all of it had spiky hair. The Nag's Head was doing well and I was putting bands on at High Wycombe Town Hall. Punk had exploded out of nowhere at just the right time and, despite the best endeavours of media and politicians, it was getting bigger by the week and refreshing the entire music scene. New bands were forming almost every day and I was putting them on in Wycombe as quickly as they were getting gigs in the capital.

I was still promoting at the 100 Club, putting on blues acts and the closest I could get to punk. I did a gig with my old pub rock buddy Nick Lowe, who had released So It Goes, the first record on Stiff, and the Yachts, from Liverpool. I put the Jam on, first in support slots and then headlining. I could also get away with booking the Vibrators and Little Bob Story, a French band who were of a similar style. Then I booked the Stranglers, but there was another fight when their number one fan, Dagenham Dave, tried to stop some of their new followers from dancing and got beaten up.

After that, I more or less gave punk a wide berth for a few months. I carried on promoting the British Blues Festivals, usually featuring Jo-Ann Kelly or Brett Marvin as headliners, and put together a version of Brewer's Droop to appear down the bill a couple of times. The same acts also performed what I billed as Studio 51 Revisited nights, remembering Ken Colyer's club where Brett and his band used to perform on Sundays. We had a bonus when Dr Feelgood played two nights as a warm-up for a British tour where they sold out the Hammersmith Odeon twice over. Those gigs, to put it mildly, were a bit warm as the Feelgoods took the opportunity to introduce their new guitarist,

Gypsy Mayo, who had taken over from Wilko Johnson. Roogalator, a pub rock band finding themselves in the right place at the wrong time, headlined a few shows for me, and although they were competent enough, as with all pub rock bands by then their music sounded dated compared to what was happening elsewhere.

The newspapers of the time were full of supposed riots between punks and teddy boys, in the style of the mods and rockers fights of the sixties. I had to smile when I read about the alleged violence on Kings Road and Sloane Square, as one of my biggest acts during 1977 were the rock'n'roll revivalists Darts, playing at the birthplace of punk. Their support band one night was the Stukas, who were a new wave band, the label being used to get punk away from the negative connotations that the music was being associated with.

I was also putting some good reggae bands into the club. It wasn't really my type of music but it kept the audiences happy and I was alert enough to recognise the ability of Steel Pulse on the night they supported Matumbi. They were clearly talented and I wasn't surprised when they got into the charts before the year's end.

On other nights, though, the club was getting quieter by the week. Trad jazz, which had always been its mainstay, was fading. The audiences were getting older and sometimes they'd be falling asleep while the bands were on. One night I was in there and Roger Horton asked me into his office. He was on the phone to his partner, Ted Morton, a big, bearded guy who didn't have much to do with the club, and who I rarely saw. Roger came off the phone and got straight down to business. "Ron, these bands you're putting on at Wycombe. Would they make money here?" I told him that they would, and he asked me to get on with booking them. I had an open invitation to put on as much punk as I liked and by the end of summer 1977 we were back in business. Once word got round that I was promoting punk at the 100 Club again, the floodgates opened. I started off with XTC, a new wave band from Swindon who I knew wouldn't give us any problems,

Complete Control

and the club was packed out to see them. Everyone enjoyed themselves, Roger was happy, and I don't think my phone stopped ringing until the end of 1979.

By now other venues had started jumping on the punk bandwagon. In January 1977 the Roxy opened in Neal Street, WC2, not far away from the 100 Club, and when it closed down a few months later was followed by the Vortex in Wardour Street. I wasn't particularly bothered about these venues taking away the audience that I'd created. I was doing enough punk in High Wycombe to keep me busy, and anyway, the scene in London was becoming far too violent. There were always a few who thought that being outrageous made you a punk, when in fact it was the other way round. Punk was about what was in your mind, not how many bus shelters you could destroy.

I could never understand what happened with the Roxy. They opened after Anarchy In The UK had been released and closed as a full-time venue before God Save The Queen came out. Whatever the promoters were up to, they didn't believe in hanging around although I did hear that they'd been stitched up when they opened and had to pay a fortune in rent, far more than they could ever hope to get back in takings. The time when they were robbed by two men pretending to be detectives wouldn't have helped their cashflow. As for the Vortex, the Jam got it right in their song A Bomb In Wardour Street.

I'd kept my regular nights at the Nag's and it became one of the main punk venues in the country. The Clash played there for a while before they got too big, the Damned came along and played when New Rose, their debut and the first UK punk single, had just come out. As you can imagine, that was a busy night. Little Bob Story pulled a good crowd, and everyone enjoyed them.

One of the highlights of the time was the New York weekend we put on in March. Cherry Vanilla, who had been David Bowie's publicist then made a couple of albums herself, headlined on the Friday. She asked for a private bedroom because she was feeling tired, so the landlord lent her one of his – which wasn't the sort of thing you'd normally get at a venue. She came out of there a few hours later full of herself and put on a great show, which was made more memorable as she was backed by an early incarnation of the Police, who had also played support. Looking back, I wonder if she'd wanted a private room because she was shooting up.

I should have realised what the Americans were up to by the state of the previous night's headliners. Johnny Thunders and the Heartbreakers couldn't have been anything except a New York punk band. They'd played on the Pistols Anarchy tour, or what was left of it after the police and outraged local councillors banned most of the dates, they were dressed in black leather and chains and they were into serious heroin usage. They were also possibly the best band I've ever seen, going right back to the rock'n'roll acts of the fifties. Tight, melodic, energetic, and Thunders fronted them like a dream. The room was packed and the band was brilliant. All the doubts I'd had about the music business collapsing were being proved wrong on nights like this.

Then on Sunday we had the climax of the festivities, courtesy of the infamous Wayne County & the Electric Chairs. Wayne was already a legendary figure in New York, a transvestite who was on his way to becoming a fully-fledged transsexual. I loved the outrage that followed such a character, but underneath it all he was a nice guy. He told me some of the most amazing stories about people on the scene in the States – and as some of the main characters are still alive, they still can't be repeated - then showed me how to turn man boobs into a proper cleavage with the aid of appropriately placed sticky tape. He came on in his Trash Queen persona, covered in dustbin rubbish, and the crowd loved him. Wayne moved to London and I was happy to book him again. Even though his music wasn't all that good he knew how to entertain, and that's all I ever wanted from my acts. Keep the customers happy and you'll always have an audience.

I was knocked out to have brought over the best of the New York scene that had first alerted me to punk. They were so different to what was happening in Britain; our bands were all

Complete Control

pretty much the same at this point, while over there the word 'punk' was a much wider term. As for the stars of the show, Cherry is now in her sixties and living in California, Johnny Thunders died of a suspected heroin overdose in 1991, at the age of 38, and as for Wayne County, well, Jayne County still tours so you can guess what he evolved into.

The Buzzcocks came down regularly from Manchester and were better every time I saw them. The Stranglers, who I'd known for a long time on the pub scene and who had played with the Jive Bombers a year or two earlier at the Roundhouse, had become punks. That was a bit of blatant bandwagon jumping because Jet Black, their drummer, was well into his thirties and the rest of the band hardly fitted the image with their long hair and moustaches. Their music was hardly punk either, with an obvious r&b influence, long keyboard solos and lyrics that the more politically aware punks decried as sexist. But they knew their stuff and I would book them willingly, knowing that they'd pack the place out and send everyone home happy. Midway through the summer of 1977 they got into the charts with Peaches and that was the last I saw of them. Yet again I'd nurtured an act that had outgrown my venues.

Another band causing a bit of a stir were from Surrey. John Weller had introduced himself to me at the 100 Club one night and told me that he was managing a band called the Jam, who his son, Paul, was singing with. We got on well and I agreed to give them a support date a few weeks later, to see how they coped. They coped well enough for me to give them a headline spot as soon as I could. A few days later they were playing Upstairs at Ronnie Scott's, which was, as you could imagine, the smaller, first floor part of the famous jazz venue in Frith Street, not far from the 100 Club. Maureen and I would often visit the upstairs room after a night at the 100 Club and we'd usually be on the guest list. We'd found a way of sneaking down the back stairs and into the main room, which meant we could see some fine jazz musicians as well as sample the chicken kiev they served which we both liked.

On the night the Jam played we stayed upstairs and at one point in their set Paul Weller kicked in a television set. After the gig the fanzine Sniffin' Glue said, "Will Ron Watts book this band now?" I certainly did, and I was glad that I'd had the opportunity. Here was a band whose mixture of original material and soul standards helped them stand out from the crowd right from the beginning. They returned a fortnight later and I soon got them headlining the circuit of 100 Club, Nag's Head, and then the Town Hall. In fact, they recorded one of their 100 Club gigs for a proposed live album and although that never came off, some of the tracks were later released on the 'b' side of their Modern World single. A year later, by which time they'd released two albums and started to get into the charts, the Jam returned to play the 100 Club for me in between the Hammersmith Odeon and touring the USA. I didn't have to advertise – it sold out totally by word of mouth. They always said that they'd return to play for me when they made it big, and give them their due, they did.

Punk wasn't all about excitement and interesting music. Skrewdriver came to play the Nag's in July 1977. They hailed from Blackpool and were a rock band who'd got into punk because that was the future, or the way to earn a fast buck, depending on your point of view. They played an instantly forgettable set in front of an audience who had learned to sort the punks from the posers and I didn't bother asking them if they fancied a repeat engagement. That was the last I heard of Skrewdriver until a few years later when, riding yet another bandwagon, they re-emerged as a neo-Nazi skinhead band. Luckily they were the only band of that ilk who I booked and an enjoyable gig a week later by those rapidly-emerging legends of the Thames Valley, John Otway & Wild Willy Barrett, put me in a better mood.

Sham 69 gave me another memorable evening. Their audience was a bit different from the usual punks, being made up of a lot of the skinheads who were starting to make a re-emergence. The first time they played the 100 Club was in the autumn of 1977, once I'd made sure that we wouldn't have any resurgence of the violence that had dogged us the previous year. I had Eric, my usual Barbadian bouncer, plus half a dozen of his mates from Harlesden working. I pulled in a rugby team to help out, and there was also Shakey Vick and a guy from Wycombe named Steve Sawney, who we called Bruv. His father owned a garage and Steve had been into punk from the start. He became my assistant, delivering posters, getting me home when I was drunk and running gigs if I was busy elsewhere. Steve and I both loved fishing, and it was a regular occurrence for us to be out until the early hours with the Jam or someone of that ilk blasting our eardrums, then get up at the crack of dawn a few hours later to fish one of the quieter reaches of the Thames.

If Bruv was my right-hand man, then another Steve, Jones, was my left hand. He had the same name as the Pistols guitarist but the similarities ended there. My Steve was openly gay, and a nice lad. He kept the local bands from the Wycombe area in order and drove them to gigs that they couldn't get to themselves. Steve became a fashion designer and now makes some of the most exclusive hats in the world, for the likes of Madonna, Kylie Minogue and Mick Jagger.

The place wasn't packed out on the night Sham played, because I didn't want it so full that I couldn't handle anything that might happen. There were a few disappointed punks outside and when Jimmy Pursey, the band's singer, popped out for a breath of air they asked if he could get them in. He looked at the crowd, looked at the size of the two guys who were on the street barring their entrance and said "Sorry lads, I'll be lucky if I can get back in there myself." But it was a quiet night, no trouble, and again everyone was happy, even though I'd been on the balls of my feet all the time, waiting for something to kick off. Another band had shown that they were headed for the top.

Punk was getting bigger and more diverse by the week. We never thought it would get that big, and now it had, we never thought it would end. Professionally, it was the best time of my life. Maureen and I continued on and off throughout the year but if she wasn't around there was always some willing punkette to spend the night with. In every way imaginable it was Christmas seven days a week. I'm often asked what the gigs were like, and the questioner is usually amazed when I say that I can't remember most of them.

There were some that stood out for one reason or another; the festival, Sham 69 or the Jam, but most blended into one mad, adrenalin-fuelled rush. Things that would have made front-page headlines in most towns were everyday occurrences on Oxford Street and London Road throughout 1977, and I got blasé about the whole thing very quickly. Seeing the Clash play at the 100 Club might have been one of the highlights of your life if you were in the audience, but for me it was just another day at the office. Like a top footballer who plays so many big games he can't recall one cup final from the next, I can't remember if it was Billy Idol who was dragged into the audience one night or TV Smith of the Adverts, whether someone spilt their head open diving off the stage when 999 were playing, or if it was during a Siouxsie & the Banshees gig.

People, and in particular the sort of people who write for newspapers, would turn up looking for outrage, but they were usually disappointed. There were no orgies, very little drug taking, few fights. For the most part, customers at my promotions during punk's glory days were exactly the same as they were at any other time. A group of youngsters enjoying themselves, having a drink and dancing. If they wanted sex, Soho was just around the corner from the 100 Club and, as for violence, there were probably more fights every week in the ordinary pubs of High Wycombe than in the two years I promoted punk. But 'Group Of Young People Listen To Loud Music Then Go Home' wouldn't sell many papers. In the same way, a lot was made of Eater and their 14 year-old drummer, Dee Generate. Young Dee, or to give him the name he was born with, Rodger Bullen, was described as a typical example of the way punk was breaking up the family unit. Nobody pointed out that his dad used to take him to gigs and help set up his drum kit, and I wasn't going to tell

Complete Control

them. After all, when you're 14 you wouldn't thank anyone for informing the world that your dad drives you everywhere.

One afternoon I was in the club sorting things out for the night's gig when a group of Japanese tourists came bursting down the stairs, taking photos of everything in sight. Tourists could be a pain at times but we knew that if we were friendly to them they'd more than likely turn up at night when they had to pay to get in, so they were tolerated if the band weren't setting up and if they kept out of our way. One of them asked me who I was, and when I said "Ron Watts" they all screamed "Ahhhh, Sex Pistols!" They were beside themselves; the Japanese are famed for not showing any emotion, but in my experience once they like you, they're devoted. Crack the Japanese market and you're set for life; they're the most passionate fans a band could wish for. Unfortunately, I couldn't imagine any of the bands I was ever involved with going down well in Japan, although the Brewer's Droop album that Mark Knopfler played on sold in large numbers over there, much good it did me.

One man who didn't like the way things were going was the Stranglers' biggest fan, a guy from Manchester named Dave, who they called Dagenham because he used to work at the Ford plant there. Dave had been with the band from their early days and as they got bigger he couldn't handle the fact that he was having to share them with other people. One night at the 100 Club he flipped and started a fight with their new fans, who were called the Finchley Boys, trying to stop them from dancing. His girlfriend left him and he killed himself in February 1977 by jumping off Tower Bridge. It was a sad end and the band commemorated the story in the song Dagenham Dave on their No More Heroes album which came out at the end of the year.

By now the press were in full flood, falling over themselves to get the inside track on this strange new sensation that was eating up the kids, as one columnist put it. They'd looked down their noses at punk at the start, thinking it would be forgotten within a few weeks, so now they were having to catch up. The Pistols began the phenomenon with the Bill Grundy incident, when they'd sworn live on prime-time TV, and since then they'd been fired by EMI, signed for A&M, been fired again a fortnight later and created all sorts of headlines, many of which had been carefully manipulated by Malcolm McLaren.

The tabloids were trying to create more headlines alongside the Filth and the Fury stuff that had accompanied the Grundy story. By now, punk had broken out of London. At times it seemed as though everyone under the age of 25 in High Wycombe was a punk. There was a wall running from the town hall to the High Street where the local kids would hang out. It was a well-known place to score drugs so it became known as the Wall of Dreams. By the middle of 1977 the hippies had vanished and the wall was almost exclusively colonised by punks.

One guy who wasn't punk, but typified the way in which the movement had opened doors for new talent, was Elvis Costello. He played the Nag's in July 1977. His first album, My Aim Is True, had been released the week before and had caused such a buzz that he broke the house record, giving us one of our best-ever gigs. A full house, a great musician, with everyone in the audience knowing that he was destined for better things and they'd soon be able to boast that they'd seen him playing in a pub. It was the sort of night promoters dream about.

Things were different in London, though. The high profile that punk had gained in the media had inevitably led to a backlash and a lot of punks were attacked, Johnny Rotten and Steve Jones amongst them. The tabloids were building up a war between punks and teddy boys along the lines of mods and rockers a decade earlier, but punks were never violent people. Despite their intimidating image, most just wanted to be left to live their lives in peace, although the world wouldn't let them. It makes me smile now to think how much punk was seen as a threat to society back then and how much it ended up giving to society in terms of the freedom of self-expression and fashion which is still being felt today.

Chapter 17

God Save The Queen

1977 continued at a hectic pace. I was doing 18 hour days and, though the music was great, it could be a bit much. There would be on average fifty letters to answer, tapes to listen to, constant phone calls, a gig most nights, either promoting or occasionally watching a new band. One week I had a rare Saturday night off and it was all I could do to walk round to the local chippy for chicken and chips, then sit at home watching television and drinking a couple of beers, happy to be on my own.

On the 7th June 1977 I was living alone, despite Maureen being heavily pregnant with our second child. I saw her in the street and commented, "Me and Bruv are off on a boat trip this afternoon." She replied, "I don't know why you're involved with all that punk stuff," to which I said, "They're my babies. I'm looking after them."

Late that afternoon we boarded a boat at Westminster Pier. I didn't notice many press on board, just a couple from the music papers, but it was mostly close friends of the bands. Some of the Bromley contingent were there, as were Chrissie Hynde, Billy Idol and Jordan, who worked in McLaren's boutique and had begun managing Adam & the Ants. Also in attendance and looking out of place was Richard Branson, whose Virgin label had just signed the Pistols. I deliberately sat next to my old adversary Sid Vicious, who was now a fully-fledged member of the band, having replaced Glen Matlock on bass the previous February despite the fact that he couldn't play a note. He was now shacked up with Nancy Spungsten and I chatted as amicably as I could, asking them both how they were. This was the last time I ever spoke to Sid.

He got up and went with the rest of the band to the back of the boat, where they began to play. We'd gone well beyond the Pool of London and out towards the docks, then turned round as the band started up. By the time we reached Parliament they were into God Save The Queen, which was their new single, out on Virgin after A&M had refused to press it. I didn't see what was going on, but the captain of the boat must have called the police. Despite what was said late I don't think Malcolm McLaren put the captain up to it; he didn't need to. By this time the Pistols were front-page news without any prompting from their management. It's my belief that the captain was freaked out by the whole thing and radioed for help.

The power was cut, forcing the band to stop playing. I noticed one police boat, then eventually four, at a distance at first then pulling up alongside us and forcing us to head for the shore. It was all done very professionally and I couldn't help thinking that they'd obviously rehearsed this manoeuvre ready for when they had to deal with the type of high-level criminals they obviously believed us to be.

The bar had been closed by now, but it had been in full swing for hours so as we were filing off the boat with yet more police guarding the quay, the inevitable happened. McLaren, who was a few feet away from me, shouted "Fascist pigs!" and an inspector ordered his arrest. This led to a lot of pushing and shoving, with no-one really knowing what was going on, but when everything calmed down there had been ten arrests made, including McLaren's partner Vivienne Westwood and the Pistols' art designer Jamie Reid.

I was probably the oldest one there, almost certainly the soberest, and everyone turned to me for guidance. "Okay," I said. "I'll do what I can." And I did. I went to find a pub.

I contacted the Fleet Street boys, so that whatever happened, the arrests were well-known enough to ensure that no harm came to the miscreants and we trooped into an eerily-deserted pub. Those arrested were held for a couple of hours, and I think that in the end Malcolm was fined £20 for insulting behaviour. It was all a big fuss over nothing, but the tabloids had their headlines, another fire of moral outrage was fuelled and the public

God Save The Queen

got their ration of scandal. Just another day at the office, but it was to prove the last time I ever saw the Pistols play live.

By now they were banned throughout the country so they did what became known as their secret SPOTS tour, although they only played one gig under that name. This was to have one amusing side-effect, as by now Brent Marvin & the Thunderbolts, wanting a change of image, had changed their name to the Blimps. Due to a cock-up somewhere along the line the posters for their forthcoming Nag's gig had them billed as the Bumps, which sounded enough like Spots for someone to put two and two together, add the name Ron Watts as the hidden factor, and spread the word that the Pistols, the biggest band in the country, would be playing a pub in High Wycombe. I was a bit confused when loads of heavy-duty punks turned up to watch a blues band, but they enjoyed themselves once they found out that they weren't going to be watching the Pistols and it just showed how volatile the punk phenomenon was becoming. The slightest thing would set it off.

As for the real Sex Pistols, the rest of their story is well-documented. They released a couple more records, courted a bit more notoriety with the album Never Mind The Bollocks, went off to America and imploded. Apart from a few court cases and the farcical Great Rock'n'Roll Swindle episode (I'm in the film, in the bit about the boat trip), that was the last anyone saw of them for almost twenty years, but in the short time I'd known them they'd changed the music scene forever.

I was promoting virtually the same acts at the club as at the Nag's, or sometimes the Town Hall. By now a lot of the bands had outgrown other pub venues but continued to use the Nag's as a warm-up for bigger tours. There was a bit of jealousy from promoters who wanted to know why bands were playing for me and not them, but I'd been the one to take a gamble on these lads when they were unknowns so it was only fair that I should get some rewards. My biggest worry was that with hundreds pogoing away upstairs, the floor of the Nag's would collapse and the audience would end up on the billiard table in the bar. Not that there was much chance of it happening – the building was structurally sound and the place was safe for live music. Some unscrupulous promoters and venue owners would cut corners and have dangerous wiring or inadequate exits – there was one place in Sawbridgeworth where anyone using the toilets had to walk through the band - but I always ensured that every venue I used was checked over thoroughly.

The Stiffs Live Stiffs tour opened at the Town Hall. What a night that was, and I'd like to set the record straight about it. In his book about pub rock No Sleep Till Canvey Island, Will Birch quotes the Stiff publicist Paul Conroy as saying that I was complaining about the size of the guest list, and referred to me as having "been doing the local Nag's Head," intimating that I was out of my depth promoting their tour. I'll admit that I wasn't happy at the sight of dozens of Stiff employees, journalists and hangers-on demanding free entrance and eating into my takings, but I'd worked with bigger and better artistes than Elvis Costello and Ian Dury, good as they were.

Chelsea performed at the Town Hall, which was a big venue for a band who hadn't created much press attention, and like one or two others they'd have been better off playing the Nag's but they probably thought a pub venue was beneath them. Their singer, Gene October, had been around the punk scene almost from the start and I'd never met anyone so desperate to be a star. He'd have done anything to be famous, but despite an appearance in the cult film Jubilee he never got any bigger than singing in a band that did the circuit for a few years without ever having much success.

The Damned came over and played regularly, as did a new band called Adam & the Ants, who were causing a stir with a stage show that had a heavy emphasis on sex. The Tom Robinson Band did a lot of business throughout the year as well. When he first got airtime in America, Tom would always say, "I'm big in High Wycombe." He was a lovely guy and always put on a good show. One of the most memorable events of the year took place at the 100 Club when Tom headlined, with Glen

Matlock's new band, Rich Kids, supporting. One of the hottest new acts of the time backed by someone who had just left the most notorious band in the world. These days it would have filled any venue in London, but in 1977 it seemed entirely natural that they chose the 100 Club, and they gave us yet another packed-out night to remember.

The success Tom got towards the end of the year with 2-4-6-8 Motorway was well-deserved and he moved onto the big Odeon-type venues for a while, although I still wonder whether he was quite as he made out. Tom was one of the first openly gay men on the music scene and his song Glad To Be Gay was released on the follow-up E.P. to 2-4-6-8 Motorway, but I wasn't sure whether that was just to cause a reaction. He certainly used to mention girls a lot.

Motorhead came along at the same time as punk, which was fair enough as you couldn't separate them in either attitude or musical ability from bands with a lot less hair. They were loud, they were fast and they didn't take it seriously. Lemmy's always been an entertainer, laughing up his sleeve as he gives the audience exactly what they want. Over a period of thirty years they've gone from playing the Nag's and similar venues to sell-out tours, Top of the Pops appearances, chart hits, and almost back to where they started out and they're still performing exactly the same kind of stuff now that they were then.

Not only did we put on the big names, there were also a lot of local groups starting out at the time. Most have been forgotten over the years, but they will all remember their part in a musical revolution. I was also in another band myself, called the Zoots. We did a few gigs, places such as the Nashville and around the Wycombe area, playing the sort of blues that had always been my first love and enjoying ourselves. It made a change from the heavy-duty punk I was involved with.

Talking of heavy duty, I was convinced around this time that Special Branch were taking an unhealthy interest in the main punk faces. One Sunday morning I woke up at home next to a young punk girl and could hear amplified voices coming from the timber yard next door. I heard one of them say "He got in early this morning with some young blonde" and was horrified to realise that they were talking about me. I can only assume that I was under some kind of surveillance and that their radios were playing over a loudspeaker somewhere. Maybe the powers-that-be thought that Malcolm McLaren and I were plotting to overthrow the government.

Maybe they were controlling the media as well. From the 100 Club festival until the Pistols went off to the States, my profile was higher than it had ever been. The press were approaching me from all angles every time there was a story even vaguely connected to punk, but I was rarely interested. The music press were usually okay, though news reporters were always looking for something sensational to fill their empty pages and punk was providing it. Janet Street-Porter came down to interview me for her television programme one morning. Unfortunately for both of us it was way too early to get any sense out of me, so she probably went away with an image of punk that wasn't strictly true. I'm sure that if I'd wanted to I could have been as big a name in 1977 as McLaren, but I never wanted to go down that route. I usually kept as quiet as I could, although when I had a gig that needed publicising I could invariably find a way of getting my name into the spotlight.

Once or twice I was asked if I fancied doing a radio show. I might have been able to make a career out of broadcasting, and it would have been less traumatic than promoting, but I didn't have the time to get involved. Besides, all they wanted me to play was punk, and at that time there weren't many punk records out so I would have had to work hard to fill a show. I could have done a blues programme, but punk was the only thing that mattered. Once the bands started recording I built up a decent enough collection to do a programme, although one by one they vanished, either given away or borrowed, never to return. I treated my early rock'n'roll and r&b stuff as though they were tablets of stone handed to me by Moses, whereas I never thought of the early punk recordings as anything special.

God Save The Queen

The music was great while the records themselves were disposable, in keeping with the spirit of the time. If only I'd been a bit more careful. Copes of that Holy Grail of record collecting, the A&M recording of God Save The Queen, went through my hands more than once. Last time I heard, one of them had been sold for over £12,000.

I wonder if the people who were frightened by punk ever realised how wrong they were. It was a movement led by a group of middle-class art students and at its height there were probably less than ten thousand punks in the country, most of them living with their parents. It was hardly the stuff of which revolutions are made. Councillors would ban gigs without realising how stupid they looked and how fascistic they were behaving. How can you ban art? What comes next; throwing people into prison because of their clothes? They'd ban gigs because they said they were safeguarding the morals of their area. Look, for example, at Birmingham, where the Clash were banned from playing anywhere in the city. If they had played one night, the band would have arrived in the afternoon, performed, and everyone would have gone home by midnight, but punk was regarded as the corruptor of the nation and the citizens of Birmingham had to be protected from it.

Meanwhile, all over the city that evening, men were beating up their wives, people were being mugged and innocent victims attacked by drunks who couldn't have a night out without starting a fight. But the city council could assure their voters that everything was fine, the good people of Birmingham were being looked after, and they got their names in the papers. Which was the main thing.

As the year came to an end I was busier than I'd ever been. I'd be putting on five or six gigs a week and I don't think any club promoter has ever booked such a wide range of acts. One night it would be John Steven's Away, a jazz-rock band who played the Nag's for me a few times. The next night would be the 100 Club and Jah Woosh, one of a number of Jamaican reggae artistes brought to Britain by producer Adrian Sherwood, who I'd helped get gigs for his acts. Then I'd have 999 at the Nag's again, the following evening would be some old blues legend such as Piano Red at the 100 Club and then Generation X at the Town Hall. A couple of days break and I'd be off again. It was hectic, it was worrying and it was the best time any promoter could wish for. I was in the enviable position of not having enough venues for the bands who wanted me to book them. As an aside, Generation X were once supported at the Nag's by a band called Deathwish, whose roadie was Dylan Jones, a regular at all my venues who later went on to be a successful writer and editor of GQ magazine. Yet another example of the talent that lay behind the 'foul-mouthed yobs' of punk.

1977 had been a miracle of promotion. I could imagine young kids all over the country cutting their hair, learning three chords and getting their moment of glory at the local youth club or village hall. It was like a summer storm – everything had been getting unbearably heavy, then we had a few splatters of rain, a sudden deluge that ended as quickly as it began and the sun came out again with everything freshened up. Punk wasn't just about forming bands, it was independent record labels, fanzines, the whole do-it-yourself ethic that had permeated the best music since rock'n'roll had begun. Punk just did it better and the effects have lasted longer. Even now there are publishing houses, record companies and fashion labels that have got the punk spirit. Punk was more than just a change in music and fashion; it was a watershed in my life. It seems as though it happened yesterday, although everything before it seems so long ago. An album from 1975 will seem old to me, while one from 1978 is modern.

I tried to help some of the local High Wycombe punk bands, advising them and giving them support slots at the 100 Club. The trouble was most of them were middle-class kids playing at being rebels. Wycombe's a nice place to live, it's no concrete jungle. It's hard to present yourself as the authentic voice of the streets when your father's a bank manager, your mother's a headmistress and you live in a nice semi in the suburbs. I tried

God Save The Queen

to help them, but you can't make a bad band good, however fashionable their music might be.

Pink Parts weren't particularly good, but the main attraction wasn't the music. They were an all-girl band fronted by Martin Stone's ex, Ruth. I'd suggested their name, and gave them a few gigs at the Nag's. They were new waveish and did alright for a while before the novelty wore off. The world wasn't yet ready for a Thames Valley version of the Runaways. The Xtraverts were one of the best punk bands from the area. Nigel Martin was their singer and I put them on as a regular support act as the Town Hall but they never made the transition to headliners.

Of course, not everyone liked punk. Some people didn't understand it, others were unable to cope as it swept them away. I was at a party talking to one guy and he was criticising punk and everything it stood for. Then someone told him who I was and he was so dumbstruck that I wasn't spitting on the floor and dressed in chains that he couldn't say another word. Another time, I was going home by train and I spotted Ian Anderson of Jethro Tull in the first class carriage. I hadn't seen him for a long time so we got chatting and as soon as I mentioned that I was promoting punk he got very abusive. Not that I was bothered about offending an old hippy.

As the year came to a close I became a father again, with Marie-Louise Watts being born in October 1977. Meanwhile, bands I'd promoted were becoming big stars. Tom Robinson, the Stranglers and the Clash were having hits and consequently playing much bigger venues than I could promote. Compensation came in the form of the Adverts, featuring the lovely Gaye on bass, and a couple of promising bands from France, Cheap Stars and Metal Urbain, who sounded like Kraftwerk had they been going to the 100 Club in 1976.

As 1978 got underway there was still a fair amount of punk around and I was still enjoying much of it. The 100 Club hosted the London debut of Magazine, fronted by former Buzzcocks singer Howard Devoto. The queues that night were reckoned to be longer than for the festival, although the music wasn't the same quality. Adam & the Ants played there, as did the Rich Kids, who were causing the sort of stir you'd have expected considering their background. They could have been massive, but their record company put pressure on them to go out and play before they had enough songs for a decent set.

What had become tagged new wave, though, was gaining ground. Bands such as the Police, Squeeze and Chrissie Hynde's band the Pretenders were forming and beginning to do well on the live circuit. One band I missed putting on was Blondie, fronted by the legendary Debbie Harry, which was ironic as their bass player, Nigel Harrison, was a local lad and a Nag's regular.

XTC also performed regularly for me. I'd first seen them at the Plough, in Shelbourne, Wiltshire, near to where my family originated. I'd often pop over there on Sunday evenings as the landlord was very enthusiastic about promoting bands and would put them on in his bar – unthinkable for a village pub at the time, so he had all the decent new talent in Swindon and the surrounding area. XTC weren't anything remarkable at the time, yet I could tell they had a certain quality about them and they plugged away getting bigger and more appreciative audiences until they suddenly changed style and became pop stars.

On a slightly different tack were the Pirates. They'd started out backing Johnny Kidd, one of the first British rock'n'rollers, until his untimely death in a car crash in 1966, then reformed in the mid-seventies and were doing well as a result of being loosely involved with new wave. Their audience was a good cross-section. Punks got into their high-energy live shows while the blues fans and rockers loved the old Pirates stuff, the blues and rock-'n'roll covers and Mick Green's amazing guitar playing, which had been an inspiration for many a young musician. Mick is an absolute legend, who later played with Paul McCartney amongst others and is still working now, despite suffering a heart attack whilst touring with Brian Ferry in 2004. They played the Town Hall and gained a new fan in two year-old Stuart Watts, who arrived with Maureen as they were coming offstage and was bowled over by the Pirate costumes.

God Save The Queen

One unwelcome group that had started to come to my attention were members of the far-right British Movement, who had started to infest the High Wycombe gigs. I'd always let them in, although I refused to let them recruit, but a bigger than usual mob of them turned up one night at the Town Hall. They stood by Gerry, who was a black bouncer I used, a middleweight boxer who knew how to handle himself. I went over with another of my lads and the three of us faced around twenty of them as they chanted, "Kill the nigger." I told Gerry to get a few of his mates, and around ten minutes later he came back with a dozen or so black lads. I put them on Gerry's position and the master race went quiet. They came back a few times after that, and we'd sometimes see leaflets and stickers around the building, but they were never as vocal again. I've always been against violence and I wasn't having any racists spoiling my gigs.

We also had a regular diversion at the Town Hall courtesy of one of my little helpers, who we christened 'The Shagger.' Very often when the lights went up at the end of a gig we'd find him at the back of a hall getting down on it with some young punk girl, the two of them going away like rabbits. I don't know what sort of girl would behave like that in public and I knew that he didn't have any morals.

I was still the first port of call for any agent who wanted to book a blues act into London. The friends and customers I had who were fans of the blues weren't concerned that I was now doing so much punk. I was putting on the music they enjoyed and anyway, the profit from the punk shows was subsidising the blues nights. It was a labour of love for me and they appreciated what I was doing.

There was plenty of clichéd stuff that I avoided. A lot of soul packages were doing the rounds at the time. Winds of Change, from Wycombe, had been down that road years before and it hadn't worked then. John Leyton, who had been a singer himself and began promoting High Wycombe Town Hall, thought melodic pop was the thing to pull in the crowds, despite punk being at its height, and booked a band called White Plains to play a

Saturday evening. He took out a lot of local advertising and on the night of the gig I went along out of curiosity. The audience consisted of two girls, and the band went on and played a full set in total silence. The girls were happy enough, though. John had set up some competitions for the audience so they won all the prizes.

On Valentine's Day 1978, Siouxsie & the Banshees played at the 100 Club. They'd become one of the top bands in the country and an appreciative audience lapped them up. Had I been inclined, I might have realised that it had been a Valentine's Ball two years earlier when I'd stumbled across the Sex Pistols, and wondered how things would have turned out had I stayed at home that night.

Chapter 18

Blank Generation

While punk was at its height I was meeting some of the most memorable characters I would ever get to know. The most infamous, of course, was Sid Vicious.

History has been kind to Sid. He's seen as some sort of lovable rogue, a cartoon character manipulated into being the aggressive face of the movement when he was really just a bit of a harmless goofball. He certainly had the iconic punk look, with the leather jacket, chains and spiky hair that most punks got into once the fashion crowd had left the scene. The truth is that Sid was a hapless, malevolent, prat, who was once described as having the classic profile of a serial killer – above average intelligence, an obsession with death and a craving for notoriety. He couldn't fight to save his life, which was why he always had to use weapons or have someone on hand to back him up. I don't think he ever realised that stabbing people wasn't just a bit of harmless fun.

I first met Sid that night at High Wycombe Tech. He never really hung around with the Bromley Contingent, who kept him at arm's length. They were very much the arty side of punk, while Sid was straight from the gutter. He made himself known amongst the crowd by arseing about and threatening anyone who he didn't like the look of. Rotten kept him in check, but I realised early on that I'd have to keep an eye on Sid if I was going to work with the band.

He never missed a Pistols gig in the early days and became very close to Rotten, which surprised me as John never suffered fools. Maybe Sid had a bit of sense underneath that stupidity; there had to be something in there for Rotten to take to him. Sid just couldn't control himself, though, as was shown by the incident when he started on Nick Kent during the band's residency at the 100 Club. Maureen and I were standing on the door when someone came running up the stairs and shouted "Sid's attacking people." I went to see what was going on and Nick Kent was there, covered in blood. I was told that Sid had hit him over the head with a bike chain, so I grabbed Sid and held him up in the air until he promised to calm down.

I was in a dilemma. As much of an idiot as he was, I knew Sid was important to the band and they liked having him around. I also knew that someone like Nick Kent, who was one of the NME's top writers, could cause the whole punk movement serious problems if he was annoyed. In fact, the incident caused him to stop covering all music for months, while Sid, as he was called, was from then on known as Sid Vicious.

I had a word with Malcolm McLaren, who thought Sid deserved banning from the club. But he also knew having someone like that around helped the Pistols image, and the band's image was everything to Malcolm. In the end I let Sid stay, but a couple of weeks later he was up to more trouble, threatening a group of punks with another chain. I threw him out and banned him. Maybe I should have kept his weapons – they'd have been worth a fortune now and the money I could have got for them might have partly made up for all the problems he caused.

Sid's mother, Anne Beverley, came to see me, and begged for her darling Sid to be allowed back into the club. Like many a bully's mother she was in denial about what he was like; in fact in her own way she was just as inadequate as him. She'd brought Sid up with a succession of Ibiza beach bums and in North London squats until he was little more than feral. That might have explained some of his behaviour, but not all of it. He had a go at Stinky Toys for being French and said that only English bands could be real punks. He started on the Buzzcocks fans for not coming from London and the Damned for being South London lads when proper punks were from North London. He'd probably have attacked someone from the next street if he got it into his head that he lived in the only punk street in London. Sid was a mindless hooligan, plain and simple.

Blank Generation

The only time I saw him after the festival was on the Pistols boat trip the following summer. By then he'd been let out of the remand centre, joined the band and got hooked up with Nancy Spungsten, and my, what a pair they made. She looked unclean, she was over-made up but at least she was quiet throughout the journey. Sid was devoted to her, and kept her away from the rest of the band, but whether his feelings were reciprocated I don't know. After all, Nancy was a junkie prostitute from New York but then again, love's blind. In fact, the only saving grace Sid possessed was that he was devoted to Nancy with all the infatuation of first love.

The question I've been asked many times is, did he kill her? Well, he was obsessed with knives, he liked hurting people and from what I was told he was out of it for most of the time he was in New York. I don't know for certain, so you just have to draw your own conclusions.

His mate John was a different matter entirely. From that first time I met him, when I showed that I wasn't intimidated by his appearance, we got on well. As a frontman he was in a select group; brilliant, unique, as good as Robert Plant, Bowie, Jagger, anyone you could name. I'd led Brewer's Droop in a piss-taking way, but Rotten did things much differently. His control of the audience, the way he'd stare at them, his manner, it was like nothing anyone had ever done before. He meant it as well; he lived the life 24 hours a day, which led to the problems he encountered during the summer of 1977, when he got beaten up a couple of times. It was no surprise when the Pistols and their followers had so much trouble. If you go as close to the edge as they did, you're challenging the rest of society and there's bound to be a backlash.

Rotten had his hangers-on, people such as Wobble, who later joined Public Image Limited, and Sid. Maybe that was as backup whenever he got into trouble, or to help with John's own sense of insecurity. Despite what Malcolm might say, Rotten was never manipulated. He was always his own man and the two of them had a mutual need. John was doing it onstage, Malcolm was getting publicity the rest of the time. Towards the end of the band's life they didn't need each other and that's when things started to fall apart.

After that, with PiL, John got too arty and became what he'd set out to destroy. The music wasn't very impressive – I'd listened to real avant-garde and I could see straight through what he was trying to do. Johnny Rotten, or John Lydon, whichever name he uses to suit the occasion, is a modern English eccentric now. Him and Ozzy Osbourne have become two of a kind, as threatening to the Establishment as Elton John. How long until it's Sir John Lydon?

The rest of the Pistols were ordinary London lads. They didn't look like punks, but they were fine. I used to go out drinking with Paul Cook and Steve Jones at the Horseshoe on Tottenham Court Road and one afternoon they told me about the flat they were living in on Richer Street. This used to be a well-known meeting area for musicians back in the dance band era and there were still sheet music shops and instrument repairers based there. The band were permanently skint, so one day they went round to see McLaren at his flat in Camden, knocked on the door and could hear him screaming. The door was open and inside there was Malcolm tied up, naked in a wardrobe. It turned out that Vivienne Westwood had tied him then gone out for the evening.

Sexual deviancies apart, I found McLaren to be very straight. He hadn't had much experience of the music business when we first met, so he tended to go along with my suggestions for developing the Pistols and punk in general. Luckily for both of us, more of my ideas worked than didn't. Malcolm found it hard to get used to the casual way we did things in Britain. Some of my biggest promotions were still done without a contract ever being signed. I'd call the band's agent, agree a fee and a time, and that was it. I'd sometimes ring him back a few days before the gig, to remind him what time his band were due to arrive, and that was all the agreement we needed. There was hardly ever a problem. Malcolm thought that this was a bit odd but he never interfered

Blank Generation

and, unlike some managers I had to deal with, he never tried to get in my way on the night of a gig.

As I said before, Malcolm was always dressed very stylishly and knew the importance of creating a good image. Despite what people say about McLaren, he was never overbearing and he always seemed to be looking out for fun. There was always a twinkle in his eye. I wish he'd stop staying that he promoted the punk festival, though. That was my idea and mine alone. I took the risks and I did the promoting.

For all the criticism they got at the time, the Pistols were never meant to be technically brilliant. They were good basic musicians who worked well within their limitations. They were never Cream, but at the same time they were better than they were ever given credit for and by the time they got back together and toured in 1996 they were superb.

Someone once described the Damned as a 'punk cocktail band'. They get dismissed as a bit of a joke now, although at the time they were huge. As everyone knows, they were the first punks to sign a record deal and New Rose was a fantastic song. Their original guitarist, Brian James, seemed to be the boss of the band and he was certainly the best connected. He was always with a journalist or someone involved with the media.

Dave Vanian, their singer, was very withdrawn off-stage, in contrast to Johnny Rotten, so I never really got to know him. In fact, I did most of my business dealings with the drummer, Rat Scabies, who was a very good and under-rated musician. As for Captain Sensible, I well remember the incident at the Mont de Marsen festival in France, when he jumped offstage and caught his balls on some scaffolding. That summed the Captain up – a lunatic who was always getting into scrapes. I wonder if he got over that French accident. Has he got any children?

I managed the Damned for a while, right back when they first got started. Management wasn't something I ever enjoyed but I did it as an occasional favour so I agreed to help the band out. I met publishers with them and got them a few gigs, which caused me some problems when they played at the White Swan in

Luton. It was probably the first punk gig in the town and at three in the morning I was woken up by a phone call. At the other end of the line was a Damned roadie. "Ron, the band are in Luton nick. Something's gone off in the town and they've been done for kicking in some shop windows." There wasn't much I could do at that time of day so I went back to sleep, and when I got up and rang the police, they told me the band had already been released without charge.

It was becoming a familiar tale. Something happened in a small town and the police went straight for the strange-looking people who were nearby. Punk was so new that to the constables who went to investigate the incident, the band might as well have been spacemen. They'd read about these aggressive punk rockers who were a threat to society and here were some on their doorstep, so the policemen did the only thing policemen could do. They arrested them.

My time as the manager of the Damned came to an end a week after the Luton incident, at the Nag's. Brian James was trying to antagonise the crowd, shouting, "Call yourselves punks?" I'd had enough of this so I shouted back, "Keep it up and I'll fetch me shotgun. We'll see how much of a punk you are then." The Damned may have been good for business but the crowd at the Nag's had been with me longer than the Damned had. Next morning we decided that our association would cease and they signed with Jake Riviera.

The Damned had quite a big rivalry with the Pistols in the early days. They didn't think much of Anarchy in the UK when it came out, but eventually both bands saw that they had different roles to play. The Pistols were always at the cutting edge, but the Damned were able to fill the void when the Pistols couldn't play anywhere.

The third of the great punk triumvirate were the Clash. As I explained earlier, they'd come from a different background because they were a bit older and had been in other bands before they formed. They weren't as early as the Pistols or as quick to record as the Damned, but when they got going they soon caught up with the others. The first gig of theirs that I promoted was a busy one, because word was spreading about punk and how good this particular band were. The Clash were more musically literate, and they could do their stuff with a bit more subtlety than the Pistols.

Even though I'd known Joe Strummer from the 101ers days I rarely got the chance to talk to him, or any of the other band members, very often. As soon as we got together their manager, Bernie Rhodes, would be straight over, making sure I kept my distance. He might have thought I wanted to take them away from him, even though I wasn't interested in management or influencing a band's direction. But that was Bernie. To hear him talk he'd invented punk, run the festival, organised the Jubilee boat trip and financed the Pistols' American tour. Maybe it was him who really killed Nancy.

One thing about Joe Strummer is that he knew once the Clash was finished, that was it. He resisted the pressures on him over the years to form the Clash mark II, and although when he did get his final band, the Mescaleros, together they played Clash numbers live, on record they had a very different style. That's my philosophy on music; something ends and it's time to move on. If you split up with a woman you don't start looking for another one who looks and acts the same. Music's no different.

Joe's death in 2002 was a great loss and although it was a shock, I get the impression that he knew he was ill. It says everything that shortly before his death Joe played with Mick Jones at a Fire Brigade Union benefit. They could have earned millions by reforming the Clash and touring America but they stuck to their principles, and that's something to be respected.

In their early days the Clash were adopted by Caroline Coon. She was a lovely lady, a bit of a middle-class hippy, but I admired her for her work during the sixties with the drugs charity Release. In those days prison sentences were routinely handed out for possession of the smallest amounts of drugs and Caroline's work in that field did much towards changing peoples' attitudes and a more realistic approach to the supposed problem being sought. She very quickly became enthusiastic about punk and the Clash were her boys. Caroline moved in with their bass player, Paul Simonen, and tried to turn him into the sort of neatly-turned out rebel who would riot in the streets in the afternoon then take her to the opera in the evening. I was grateful, though, for the nice mention Caroline gave of me in her book, The New Wave Punk Rock Explosion.

Other characters came along as the scene progressed but few of them made as much impact as the big three, however much they might have wanted to. Gene October, for example, was desperate to be famous. He was one of the original Bromley Contingent and put together a band he called Chelsea. They were okay, nothing brilliant, but they were the sort of act I'd put on if nobody better was available because I knew they'd pull a reasonable crowd and put on a decent show.

Gene desperately wanted to be a star and he was using punk as a short cut. The first single they released, Right To Work, wasn't about unemployment as everyone thought, but Gene complaining he couldn't get an Equity card to work as an actor. He made his wishes too obvious, though, and the punks could see through him. Gene had a part in the punk film Jubilee, which starred Toyah Wilcox, but that was the end of his acting career rather than its beginning. Chelsea stayed together for a few years, playing the usual venues. They're probably still going now, working whatever passes for a punk nostalgia circuit.

Billy Idol came out of the same crowd as Gene, and indeed, he was a founder-member of Chelsea, but was much more talented. He looked good and right from the start when he turned up to watch the Pistols he oozed charisma just by being in the audience. Billy was a throwback to the heartthrobs of the sixties and he knew how to use his looks to good advantage. One night at the Nag's we were talking while the band were setting up their equipment and he made it clear to me that he was using the punk scene as a stepping-stone to greater things.

Full marks to Billy, he knew how to get on and he had the talent to do it. Generation X had some chart success, then after they split he went quiet for a while before emerging in California as the longest-lasting and highest-profile of any of the punks. Billy lasted so long because he became the acceptable face of what had once been a threatening, rebellious movement. He took the pop star looks of the sixties, music from the seventies and added them to eighties fashions, and he exploited the fact that once you're big in the States you can live off that forever. Some people have such a burning ambition to make the big time that they'll continually change fashions in their pursuit of stardom, always trying too hard to fit into the scene. Others use the natural talent they possess and adapt it to whatever's the in thing at the moment, yet at the same time retaining their individuality. Gene was the former, and he failed. Billy was the latter, and he's still doing well.

Siouxsie was the final Bromley member to become famous, although it took her longer than expected. After the festival and the Bill Grundy incident she got a lot of press, but the Banshees didn't start playing straightaway and when they did they were more a Roxy and Vortex band, although we'd still see her occasionally at the 100 Club watching others.

Siouxsie and the rest of the Bromley Contingent were different from the rest of the crowd. While punk soon became a uniform of spiky hair and leather jackets, Siouxsie and her friends continued to look their best. I always complimented them on the way they dressed. It must have taken them all day to get ready and they always made an effort to look the part. When Siouxsie said that she was putting a band together I was happy to put them on at the festival, but even though they were different to everything else I recognized what they were playing as the sort of thing I might do.

The Banshees had a strange career. For some reason they missed out on a record deal when the labels were signing up every band who were vaguely punk and there was a big 'Sign The Banshees' graffiti campaign by their fans. Then by the time they joined Polydor in 1978, punk bands were last year's model and they were too heavy for the new wave that had become the big thing. The Banshees eventually became the darlings of the goth scene, but that was another story.

Jimmy Pursey and Paul Weller were a million miles away from Siouxsie in attitude, dress and even the fans they attracted, which showed how wide-ranging the best punk was in 1977. They also seemed different to each other at first glance, but they had a lot in common, even sharing the same record company. Pursey had been around the 100 Club from the early days. He was from Hersham, a well-off town in Surrey, but the band he put together, Sham 69, was full of East End images, singing about borstal, gangsters and rioting. Despite the mock-Cockney affections I always found Jimmy very earnest, and he sincerely believed in what he was doing. He was similar to Paul Weller in that they both reminded me of the old-time blues singers who would drill their bands until they were word-perfect.

I had a lot to do with the Jam. John Weller, Paul's dad, asked me to do their pre-publicity for the first American tour, but I had to decline as I didn't have the time to spend weeks away from my venues. Paul was very insecure then; for example, he didn't want to go to the States as he thought his girlfriend would leave him while he was away. On stage, though, he was a king.

I noticed early on that the Jam attracted more girls than any other band I promoted. We did one gig with them and sold advance tickets, which we didn't often do. The amount of girls in school uniforms waiting in the queue was amazing; we probably broke the law by selling to them. The girls were all over Bruce Foxton, for some reason, which pissed off Weller, who thought that as the singer, they should go for him. For a three piece the Jam were a sensation. It was very brave of them to be doing the sort of soul covers they were playing – Wilson Pickett and Arthur Conley stuff – when everyone around them was singing about rioting and political events. They went down a storm, though, and I'd say that after the first wave of bands who had kick-started everything off, the Jam were my favourite live act. Elvis Costello and Ian Dury made the best records but by the end of 1977 the Jam were the top live attraction

Sham, on the other hand, attracted skinheads almost from the start. They pulled in the sort of fans who would go to see the band on a Friday night then watch football on Saturday afternoon, and considered the weekend a success if they didn't get arrested at either. Jimmy might have claimed that he didn't want that sort of crowd, but with songs like Borstal Breakout and We Gotta Fight, what did he expect? Sham had a successful career for a few years. For a time they were selling more records than the Jam, and the record label Polydor, to whom both bands were signed, were talking of Pursey as a solo star of the future. But Sham could never shake off their more troublesome followers, their gigs got increasingly violent and Pursey split them up, almost killing himself in the process. Poor Jimmy; his heart was in the right place even if his head was often in the clouds.

One of my most fondly-remembered bands were X-Ray Spex, and not particularly for the music. Almost thirty years on I'm still in love with their singer, Poly Styrene. She was a lovely girl who was into the music from the start, although I didn't notice her until she got the band together. Even then I didn't promote them until they had their first record out and I could be guaranteed of getting a decent crowd. I let them build up a following at the Roxy and the Man on the Moon in the Kings' Road before offering them a gig at the 100 Club once I knew they'd fill the place. This was a luxury that I was getting by the end of 1977, and it was one I reckoned I'd earned. After all, I'd put these bands on when nobody else wanted to know them so why shouldn't I let someone else start taking the risks? Bands wanted to play the 100 Club, it was the most prestigious punk gig in London, so I could afford to pick and choose.

Poly turned up for her first gig at the club full of bravado, and totally unflustered. She had a brace on her teeth and carried a plastic shopping bag – a total contrast to the leather-clad punks who made up the band's audience by this time, but in keeping with her previous life as a South London checkout girl at Woolworth's. The band was a move away from the mainstream, as well. They had Laura Logic playing saxophone, so they were a mile away from the Sex Pistols/Ramones copyists that most bands were trying to be as the year wore on. X-Ray Spex reportedly signed a record deal after they'd played just three gigs, had a few hit singles, toured the bigger venues for a while and faded away, all within a couple of years. That, to me, was what punk was all about. Get in, get out, and quit while you're ahead.

The Rezillos were another band with a girl singer. They didn't appear on the London scene until well into 1977, although I suppose it had taken a long time for punk to get up to Edinburgh, where they were from, and bring a band back with it. They were one of the last of the first wave of punk bands, if that makes sense, and they played the Nag's for me. Their singer, Fay Fife, had an interesting habit. She'd sort the business side of the gig out while getting undressed, so we'd be talking money while she was in an extremely lewd state of undress. Whether she thought it'd take my mind off business or not, I don't know, but she had a good band and although they never sold many records - in fact, they spilt up during their first major tour - the Rezillos' music has stood the test of time more than most of their contemporaries. It still sounds fresh today.

I'd first come across John Peel when Brewer's Droop had done a gig with him at Woolaston, Bedfordshire, in 1970. He was in his hippy phase then, so he didn't like a bunch of lunatics like us very much, but by the time 1977 came round John was the alternative scene's favourite broadcaster, a title he held until his untimely death in 2004.

I'd often see John and his producer, John Walters, as they worked in Portland Place, just around the corner from Oxford Street. A lot has been said about how disc jockeys create trends, but although you might think I'm biased, it's almost always the promoters who start things off. It's rare that a band will get a record deal without first getting a good live reputation and all the greats learn their trade on the road, so anyone who's putting on gigs at small venues, whether it's a pub landlord, a club promoter or the social secretary of a university, will know what's happening long before a broadcaster has any idea. Punk was no different to any other movement; the Pistols played the 100 Club six months before Anarchy in the UK was released and the festival took place a month before the Damned's New Rose came out. John Peel was a great broadcaster, he did a lot to help all types of music and he fully deserves the tributes he continues to receive, but punk had been going a long time before he began covering it.

Punk wasn't just about the bands that were forming, it was the entire structure of a movement. If you weren't a musician, you could still be involved – you could write about it, be a fashion designer, start a record label, you could do anything you wanted to.

This was the best time for new bands that I've ever known. Everywhere you looked there were new venues for them to play, media to publicise them, record companies wanting to record them. A lot of the bands I've mentioned hadn't been formed when punk first started to take off, in fact some of their members could barely play their instruments, yet they were doing the concert hall circuit within twelve months. I was asked to promote them on large tours, but I wasn't interested. If you put a band on at an Odeon or Apollo it stops becoming music and it's a business. I wasn't interested in dealing with PA companies, security firms or press agents. Throughout 1977 I was busy enough booking bands and enjoying myself.

Chapter 19

Cor Baby That`s Really Free

As 1978 went on punk started to fall by the wayside, although new wave bands were beginning to do well. I was putting on bands at the 100 Club who were showing how punk had changed, such as Penetration, from the north-east and with a very talented singer in Pauline Murray, plus Wire and Alternative TV, whose singer, Mark Perry, had been one of the early members of the Pistols audience. Adam & the Ants were regulars, while I also threw a few different options to the paying customers in the shape of rockabilly band Whirlwind and a few reggae acts.

Punk definitely had an air of last year's thing about it. The fashion crowd had moved on and the gigs were often like being at a party when most of the guests have gone home and everyone who's left is either too tired or too drunk to leave. But it had helped the mood of the moment swing back to rock'n'roll basics and in its wake a lot of talented musicians were able to make their mark. My old pub rock sparring partner Nick Lowe, for example, had a few overdue hits, as did his buddy and former Brewer's Droop producer Dave Edmunds.

The audience at the Nag's was very much into new wave and it remained a strong venue for the music throughout the year. Mick, the landlord, was right behind me. He was a red-haired bloke who, like me, had an up and down marriage but he knew that the shows I put on would sell out. He wasn't too keen on the firework display we put on for him, though. WH Smith had been selling fireworks cheaply during the summer, so we bought a load of boxes and set them off in the bar one Saturday night. Mick took it all in his stride as rockets went flying past him, but eventually, as the bar filled with smoke, he made us take them outside. He said it had got so dark his normal customers couldn't see what they were drinking.

I was still promoting blues gigs, although they tended to be less frequent, and only if I fancied the acts. 1978 was one of those strange years when there was no real underground scene. The punk bands had all got big or melted away and nothing was coming through. I knew that if I was going to do anything to build on my successes of the previous two years, I'd have to start looking for bands that were out of the ordinary.

John Otway and Wild Willy Barrett certainly weren't ordinary. Otway had been around the local scene in Buckinghamshire forever, although he was still only in his mid-twenties. He must have been playing folk clubs when he was 14. John came up to me in a pub one night and said "Ron Watts. I've known you a long time," and mentioned a pub where I'd promoted years before, the Derby Arms in Aylesbury. I'd put a few local blues acts on there, but I didn't use it very often because it was twenty miles away. I was usually busy at weekends back then, so I only got to do the Derby on quiet nights early in the week and I'd more or less forgotten it but Otway had remembered me from there.

Wild Willy had been around the scene for a long time as well. I'd refused to let him into one gig many years earlier, when he came up to the door with a guitar and said he was one of the acts. They'd had their hit, Really Free, at the end of 1977 and were a reliable draw, even if they were insane.

Wreckless Eric was similar to Otway, being a quirky performer with a nice line in ironic lyrics. That's where the similarity ended, because while Otway's eccentricity was a fun thing which rubbed off on the audience, Eric was a miserable sod who thought his songs were up there with the works of Bob Dylan and hated being regarded as a novelty act.

It was at this time that I put one two of the worst bands I've ever promoted. I'd never really liked Adam & the Ants and one night I called them "boring young farts" over the 100 Club PA. Next time they played, at the Town Hall the following February, Adam singled me out. "Are you Ron Watts?" he said. "No, I'm Micky Spillane." Hardly cutting wit but it confused Adam. He

Cor Baby That's Really Free

was dressed like a pantomime act, they performed like one, and the turnout was so low they would have been better off at the Nag's. Two years later they were the biggest band in Britain, with hordes of screaming girls packing their gigs. Ah, well.

The Slits were without doubt the weakest band I ever put on at the Town Hall. They drew a good crowd, but their music was so bad. The singer, Ari Up, said as she walked onstage "Do you like reggae? Well you won't like us then." I didn't.

After playing, producing, promoting and managing, the next logical step was to start a record label. Punk had made it easier, as there were independent labels springing up throughout the country. My old soul-producing mate Joe Farquarson and I set up Hubcap Records and the first band we recorded were Brett Marvin & the Thunderbolts, or whatever they were called after the Bumps fiasco. Their material was never released and it's probably still gathering dust somewhere.

The next band we got involved with were Sore Throat, who I'd been promoting for some time and who recorded a single for us called "I Dunno." It didn't do too much except in their North London homeland and I ended up giving copies away when they played the Town Hall at the end of 1978. They weren't much of a band – wannabes pretending to be working class so they could ride the new wave bandwagon although I was always able to call on them when I needed a slot filing quickly and they eventually played for me more than almost any other act.

Having the 100 Club was a big help in putting on the best local bands at High Wycombe, as it meant that I could also offer them a date at a prestigious London venue. Hook Line and Silverfish were from Wokingham. I loved their name, and I booked them into the Nag's almost on the strength of that alone. They brought a good crowd with them and the locals liked them so I put them on at the 100 Club a couple of times. They took a couple of hundred fans with them and as usual, the fact that there was already a lot of people inside the club made others turn up. I've often noticed this. If you have an empty venue no-one ever walks in on the off-chance, but if the place is full they get drawn by some magical force. So we had a couple of good nights but the band did nothing after that. They'd had their moment in the spotlight, though.

I pulled that trick a few times; get a band with a local following and hire coaches to take their fans to the 100 Club. It was usually a big success, with the club doing good business on what would have been a quiet evening and the audience having a night out at a world-famous venue before being dropped home virtually on their doorstep. Very often I'd put them on at the Nag's on the Saturday and use the opportunity to drum up trade for their 100 Club gig two nights later. Sometimes, though, I'd put on a band whose following would get a bit over-excited. When Moscow State Circus played, their fans thought that the right way to behave was to get drunk, fight, take drugs and make general nuisances of themselves all night. They wouldn't have dared do it on their home turf, but this was the way they thought they had to behave in the big city. The band didn't get a return gig and I didn't book them for the Nag's again even though they carried on playing other venues in the area.

Putting on the best blues acts didn't always mean the biggest names. Big Joe Duskin, a pianist from Birmingham, Alabama, had promised his father some time back in the 1940s that he wouldn't play anything but church music while the old man was alive. As Pop Duskin was 79 at the time Joe probably didn't think this too much of a hardship, but dad lived to be 105. Joe's best years were lost and he never managed to catch up with his contemporaries. If he'd been able to record in the fifties, his goodtime style would have made him a star, but it wasn't to be, although I brought him over to play at the 100 Club and he's still recording now. Longevity obviously runs in the Duskin family; their insurance man must be happy.

John Jackson was an acoustic country blues guitarist from Virginia. He'd come on stage dressed in overalls and pick at his guitar before going off into a monologue about how "Back home ah gets up in de mownin', ah waters de mule then ah goes out an' ah ploughs dem fields." Bollocks – he lived in a town and worked in a factory. Then he'd go on; "Ah gets home to ma supper o' cornbread an' chitlins, ah goes out onto de porch with ma buddies and we pass de moonshine jug around an' we sing us these little ol' songs ah'm a singing fow all you good people out dere tonight." And all the time he was winking at me, then when he came off stage he'd whisper, "Ron, all that bullshit went out thirty years ago." It was as authentic as when the diplomat's son and art student Joe Strummer sang about White Riots and Garageland. But both of them knew their audiences loved it.

I always regretted the fact that by this time there weren't enough blues fans in the Thames Valley area to make some of these acts worth bringing to the Nag's. Someone like Homesick James would have pulled a decent crowd, but Joe Duskin or that great showman John Jackson weren't enough of an attraction, even though they'd have gone down a storm. The 100 Club was different. Such was its reputation even an unknown blues act would bring in a crowd. Enough people realised that if an act was playing the 100 Club they must be good.

Piano Red, or to give him the name he was born with, Willie Perryman, was a deeply religious man, whose brother Rufus, known as Speckled Red, was also a pianist. They were both albinos and extremely near-sighted, but Piano toured Europe several times, his barrel house and ragtime style going down well at the 100 Club. I'd managed to get him by persuading his son what a fine fellow I was, and to prove my credentials, I took Piano to church one Sunday morning. The place we went to, St Lawrence's in West Wycombe, had been used by the Hellfire Club, a bunch of debauched eighteenth century aristocrats, and was in the centre of a Neolithic circle. I explained that it had been a place of worship since prehistoric times and Piano, almost blind, wanted to walk around the grounds and feel the landmarks that had stood for thousands of years.

Many of the American acts that came over to play in England were fascinated by the heritage of the country, particularly back in the sixties when they loved seeing the war damage that remained – the bombsites and the old aerodromes. I suppose they'd watched all the war films and then wanted to see the real thing. I played up the historic aspect for them, taking them to Windsor to watch the Changing of the Guard, which few people realise takes place at the castle throughout the year. They loved all that pageantry.

Piano Red was often billed as 'The Real Dr Feelgood', and that caused a few problems when he played the 100 Club. The Canvey Island band's manager rang me demanding to know why I was advertising that his boys were playing a gig they knew nothing about. My reply was straight to the point, "He's been called Doctor Feelgood since 1940. Where do you think your band got their name from?" and the phone went quiet. I'd often worked with the band, but I wasn't going to let their manager cause problems for one of the authentic bluesmen. A few people turned up on the night expecting to hear Lee Brilleaux singing, but they were perfectly happy when the situation was explained to them.

Chapter 20

Ghosts Of Princes In Towers

The 100 Club was still going strong, and there were still a lot of bigger bands who wanted to play there, when Roger dropped another bombshell. He'd been getting flak from the Oxford Street Traders Association again regarding the queues across their doors and the fact that their customers didn't like having to walk past those horrid punk rockers to get into the shops. I could see the traders' point – they were paying big money and they didn't want to lose trade from early in the afternoon, which was when the punks would often start queuing for the big bands. They were very influential with Westminster Council and in those days the councillors regarded rock clubs as the lair of the devil rather than as the money-spinning tourist traps they later became.

The Roxy and the Marquee never had the sort of problems with the neighbours that the 100 Club suffered, because they were situated away from the main shopping area, but I think Roger was worried that he would be closed down if the complaints got too loud. I don't think he liked having to re-paint the toilets because of all the graffiti every week, either. He told me that I had six weeks notice and I couldn't put any more punk bands on after that. I'd just had the Jam and the Tom Robinson Band playing there and the Nag's while they were in the charts. Both were brilliant gigs that sold out completely by word of mouth. The bands were happy to break away from their busy schedules to play for me, and I'd never seen either venue look as busy as on the nights they were there. We couldn't find enough staff to cope.

I was naturally upset; things had been going well and now I'd lost my flagship. I went back to promote the club later on but it was never as successful. Looking back, I helped make the 100

Club one of the best-known live venues in the world. Before punk, it was a trad jazz venue with an ageing clientele. Now, people travel from all around the world to play there. The Stones chose the club to do some gigs in 1982, and modern bands such as Metallica and Oasis have played it.

I still had the Nag's, though. The Police played just as they were beginning to break through. Sting wasn't what I expected. He had a very aristocratic air, which was surprising in a former schoolteacher from Newcastle. With their blonde hair and aloof manners, his band looked like a bunch of Vikings. Their later success came as no surprise, even if Sting did keep his love of jazz quiet at that time.

I also promoted an Irish band called U2 at the Nag's. They were pretty much unknown, but word of mouth had done its job and the pub was heaving when they performed. That was one of the great things about my customers; they were up on which bands were causing a stir around the country before anyone else caught on. U2 were as you'd expect. They put on a storming show and everyone could tell that they would make it.

Bono in particular was showing signs that he would develop into one of the most charismatic frontmen in music, probably the best new singer I'd seen since Rotten. Terri, my eldest daughter, was there and although she doesn't remember the gig, she still tells people how she watched U2 in a pub. Putting them on that early in their career didn't do my reputation any harm, either.

I've always liked Reg Presley, the singer with the Troggs. We look similar; maybe we're related. He was born in an area of Hampshire not far from where my grandfather was born in Wiltshire, so it might be that there was a bit of cross-border invading a few generations ago. I'd first promoted Reg and his band at the Nag's in 1973. On that occasion he lost his octavia, a rare wind instrument, and tore the place apart looking for it. Reg went onto the stage and belaboured the audience, demanding that whoever had taken it give it back immediately, then it was found in the dressing room. His band filled the venue and I booked them for the 100 Club, which Reg was delighted with. "I've been told this is the place to play, no doubt about it," he said to me afterwards.

I put the Troggs on regularly at both venues, but only once a year. There was no point in over-exposing them. Ronnie Bond, their drummer for many years, would invariably go missing whenever they played the Nag's and I'd have to track him down by searching all the pubs on London Road. Poor Ronnie died as a result of his drinking, in 1992, but for Reg the nineties were to be much happier. He'd been jogging along as a cabaret artiste, still pulling in the crowds with the sixties revival packages, when Wet Wet Wet's version of the old Troggs song Love Is All Around got to number one for an eternity and Reg picked up a fortune in royalties. He spent most of it on research into crop circles, which made him happy, and he continues to play to packed houses with an incarnation of the band forty years after they started out. Sometimes the nice guys do win.

We had an interesting couple of nights at the Nags, first with the Skids, who were yet another band with obvious massive potential. Richard Jobson was a dynamic singer, not blessed with the greatest of voices but he could handle a crowd. They also had Stuart Adamson, a guitarist who went onto even greater things with Big Country before sadly committing suicide in America. That was a real tragedy; Stuart had so much talent, yet he couldn't cope with his situation. I also promoted the White Cats, featuring Rat Scabies, although in keeping with the time he'd gone back to his real name of Chris Miller. The band were nothing special and it wasn't long before Rat/Chris was back with the re-formed Damned. Dave Vanian, another of Rat's Damned colleagues, briefly joined the Doctors of Madness. They'd been around before punk and were always very theatrical. A couple of their albums were highly-rated by the critics, but when they played the Nag's I thought the best thing about them was their name.

A few days in the autumn of 1978 showed how schizophrenic music promoting had become. Wayne County played the Nag's, with Motorhead at the Town Hall the following night, and I'd have paid good money to see their respective reactions if they'd been on the same bill even though I reckon that Wayne/Jayne would have scared all the big tough Motorhead fans away. Then I had punk originals 999 at the Town Hall with folk-rockers the Strawbs playing there two days later. But they were all crowd-pullers.

As the year progressed, power pop was supposed to be the next big thing, and I promoted stuff like the Smirks, who were a Manchester band in the style of Jonathan Richman, then the Records and the Pleasers, who wore Beatle suits and made utterly forgettable music. In a different vein I put on Pere Ubu at the Town Hall and they were great. The best way to describe them is avant garde punk. Their singer was wearing a shiny grey suit and as the gig went on it got progressively darker the more he sweated. This was a band I really enjoyed and it was one of the few times where I stayed and watched the entire set. Even if I liked an act, there was usually some sort of distraction while they were playing, whether it be members of the audience making a nuisance of themselves or technical problems, but luckily this was a night when nothing went wrong and I was able to enjoy some wonderful, innovative music. It was one of the most memorable nights of the era and I was proud that a place like High Wycombe was so receptive to such unusual stuff. Most small towns were musical backwaters where the locals were only interested in whatever was on that week's Top of the Pops, with a token live venue churning out third-rate rock covers, but the bohemian side which had made Wycombe such an attraction in the sixties was still flourishing.

Although I'd been upset to lose the 100 Club just when it was taking off again, punk had been fizzling out anyway. The club scene slowed down in the summer of 1978, as it does every year, and when things livened up once more the name bands had gone on to bigger things. All that was left were the ones who were moving in ever decreasing circles, their audiences were getting smaller and the venues that had been falling over themselves to

Ghosts Of Princes In Towers

promote punk twelve months earlier were now pretending that such a thing had never existed.

As 1979 came around I began to use a new talent named Joe Jackson, who supported Ian Gomm at the Nag's and was so impressive that I gave him a headline spot as soon as I could. Joe was a nice guy who wrote great songs and was another who deserved the acclaim that he received over the next couple of years. I wasn't at all surprised when scarcely more than a year after he played a support set at the Nag's he was selling out the Hammersmith Palais, with the High Wycombe connection strengthened by his choice of support act – my old workhorses Sore Throat. Not quite so memorable were local acts TV Surf Boys and the Flobs, who somehow got me to put them on at the Nag's and that was as far as our association went.

XTC played the Town Hall while they were on the verge of making the breakthrough into the big time, while the Tom Robinson Band were, sadly, on the way down when they performed at the same venue. The mod revival was beginning to take off and I booked the VIPs, Squire and the Merton Parkas into the Nag's, the latter band playing the Town Hall for me after getting into the charts with their greatest hit You Need Wheels, then the Nag's again as the revival faded away. They were all decent enough, even if I had heard their brand of speeded up sixties music twelve months earlier when it was called power pop. The line of scooters parked outside whenever a mod band was in town looked impressive as well.

On a more challenging note the Psychedelic Furs and Doll By Doll played the Nag's. It wasn't my sort of music but I was interested to see how they had taken punk's approach and fitted it to their own identity, even if their clothes and attitudes were far remove from the vitriol of Rotten and Strummer. Another interesting night was the appearance of the Jimmy Norton Experience. Featuring Glen Matlock, his Rich Kids sparring partner Steve New, future Banshee Budgie and Danny Kustow, highly-rated former guitarist with the Tom Robinson Band, life should have been promising for this new wave supergroup, yet they hardly had time to finish their set before they'd faded from view.

I was forever being promised the Next Big Thing and often gave them a gig just on the off-chance that they might show a bit of promise. To judge how successful I was, can anyone remember 64 Spoons, Funboy 5, NW10 or Angletrax? I even put on a bunch of old blokes named Brewer's Droop, who performed their definitely, absolutely, this time we really mean it, final couple of gigs.

Nine Below Zero were never the coming thing. They weren't new wave, punk or anything other than a good rocking r&b band. They'd walk onstage to the Sonny Boy Williamson track Nine Below Zero played over the PA and do a set full of blues standards and their own original stuff. Their singer, Dennis Greaves, led the band well and played decent guitar, and although they're still going strong now the closest they ever came to chart success was when Greaves left the band in the mid-eighties and had a couple of hits with The Truth. They weren't doing much other than what had been done before, but they did it well and the audiences loved them for it.

During this time as with every other, there were artistes who should have become bigger. The Headboys were a very classy pop band who played the Nag's and seemed en route to Top of the Pops and stardom, yet never did more than a couple of songs that didn't so much hit the charts as scrape the bottom end of the Top 75. Any Trouble had a lot of press attention early on, and again their show at the Nag's was well-attended and well-received. I think that their problem was that they were signed to Stiff, which by then had moved away from the new wave anthems of Elvis Costello and Ian Dury and was being seen as a novelty label, which put off serious record-buyers.

Things were starting to take a downturn and they were to get worse. Mick Fitzgibbons wanted to leave the Nag's, he'd made his money and he started running the place down. He'd taken another pub on the quiet, although he was telling everyone that he'd got a job in a bonded store at Heathrow. Mick installed a manager, a lad named Woody who had been working in a factory and wasn't interested. I was still promoting, but I'd also got a day job, as a quality engineer in a plastics factory. This lasted a couple of months then I saw an advert for a nightclub in Cippenham called Alexander's, that an acquaintance of mine named Barry Mason had opened. I knew him from the Black Prince at Bexley Heath, where Brewer's Droop had played back in the old days, and he was a friend of Roy Tempest, which says as much about him as anyone would need to know. I applied and got the job, managing the door and doing promotions. I'd never been involved in a disco before, but it was interesting to see a different side of the business. The disco crowd were flash and tried to make out they were better than the music fans, although in reality they were a lot more workaday.

Chapter 21

Career Opportunities

My marriage had finally ended. As the money dried up so did Maureen's interest, or so it seemed. I'd made a lot of money in the punk era, but I'd spent a lot as well. Like many people before me I thought I'd found a magic formula and it would last forever, but reality was now slapping me in the face with a vengeance. The 100 Club was gone and the Nag's seemed on its last legs. It was dirty, no-one was answering the phones and there was an atmosphere about the place that was putting off the punters. Woody's only interest seemed to be in shagging one of the barmaids. I persevered, but it was a losing battle. I was back living with my parents at one point, not exactly where I'd expected to be by now. At least it was only about a quarter of a mile from Alexander's.

I chose Thursdays as the main live night at Alexander's, with blues on Sundays. The place was geared up for live music – they had a big portable stage which Peter, the manager, used to help me pull into place every week. The acts were a few old mates, such as Jo-Anne Kelly's Spare Rib, as well as some solid, reliable names. Red Beans & Rice were one of the bands we put on, and although they were a bog-standard blues band from South Wales, in one aspect they were unlike any other act I've ever known. Their roadies would turn up with the gear, then the band would arrive by train. They'd do the gig and sprint back to Burnham station for the last train back to Cardiff. I never found out why they always caught the train when they had their own transport. Maybe they liked British Rail sandwiches.

A new landlord took over the Nag's. His name was Ray Russell and he'd wanted the pub for a long time. Ray had been in the furniture trade and he was attracted to the place more because of its proximity to the Rye and the surrounding parkland than as a music venue. The pub was in the doldrums and on his first night in charge, Ray didn't see a single customer until 10 o'clock. In fact, he wanted to turn the upstairs into a snooker hall but I didn't know that when we first met and I filled him in on its history.

Ray told me to carry on promoting but unfortunately he brought his own prejudices and phobias with him. He didn't like punks so he barred me from booking punk bands. Word soon got round the town that if you wore the wrong shirt at the Nag's you wouldn't get in. You can't do that at a live venue so I realised that Ray needed encouraging and showing the ropes.

I told him that it would be a good idea to have music in the bar to get customers in and I formed the Nag's Head All Stars, with John Mackay, Bobby Walker and a great local singer named Paul Sharman, plus some of the best other local talent. I played with them at the start and they soon started drawing a crowd on Fridays and Sundays, which showed the landlord how he could do well out of live music.

Getting the Nag's back up and running properly was a massive job. I had to start putting on things I wouldn't normally have bothered with and had to stay outside the current trends because Ray didn't want them. In some ways he was right. There was a violent edge to a lot of the music at that time, with skinheads looking to cause trouble, punk becoming more ghettoised and two-tone attracting a volatile audience. The second wave of punk was well underway and I booked the UK Subs and the Angelic Upstarts into the Town Hall as well as giving the Ruts their debut, supporting Wayne County. I've no doubt these bands were genuinely into the music, even though Charlie Harper of the UK Subs made one or two of the Stranglers seem young, but I couldn't see the point. It was all two years out of date and bringing in a very nasty audience. Sham 69 had just split up, destroyed by the pressures of riots at almost every gig, and their followers were looking for another band to latch onto.

The Damned were another punk band I booked into the Town Hall. At least they'd made the effort to change their style a bit,

Career Opportunities

but the night ended up with some problems. The band, who probably hadn't forgiven me for the way our business partnership had ended three years earlier, refused to leave the stage and the caretaker of the hall called the police, who were stationed next door. They arrived and lined the side of the hall, with the band finishing sharpish and their fans filtering out, although by now the average age of a Damned fan was about 15 so there was never any danger of a riot ensuing. The band were on a percentage of the door take and reckoned I'd fiddled them, even attempting to sue me. Things were eventually sorted out although that was the last time I had any dealings with them until running into Captain Sensible, both of us a lot older and wiser, over 25 years later.

Arrogant were a local new wave band, and they were aptly named. If their talent had matched their opinion of themselves they'd have got a lot bigger than playing the Nag's. Protex played a similar type of music but were completely different. They were from Northern Ireland and loved the opportunity to perform at some of the well-known English venues. Again, they did well at the Nag's, but although Protex toured the mainland for a couple of years they never got past the pub and club circuit and eventually returned home. Patrik Fitzgerald, a poet who had been involved on the punk scene almost from the start, performed at the Nag's one New Year's Day. I probably thought it was a good idea to have a quiet headliner due to the amount of hangovers that would be in the room. Patrik was very funny but I didn't think it would be a good idea to book a repeat for a long time as you can't tell the same stories twice, and although I was asked, I never got round to using him again.

In 1980 another club opened in High Wycombe to cater for the punk crowd. Called the Flyover Club, it was based in the old concrete bunker where the Twynight had been situated many years earlier, underneath the road in the town centre from which it took its name. I didn't fancy the idea of sharing my audiences so I made myself busy for a few weeks putting on more punk than usual and the new venture didn't last long. It might sound mercenary, but I'd spent years building up the very crowd that they were trying to take away from me.

Ray Russell wasn't all that interested in the bands themselves and preferred to let me get on with running the music, even if to listen to him he was one of the great promoters of the world, up there with Bill Graham and Harvey Goldsmith. He had a two page spread in the local paper, talking about the Nag's but not mentioning me at all. Another time, he had someone from the brewery down and I was introduced as "Ron, the bloke that helps me out."

This was about my lowest ebb. I was skint, I'd lost my biggest venue, with another looking as though it could go the same way any minute, and as the eighties began we had a recession to contend with. Unemployment was rising all the time and people couldn't afford to go to gigs.

Luckily I still had Alexander's, and a boss who knew the music business. Barry said to me, "Come on, we're going flyposting." I was used to going round town in the middle of the night when nobody could see, but Barry marched over to his Rolls Royce, filled the boot with posters and we'd start on Monday morning. He posted everywhere; shop windows, advertising hoardings, even opposite the council offices in Reading. If anyone who looked official asked what he was up to, he'd always manage to sweet talk them and send them away with a pile of tickets for the club. He even did it with a couple of policemen. Barry never shinned up trees in the park, though.

I was at Alexander's for 18 months and sometimes I managed to get back to the cutting edge. We did new romantic bands when that scene was just starting; Spandau Ballet played one of their first gigs for us. A good crowd came down from London for the nights, but the locals weren't into the scene and there weren't many bands being formed so from our point of view it quickly fizzled out. The new romantic look was always more about dressing up than the music and neither aspect had any lasting effect. The whole thing was false, like dressing for a party, and appealed to people who wanted to suspend their belief for the

Career Opportunities

evening. The music soon came and went and you don't exactly see many pirates walking down the high street these days. I did, though, meet another interesting character, or rather make his acquaintance once again.

Boy George was a regular visitor to the 100 Club when punk was at its height. Actually, that's not strictly true. He was a regular visitor to the top of the stairs, where he'd come along most nights and chat to us. George was always talking about forming a band and I think we were part of his rounds; his night out was to tour the clubs talking to the door staff. I think he was trying to get an invitation inside. George was a respectful young man, always very quiet and well spoken. He wasn't as outrageously dressed as he became later on, although that's not saying much.

One of the strangest, and saddest, incidents while I was working at Alexander's took place on New Year's Eve. The weather was freezing, as it had been for days, so frost was lying thick on the ground. The club was filling up at about 10pm when two girls came to the front door and as they were paying, told me that "There's a bloke round the back looks like he's been beaten up. He seems to be badly hurt." Although strictly speaking it was nothing to do with me I didn't like to think anyone could get into trouble while I was working so I went round the back with Pete, the bar manager. We both expected to have to deal with a gang, but there were only two people there, looking at a man who was lying on the floor dressed in just his underpants and socks. We called for an ambulance and he was taken away, suffering from a broken leg and arm. I later found out that he'd been shinning up the drainpipe into the men's toilets, trying to get in without paying, and he'd lost his grip on the icy pipe. The reason why he wasn't properly dressed was that his friends had smuggled his clothes into the club and he intended to put them on when he got into the toilet. He'd probably run out of money over Christmas and couldn't afford the entrance fee to the club, but how he thought he'd be able to climb up an icy drainpipe I don't know, especially when he was drunk. He must have been drunk, because he surely wouldn't have attempted it sober. For the sake of five quid, which was how much we were charging to get into the club that night, he almost killed himself, but I'm glad to say he made a full recovery. Stupidity might be punishable, but it isn't a capital offence.

I really didn't enjoy working at the club. It was situated just outside the town, on the A4 Bath Road, a quarter of a mile from an industrial estate, and it worked at much the same level. It was another industrial outlet, catering for people who led automated, robotic lives. They were given a rudimentary education, pushed into a job where they didn't have to think for themselves, then at the weekend they were let off the leash and were so relieved at their taste of freedom that they just wanted to get out of their heads. They'd all dress the same, buy the same drinks, act the same, then end the night in the same way. The audiences at live venues can think for themselves and they seek out the best forms of entertainment. The disco crowd had to be told how to enjoy themselves and were too stupid to act independently.

We'd had Bill Clinton, and in 1982 Tony Blair made an appearance at the Nag's. He was Labour candidate in the local Beaconsfield bye-election and came to the pub early one evening. His agent introduced him and I showed them both around. Blair was an enthusiastic music fan; wandering round this famous venue he looked like I would if I'd been shown around a Mississippi juke joint where Robert Johnson had once played. Again, I'd like to say that I was touched by a feeling that here was a man who would one day become a world statesman, but I couldn't get over his air of superiority and the feeling that even then he was doing us a favour by gracing the place with his presence.

My dad died in 1982, after a long illness. By this time I had a full-time job as a quality engineer and I was buying a flat in Slough. Things had come full circle. I was back in proper employment and promotion was a sideline, although ironically I was putting on some of my best-ever gigs.

Unfortunately, Ray didn't seem to improve. He'd do stupid things like blocking the access drive at the side of the pub with

Career Opportunities

his car and refusing to move it, so that the band had to park in the road. It might have only been another fifty yards but they'd have to make several trips and when you're carrying gear that's not nice. Another time he threw someone out of the pub for wearing patchouli oil, because "it's covering the smell of something else." He was annoying the bands, he was annoying the customers, and I was regularly told, "We'll play for you, but you'll have to find another venue." I was losing quality acts and my reputation was suffering through no fault of my own.

Alexander's was gradually fizzling out, which happens with most nightclubs as trends change and a place that's fashionable becomes out-dated. I went part-time there and I decided that it was time to get on with my life outside of the music business. I enrolled on a course in maintenance fitting and from then on things got better for me. I'd done similar work before, but I needed formal training.

I felt like a 40 year-old apprentice, although with so many people unemployed and industries closing down there were plenty in a similar situation. And from that course, I started to build back and get my life sorted again. I hadn't got a home of my own and my venues were hanging by a thread – I was now doing a few 100 Club blues gigs again and the Nag's occasionally, yet I was still supposedly loaded. I got a job and I'd hear comments such as "I never thought we'd see you working here." It was the typically English thing – people were happy to see me down. They'd love to have done what I had, but they didn't have the nerve or the ability so they didn't want me to make a success of it, either. What they didn't seem to realise was that promoting is a gamble. It isn't just about finding a decent band and then counting the money, there are many factors out of your control. You can put on a great band and still do badly because it's belting down with rain or there's a better band playing in the next street. We ran the 100 Club throughout the three-day week and the IRA bombing campaign during the seventies. That had an effect on crowds but I survived. Now there was a recession, and even people who were still in work weren't sure they would be in a month's time so they were economising, and a night out was the first thing they stopped.

Things started to improve, and ironically they got better at a time when I felt everything else was at a low ebb. The youth cults that had been driving the music scene since the sixties were starting to fizzle out and inspiration was coming from morose young men writing poetry in their bedrooms. It might have made gigs safer but it was dull and boring. The great bands I'd help nurture from the start – the likes of Thin Lizzy, Slade and the Jam – were splitting up and success for their replacements seemed more about having the right haircut than possessing talent. I could have got the Nag's back on the circuit but Ray wasn't interested so I had to look back to the bands I'd worked with before and who I knew could attract the type of crowd he wanted. Some weeks I'd have three bands at the Nag's and more at the 100 Club, other weeks I didn't do a thing. I put on bands that I knew my audiences would enjoy, on nights when I knew they'd draw good crowds. The pressure was off and I was enjoying myself.

The Nashville Teens were a sixties band, although they were a long way removed from the frilly shirt-wearing cabaret material that their contemporaries were playing, and they pulled in a good crowd. I'd stumbled across them due to my association with their manager, Andrew Kilderry, who I'd known since Brewer's Droop played their early show at his 1832 club in Windsor. He suggested that they'd go down well at the Nag's, and so it proved. The only original member of the band was singer Ray Phillips, one of those lucky bastards who looked twenty years younger than he was, and who was now working in a factory as well as playing gigs. The band ran through a set of blues standards and biker favourites, Born To Be Wild and that sort of stuff. They knew their audience, they were good at what they did and they soon became a favourite at the Nag's, playing there by popular demand every couple of months.

Ray Dorset played a couple of gigs with his band the Insiders, then again when he reformed Mungo Jerry, round about the time

Career Opportunities

his song Feels Like I'm In Love was a number one for Kelly Marie, earning him a considerable amount of royalties. Again, he'd been in the business long enough to know what the audience wanted and they got the hits.

My acquaintance from two decades earlier, Long John Baldry, played, as did Nightshade, a reggae act from Reading, who regularly packed the place. Tom Robinson, then at a similar low ebb to me after his band broke up, played the Nag's a few times and went on to some well-deserved solo success afterwards. Brewer's Droop really, really meant that the Saturday night they played would be their last gig.

The Magic Mushroom Band, a bunch of hippies from Bracknell, came along and did great business. They were very lively and original, even though Ray managed to upset them. He reckoned they'd dented his car while unloading – the car that you'll remember wouldn't have even been parked there if he'd been in the slightest bit helpful. Ray demanded £100 damages from the band's money and I had to hand it over to him, then explain to them why they were being short-changed. Naturally they weren't happy and another good draw was lost to the Nag's.

Lee Kosmin was the sort of act every promoter needs. He was a good singer and had a decent band. What was more attractive about Lee from my perspective was that he would fill in at short notice. It's reckoned that Queens' Park Rangers were on Match of the Day so often in the seventies because their ground at Loftus Road was close to the BBC's White City studios, so whenever a match that was due to be featured was postponed a camera crew could be dispatched to film QPR. In a similar way, Lee Kosmin played so many gigs at the Nag's because I could always get hold of him and knew he'd entertain the crowd. I remember the Idiot Dancers because of the name, which reminded me of what we used to get up to at festivals all those years ago, but their music was a heavy industrial sound totally different to the hippy stuff of the early seventies.

Dana Gillespie, a blues singer who was friendly with many of the rock aristocracy, became a house favourite. Steve Gibbons, who'd been on the scene for years and had been in the charts a couple of years earlier, played regularly, as did Caddyshack, a local blues act. Lazy, a heavy metal band, were a good draw and had a stunningly pretty manager. The Hamsters were just starting out and later became one of the biggest attractions on the live circuit. The type of music was as wide-ranging as anything I'd ever put on. There were US blues masters Big Joe Louis, Los Angeles saxophonist Jay McNeely and Luther Allison, who performed one of the greatest sets the Nag's ever saw. Anyone privileged to be at that gig will remember the way Luther played and it's still talked about every time I go back to the town. Tony McPhee's Groundhogs played regularly, as did Sledgehammer, who were Slough's premier heavy metal band, for what it was worth. At the other end of the scale were Ozric Tentacles, a new age hippy band who are still going strong to this day.

Howard Jones had been around the local scene for ages, playing in a variety of bands. When he did his solo stuff I could see that he was going to get big, because more and more people kept turning up. He eventually had a few hits and still plays eighties revival tours. Howard was probably the last big name that I broke at my venues. Marillion also did some gigs for me in their early days. They were living in Aylesbury and I was able to put them on a few times before they started playing halls. I wasn't too keen on their prog rock stuff, as the original had almost killed off live music ten years earlier. Still, it pulled in a crowd, and by now I figured that I was selling music, not eating it. I didn't have to like a band to use them

The eighties had started off badly but once the decade had got going for Ron Watts, I enjoyed it. Things were looking up again. I was working, earning money and putting on some good acts. In fact, for a time I was busier than ever. I wasn't at the whims of fashion any more and I could book acts regardless of what they looked like.

Chapter 22

New Song

Ray Russell was still running the Nag's, but I'd managed to turn it round despite him. John Otway asked if he could play; I got in touch with the local press and they did us proud with a big spread about "Otway Comes Home." It turned into one of the biggest nights the Nag's ever witnessed. The pub was mobbed; even the wall heaters were wrecked as people were standing on them to get a better view. As a result John started a Monday night residency that did good business for a while.

Ray was happy while I was promoting safe sixties stuff that he could relate to, but there were also some good rock acts coming through. It was towards the end of what had been dubbed the New Wave of British Heavy Metal and some of the bands were a lot more tolerable than their predecessors – they'd caught a bit of the punk spirit. Dark Star played at the Nag's and their blend of melodic metal captured the mood of the crowd well. Pagan Attack should have stayed in their bedrooms being frightened by the full moon. They dressed the stage with a Black Mass altar, skulls, inverted crosses, the lot. I think they were trying to be devil-worshippers but they just looked daft and most of the Nag's audience thought the same. Once you've seen Johnny Thunders stop just short of shooting up onstage you aren't that bothered by a Hammer Horror b-movie acted out by a third-rate heavy metal band. I was surprised that Lazy didn't get bigger than they did even though they were the sort of band whose success would have given me mixed feelings. I'd like them to have done well but at the same time I didn't want them to get too big for the Nag's.

Mick Abrahams, on the other hand, could have stayed in obscurity for all I cared. I'd book him because he pulled in a decent crowd then he'd turn up two hours late even though he was only coming from Dunstable. He hadn't arrived by eight when the audience started to turn up and I couldn't let them in, in case he didn't show. Then he rolled up at 9.30, no apology, just a smile and a shrug, didn't bother soundchecking and did a perfunctory hour. With an attitude like that it was no wonder he didn't become as big as his talent deserved, and Mick on form was as good a blues guitarist as this country could boast. Promoters talk to each other, we may be rivals but it's in our own best interests to find out what's going on. When you have someone who's unreliable for one promoter he'll struggle to get work from anyone else and when you have a performer behaving like Mick Abrahams you're better off going without. Then there's John Otway, who has a reputation for being an absolute lunatic but who has never as far as I'm aware caused a minute's problems for anyone.

By now I was working as chief inspector for British Plastics, on the Slough Trading Estate. I'd once sworn that I'd never return to that estate after leaving Mars, but needs must... And I was doing fine. By juggling work and promoting I was able to buy a flat in Slough and as my money was coming back, so was my confidence. It's always the same. If you're doing well it's noticeable and people want to be associated with you. I was working from seven am until midnight and, once more, a night off was a rarity. One of the reasons for this was that I was back at the 100 Club.

Bill Bryant, who had been involved with Howard Jones, asked me to help him get a gig at the club for a singer he managed named Paul Linn. I got in touch with Roger Horton again, he was happy to see me, and as a result of this initial contact I started doing two or three gigs a month for him. The 100 Club had been losing its way a bit and had been promoting some of the nasty skinhead stuff that I'd avoided at the Nag's. I started bringing decent blues back to the venue. Big Jay McNeely came back over from California, together with his light show and a saxophone that glowed in the dark. It was a bit gimmicky but the crowds loved it. One time, Jay came directly from Heathrow to the club, and went straight into a two-hour rehearsal with his band, who he hadn't met previously, then did a show that night.

I persuaded Nappy Brown, one of the early r&b vocalists, from North Carolina, to come out of retirement and play for me. With his band the Heart Fixers he'd made some of my favourite blues records and hearing him play live totally refreshed me about promoting again. Unfortunately, there was to be a sad ending to his UK tour when we heard that the wife of his guitarist, Tinsley Ellis, had been murdered. She'd left Tinsley and taken up with a drug dealer in Florida, who had killed her. It was a real blow to see Tinsley so happy then to have a shock like that. He flew home straight away and although we got a replacement and the tour continued, quite understandably the heart had gone out of the band.

I like to think I helped the 100 Club regain some of its lost prestige, although I'd missed out on the legendary night when the Rolling Stones performed their secret gig in 1982. They played the club rather than the Marquee because they'd got into a fight at the Marquee twenty years earlier that had led to their being banned from performing there, and still bore a grudge. I couldn't get to the gig because I was busy and when word got round that the Stones had played 'my' 100 Club some of the Nag's regulars weren't very happy about me not telling them. But of course with a gig like that, everyone who had advance knowledge had been sworn to secrecy. I also helped the club maintain its reputation for having the most schizophrenic booking policy in London. An average week would see a night of soul or reggae, two nights of jazz, maybe some r&b, a new band such as Big Sound Authority or the Blow Monkeys, and a couple of punk bands. With such a line-up the audiences could have been forgiven for getting confused and I often wondered if any of the old trad fans who'd been going to the club since the war turned up by mistake on a punk night. If the UK Subs were playing they could have talked about rationing with Charlie Harper.

James Booker came back; he could play but I still wouldn't have him in the house. He was a very big drug taker, which is something I've never had much time for, and he caused me problems. That guy could have been a big star but he was the original 'cause trouble in an empty room' character. He'd walk into a shop and start a riot because he didn't want to queue or he couldn't understand the English money he was getting in change. "They should have some dollars and cents in the till for when Americans come into their shop," he said to me on one occasion when he'd got into an argument buying a paper, and I've no doubt he was being serious.

As for Paul Linn, who had indirectly got me back into the club, I was asked to become involved with his management. He was similar to Howard Jones, playing keyboards and singing, but after I'd seen Paul a few times I couldn't see much of a future for him and passed on the opportunity. Maybe it was for the best – after a bad review in the local Bucks Free Press, a woman fan of Paul's sought out the reporter responsible and threw a bottle of piss over him. He got on the phone to me wanting to know what was going on and I had the devil's own game persuading him that Paul was nothing to do with me.

I was still promoting at the Town Hall until the council decided that they wanted a sole promoter and put the contract out to tender, even though I'd enjoyed a long association with them. The final choice was down to me or Dave Stopps, from the Friars club in Aylesbury, and we both went to be interviewed by council officials one afternoon. I was questioned closely about security at my gigs and my accountancy methods, which was strange considering that I'd been good enough on both levels to promote at the venue for years. Dave and I got together and decided that neither of us could be bothered with the hassle; the council were treating us as though they were dealing with the devil and we both walked away. Not long afterwards the Town Hall was rebuilt, in any case, and re-opened as a leisure complex, the Swan. It's used for arts stuff and as a theatre now.

During the mid-eighties the Windsor chapter of the Hell's Angels started turning up at the Nag's. They liked a lot of the blues and boogie music I was putting on and I was happy because they attracted plenty of women. Despite their sinister reputation the Angels were fine left to their own devices and nobody was going to challenge them. In fact, they served as an attraction because some people liked the excitement of going to a place where the Angels hung out.

We were also the preferred haunt of the Herpes Owners Club, a branch of the Bucks Bikers Club, for a time. They were into blues rock, so the Hamsters and similar bands were big favourites of theirs. The only incident that occurred with the bikers came when one of their girl members was assaulted by another bike gang one Saturday night. I didn't know the details but a lot of serious discussion took place throughout the following day, with the result that someone had an old motorbike engine thrown through their front window that night. A first and final warning had been issued and things soon returned to normal. Apart from that, we never had any problem with any of the bikers. The closest we got was when one of their prospects might occasionally overstep the mark trying to prove himself, but a word to a senior club member was all it usually took for peace to be restored.

By now I was living in Slough and working as a quality technician for Broome & Wade, who made roadside compressors. Blues was still a big crowd puller; Long John Baldrey and Johnny Mars did gigs for me at the Nag's and the 100 Club. I also put on a Tex-Mex act, Flaco Jimenez, then the Mighty Fliers, who featured a harp player from California named Rod Piazza. Rod did a sold-out Sunday lunchtime at the Nag's with his wife, Honey, playing piano. He also played with Baconfat, featuring another harp player, George Smith, who was one of the best in the world. They did good business for me at the 100 Club until the Department of Something or Other found out they were in the country illegally and they were deported sharpish. Charlie Musselwhite, a harmonica player who had recorded with, amongst others, John Lee Hooker and John Hammond, also performed. I was still able to have the edge over other promoters by offering two prestigious venues.

Plenty of local bands were doing well at the Nag's. I'd put promising acts on Thursday nights and the bigger ones on Saturdays. By now the college and club circuit was fading away but the Nag's was still going strong. Of the local bands, Travelling Shoes were one of the best. Their type of blues was reminiscent of the Allman Brothers band, and although it sounded a bit dated by this time, they played it well enough and always attracted a crowd. They could probably have got a bigger name for themselves but they were happy to stay local and I was happy for them to stay at the level where I could still afford them. Rough Justice and Spod were two more bands whose rocking blues pulled in decent crowds without ever pushing back any musical boundaries. But they kept things ticking over, and by now that was all I was really interested in. TV Smith, former singer with the Adverts, provided a night of punk nostalgia and was about the most extreme act Ray Russell would let me get away with.

The landlord was, in fact, causing me more than one kind of problem. Ray had always wanted to make upstairs into a snooker room. He even applied for permission from the council, although he got turned down. He hadn't said anything, although I had an inkling when he took me to one side and said "Carry on with what you're doing." That was nice of him. I'd been carrying on at the Nag's for about twenty years by now. And if the council had let him, I'd have been straight out the window.

The Thursday night gigs, in truth, weren't up to much. I don't want to criticise them but some of the local bands didn't have much of a clue. They'd played in front of their friends and suddenly they had a booking at one of the top pub venues in the country. They were enthusiastic, but that alone doesn't win over a crowd who were used to seeing some of the best bands on the scene. A similar thing would happen to bands that progressed from the Nag's to the 100 Club and couldn't handle an audience who didn't know them. I was happy to try to plug local talent, but the only act who came through at this time was Howard Jones. Basta Roc weren't bad, a new wave band who did a few shows for me at the Nag's and the 100 Club. They featured in a TV programme about the Nag's, although the exposure didn't do any of us much good. Wild Willy Barrett finally got the solo gig he'd claimed he was due ten years earlier. It wasn't particularly memorable. Whatever his musical ability, Willy didn't have much stage presence and he's never been the most reliable of performers. One of his solo evenings was enough. It says a lot that John Otway kept him in check when they briefly reunited for a gig at the Nag's.

Some of the local bands were memorable only for their names. The V2s were ironically-named considering one of their forerunners had almost killed me forty-odd years before and World Leaders Must Die were possibly the best-named band ever. Other acts were memorable because of their talent. The Soul Agents were from further afield – the East End to be precise. They played sixties Stax and Motown and were not only talented, they were some of the nicest people I've ever met in the music business. Their audiences would travel a long way to see them, although bands like that are only ever going to get so far and for a short time. It's inevitable that if you're playing the same stuff every night the people who go to see you will eventually move on, but for a time the Soul Agents gave me and the audiences at the Nag's and the 100 Club some good nights. The Xtravertz, Wycombe's finest punk band, got back together for a while and I was happy to give them some dates. Dog Town Rhythm were from Maidenhead. They wore suits, played a poppy mod style and had a friendly rivalry with their neighbours Caddyshack over who could draw the biggest crowds. The total number in the audience would usually be around the same, but Dog Town definitely had more women following them. So naturally I gave them plenty of work.

Rouen were a strange band. They came from Birmingham, wore white and played pretty boy pop. Unfortunately for them Duran Duran were doing all that five years earlier. I booked them into the Nag's during a furniture exhibition. The idea was that they would entertain the visitors, but nobody there was interested in listening to a live band while they were talking business, and Rouen performed their set in total silence.

Dance of the Lost Souls caused me a problem, but not because of their act. They were a decent enough band, playing indie pop at the time the Smiths had made it fashionable, and pulled good crowds, although Ray didn't like to see too many young people in his pub at any one time. Then one day the murder squad came round to see me on account of my connection with the band. One of their fans had been found naked and murdered near their home town of Chinnor, on the Oxfordshire/Buckinghamshire border. The police had a suspect and wanted to explore every possible loophole so as not to jeopardise their case against the man. In the end he was found guilty and sentenced to life.

The Directors were a good rock band from Reading. I fancied doing some gigs again and approached them with the idea of them becoming Brewers Droop mk. IX, or however many incarnations we'd had by then. They were up for it, we rehearsed together and eventually played a gig at the Nag's. Sadly their rock influences proved too strong and after one guitar solo too many I realised that we weren't compatible. We parted on good terms and they continued to play for me.

Eddie Campbell hails from the South Side of Chicago, the meanest part of town as the song goes, and he's lived life to the full. I think he used to tour Europe when things were getting a bit hot for him back home and eventually they must have reached boiling point because he lived over here for some time. That was good news for the blues audiences, because his guitar playing was as good as anyone during the eighties, when he toured regularly and I was able to promote him at the 100 Club.

Little Willie Littlefield was a contemporary of Campbell, although he's a pianist from Texas. He also moved to Europe and after hearing some of his stories of life in the South, I didn't blame him. "I'd be driving along the road and I'd pull into a gas station," he once told me. "I'd get out of the car and suddenly some big guy would come out and pull a gun on me. 'Get back in the car, nigger' he'd say. 'Just tell me what you want and gimme the money through the window.' They didn't want me in their nice white gas station but my money was okay for them." Willie was as pleasant a man as you could wish to meet and it was a sobering thought that such incidents were commonplace in a country that prides itself on its freedom and democracy.

Eddie and Willie moved from the States to Europe but Wes McGhee did the journey in reverse. Hailing from the bayous of Leicestershire, Wes suffered from problems with his record company during the early part of his career, eventually setting up his own label, and his brand of country rock has enjoyed plenty of success on both sides of the Atlantic. He was another performer who I booked into the Nag's knowing that the audience would love him even though they may not have heard of him. I felt that there was an air of mutual respect between me and the Nag's customers and I was always confident that the audience trusted me to put on quality acts, even if they were unknowns. The night Wes played was no exception and it was a treat for me to see a full country band in such an unlikely setting. He was an old friend from back in the days when he backed Homesick James and I was glad to see Wes get the success he deserved.

One band who didn't get the success they could have enjoyed were Pride and Passion, a local outfit who I always enjoyed watching even at other venues. They had a lovely girl singer and I was glad to give them gigs. I thought they'd become a big success and I remember being very disappointed when they told me they were splitting up, and not just because I'd lost a band who always did good business for me. Talent such as theirs should be encouraged, as there isn't enough of it around. They were so good I can still remember them now, years after they finished.

Dumpy's Rusty Nuts were another band you'd never forget. If the name wasn't enough, Dumpy's appearance, complete with motorcycle helmet and goggles, showed that they could never be anything other than a rocking r&b band appealing to bikers who wanted to drink and enjoy themselves to loud music. Dumpy would ring me two or three times a week, telling me how well they were going down at other gigs, even though I'd already booked him and had promised that he was going to get paid. I'd seen the type of music they did hundreds of times before, but that made it no less enjoyable. Like Brewer's Droop, their audiences appreciated a band who made an effort to entertain.

At the other end of every scale imaginable were Egor and the Worms, who played several gigs at the 100 Club. This wasn't so much a band as a performance theatre of the kind I might once have enjoyed playing with. They'd do a pop song then go off into some rambling Celtic poetry. A decent crowd followed them around, which meant that I was happy to put them on.

Chapter 23

The Final Countdown

I spent a lot of this period, particularly during the summer months, living on my boat on the Thames. It was moored at Bourne End, close to a brook that fed into the river, and I'd often wake up to see the sun shining on the water, three feet deep and crystal clear, with trout swimming happily. There was a free meal there any time I wanted but my fishing days were over. Ironically in view of my past, I was healthier and fitter than I had been for years, running two or three miles a day and cutting back on my alcohol intake.

In 1987 I decided to make a clean break and move out of the Wycombe area. First of all I went to live in Ffestiniog, North Wales. It was a beautiful place, and when I arrived I got on well with the locals. I found out later that they thought I was a lorry driver, because whenever I used to go into the local pub it was always on the same night as a big lorry was parked in the town centre. When they found out that I was living in the town, and to make matters worse I started seeing one of their best-looking girls, I got the typical speak-Welsh-when-I-walked-in treatment that has made North Walian hospitality so renown throughout the country.

I stood it for a couple of months, then remembered how Duster Bennett had always raved about this place he'd moved to; Tamworth, in Staffordshire. He'd told me how lively it was and how cheap houses were, so I looked around and ended up getting a nice house there for the same price as my flat in Slough.

Tamworth's hardly known for its musical credentials. Julian Cope was brought up there and it's where Blaze Bayley, who was the singer with Iron Maiden for a time in the nineties, comes from. I met Blaze while he was with Maiden, and when we were chatting away I asked him what he did for a living, knowing full well who he was. "I move hi-fis," was the reply from a man who looked every inch a rock god, with his long hair, clothes and demeanour. Fair play to him for not shouting his name from the rooftops.

I continued to promote at the Nag's and split my time between Tamworth and High Wycombe. Larry Johnson, an old-style delta blues guitarist from Georgia, lived in Wycombe for a while. I was doing some djing at the Nag's one Sunday lunchtime when I had a phone call from him asking "You still in business?" He'd just arrived at Heathrow and was looking for work. I booked him that night and he ended up staying in the town a while. I put him on a few Saturday nights, until he threatened to throw acid in my face after we'd fallen out because he wanted me to be his agent. Larry could be volatile - I got him onto Charlie Gillett's radio show, but he wanted cash up front to perform and because that was a non-starter he wouldn't play. That did it with him for me.

Jack Bruce also played on what was the last great night at the Nag's. He was involved with a band who were so average that I've forgotten their name; and was in the audience. When the band began their second set Jack was on the stage and as the music started up he turned round and began playing. The audience were cheering and he played a few numbers before letting the band finish on their own.

I was putting on more gigs at the 100 Club than the Nag's by this point. There wasn't a great deal happening in Wycombe, although I provided a few nostalgic memories by promoting acid rockers from the sixties the Pink Fairies, plus a couple of shows by Eric Bell, Thin Lizzy's original guitarist, which reminded me of the show Lizzy had done back in 1971. More great memories were provided by Jimmy Witherspoon's show at the 100 Club, where he rolled back the years and showed an appreciative audience what a great bluesman he was and, I hope, reminded them of the good times I'd provided at the club.

Glen Matlock brought another group to the Nag's. This time they were called Gangshow and they were another good band that lasted about five minutes. Sometimes I wonder if I've ever

The Final Countdown

promoted anyone in as many different bands as I have Glen. A band by the name of Brewer's Droop did a couple of shows, including a real festival of nostalgia at the 100 Club. Nappy Brown, Caddyshack and Shakey Vick's band also featured in what was billed as the London Summer Blues Festival and was without a shadow of a doubt the last time Droop would play anywhere, ever. You could put money on that.

By the early nineties I was starting to accept that live music was dying out. The youngsters were into rave and club stuff and it was getting to the situation that we'd endured before punk, when gigs were the preserve of the older generation. In fact it was worse, because at least back then kids were waiting for something new. Now, though, they'd found it and it wasn't anything I could get involved with. The days when customers would be queuing before we opened the doors were long gone. I was made redundant by Broome & Wade, and it was time to redesign my life again. One Thursday night in early 1991 I couldn't get back for a gig at the Nag's and I couldn't be bothered to let Ray know that there was a problem. I went down the following Saturday and Ray told me, "That's it." I'd obviously given him the excuse he'd been looking for to get rid of me.

I had mixed feelings about leaving the Nag's. I'd been there for years but in my heart I knew it would never be viable again. Ray had a succession of new promoters trying their luck but they all failed and eventually it ceased as a live venue altogether. Ray sold up, and after a time as a gay bar, it's now called the Office. Presumably that's so businessmen can spend their time after work in there and tell their wives they've been in the office. Ho, ho, ho.

When it was a gay bar it was called the Pride. That's an appropriate name, because I'm still proud of my time at the Nag's Head. It was where I really got things started and where I got hooked on the lifestyle that kept me going for so long. There can't be many pub venues that started out booking Howling Wolf and then broke someone like Howard Jones. Shakey Vick did our twentieth anniversary in 1988 and still pulled in a crowd.

The old-timers all turned out and we had a great night. But you couldn't help enjoying yourself when Vick was around. For many years he lived in Chippenham Road, Paddington, and he always kept a room there for me. I'd go round there after a gig and we'd sit until late in the night, philosophising about every subject under the sun. Vick's about 70 now and he's been a big help in every way. His band gave me a start when I was first promoting, he did the door for me at the 100 Club and helped me a lot. He deserves a long and happy retirement.

In the same week as I lost the Nag's, I rang Jim Simpson for a job reference. We'd kept in touch since the Brewer's Droop days, when we'd given him the publishing rights and not seen a penny in return, although knowing Jim and his business methods, neither in all likelihood did he. He was now working mainly as a promoter and I'd helped him put together some of his blues tours. I told him my situation and he asked, "What are you doing tonight? Can you get to Newark?" I got the train and had an interesting journey following the Trent Valley, arriving earlier than I'd wanted, so to kill time I went into the first pub and was amazed at how busy it was. At ten past six on a midweek evening the place was packed, despite there supposedly being a recession on.

Jim was in town to watch a show he'd been putting on at the Arts Centre called Lady Sings the Blues, a tribute to Billy Holliday starring his partner, Val Wiseman. Val's got a lovely voice and it was a good show. Jim then asked me if I fancied working for him, promoting the Birmingham International Jazz Festival, which had been going since 1985 and was now one of the biggest in Europe. We agreed a wage and the following Monday I arrived at the Big Bear offices bright and early ready to help promote a jazz festival.

The Birmingham festival had made its name with the quality of the free gigs. They were putting world-class acts into pubs, shopping centres, car showrooms, anywhere that could attract a crowd. Some big names were performing at orthodox venues as well. B.B King played, as did Albert Collins at the Alexandra

Theatre, which was a night to remember, or to forget, whichever you prefer.

C.J. Chenier & the Red Hot Louisiana Band were the support act and went down well, but once the interval was over it was obvious that there were problems. Albert wanted payment up front and when that didn't happen he refused to do a soundcheck. His backing band, the Icebreakers, came on and did a couple of numbers, then Albert performed for twenty shambolic minutes before going offstage. Once the house lights came up and the crowd realised that the show was over they began to first get restless, then got angry. Naturally they wanted explanations and the festival staff, most of whom were volunteers, didn't know what was going on. One or two discreetly hid their identification passes and slipped away. Being a black American bluesman, Albert had been so used to getting ripped off over the years that he'd acquired a built-in defence mechanism and the non-arrival of his wages had triggered it again. If he'd been a bit more sensible he would have realised that a festival promoter with sponsorship from major companies and the city council was unlikely to default on payment, but he probably thought the worst and behaved accordingly.

With the festival over I could tell that Jim's business sense hadn't improved, but I'd had an enjoyable two weeks. There'd been women, drink and great music. I'd got back doing what I liked; traipsing around pubs, leafleting, meeting people and persuading them to turn up at the gigs. I'd really enjoyed myself. There was a great ambience around the festival even if you couldn't take the music too seriously. Jim had always gone for showy bands rather than authenticity.

The festival had also made me realise there was a market for a blues club in Birmingham. I asked Jim to co-promote with me, and as he had a promotional link with local brewery; Ansell's, we got them to find us a venue. They came back with a few names that weren't what we were looking for; one pub had oars along the walls and hanging from the ceiling, so that was out. Another looked fine but we were told the car park was a no-go area after dark, which put us off because we were looking to attract people from around the Midlands.

Eventually we hit on the Bear, in Bearwood, three miles from the city centre and with plenty of public transport. The venue itself was perfect, boasting a large room upstairs with a separate bar and a capacity of around 300 including a quiet area that was cut off from the rest of the room. Jim, the landlord, was a lovely Irish guy and he had several equally lovely daughters.

We kicked off the first night with Mojo Buford, who had played harmonica in Muddy Waters' band, and hit the ground running. The club had started at the time of a blues revival and within two years we'd got 5,000 members. Robert Plant was one of the first to join. I'm sure he'd have played for us if we'd pushed it, but we never got round to asking him properly. Olympic swimming medallist Nick Gillingham was another regular, although we never asked him to perform. We were pulling in customers from as far away as Manchester and Derby and Big Bear's staff would be full stretched on Tuesdays answering calls about that night's performance.

One great thing about the Bear was that we put on every possible interpretation of the blues. Jimmy Witherspoon did a memorable sell-out gig, when it seemed as though every musician in the city was in attendance. My old standby Johnny Mars played, as did such American names as Chris Thomas (who later appeared in the film 'Ray' playing the part of Lowell Fulson/Fulsom with uncanny likeness) and Lazy Lester. The Hamsters were at their peak and packed the place out every time they were on. They'd got merchandising off to a fine art and earned a fortune from their t-shirts and CDs. There was cajun, with the likes of R Cajun and the Zydeco Brothers, from Derby, who always pulled in a good crowd and gave us some great nights. The Red Lemon Electric Blues Band were local and did a Blues Brothers-type act, nothing ground-breaking but they were very popular and knew how to entertain.

With the club doing well we staged the Second Birmingham Blues Festival, so-called because Jim had put on another one

The Final Countdown

during the seventies, over the August Bank Holiday of 1992. It featured, amongst others, Sherman Robertson, Chris Thomas and Shuggie Otis, son of the legendary Johnny, with his own band. There were also home-grown acts; Sonny Black and local hero Steve Gibbons being big draws. My old mate Brett Marvin came up to do a gig at the Red Lion, a well-known pub on the local live circuit, and I sang a couple of numbers with his latest Thunderbolts.

Most of the festival gigs were free but unfortunately Jim, being Jim, decided to have the showcase promotion, at the Irish Centre and starring some of the big American names, on the opening night rather than at the end, by which time word would have spread about how good the acts were. Ticket sales were poor and to make matters worse, as it was August Bank Holiday weekend, it rained heavily so the chances of a good walk-up were ruined.

That apart the festival was a big success, even if Lucky Lopez Evans got legless while watching Tony McPhee downstairs at the Bear, then went up to the main room and performed one of the most drink-affected sets I've ever seen, culminating in a 25 minute version of Rainy Night in Georgia.

Shuggie Otis played ten gigs in five days and was superb; his last show was on Bank Holiday Monday at the Junction in Harborne, which was full to capacity and not one person over honest, officer, with people who arrived late standing down the stairs and on the fire escape trying to hear anything they could. Jim got Shuggie into a recording studio to make an album, although by all accounts it was a disappointing affair and never saw the light of day due to contractual wrangles. Shuggie could have been a star, but like many others before him, whenever he seemed on the verge of making the big time he let drink or drugs get in the way. He's released a couple of albums since, and played with some top names, but never got the acclaim that he deserved.

Despite the success of the festival I never got paid for putting most of it together, and neither did several of the workers Jim relied on. We did another the following year, but it was a low-key affair featuring local bands and some gigs by slide guitarist Catfish Keith in pubs around the city centre. The idea was dropped after that, which was a shame as it made a nice end to the summer after the mayhem of the jazz festival, but proper funding was never available and we were competing with the world-famous event at the same time in Colne, which always takes place on August Bank Holiday weekend.

Chapter 24

Back In The Night

I spent the next couple of years working more or less full-time with Big Bear. The jazz festival took some putting together and we booked plenty of established names. The Blues Brothers band came over, while they were playing the Spencer Davies hit Gimme Some Lovin' as part of their set at the Town Hall in 1992 Spencer's original drummer, Pete York, was playing with Mose Allison a couple of hundred yards away at the Grand. That was when I got more evidence that as a general rule, the bigger the star, the nicer they are.

Things didn't go smoothly on the night of the Blues Brothers gig. Meals that had been brought in arrived late, there hadn't been any security booked so the festival staff ended up having to patrol the backstage area and the show ran late. Yet Steve Cropper, Donald Dunn, Eddie Floyd and all these other legendary musicians couldn't have been any more understanding about it all.

A few days later Albert King played at the same venue. Almost seventy years old, he performed a blistering set of near two hours duration and only left the stage because he could barely walk another step. He was great; his manager, who I believe doubled as his wife, made so many demands and insisted on a member of our staff standing outside the toilet so that no-one else could enter while she was in there. The Walter Trout Band supported, and although they were comparative unknowns at this time some of them were as demanding as any arena headliners. That gig had run late because the soundcheck was delayed. The reason for the hold-up was that the Town Hall was regularly booked at lunchtimes for a recital by the city organist, so none of our equipment could be brought in until three old ladies had finished listening to their own gig.

There was also the strange case of Plas Johnson. Plas had been working the studios in Los Angeles for years, played with my old friend Johnny Otis amongst others, and was best known for the sax solo on the Pink Panther theme. As studio work had dried up he had begun making a living on the live circuit and we were looking forward to welcoming this well-respected musician whose promo photos showed a youngish, typically West Coast, dude. The photos were either very old or taken by a genius, because what we got was a middle-aged man with a bad toupee and a worse attitude. He refused to play the two sets per gig that was traditional in the festival, insisting that his backing band perform the first as a warm-up, and wouldn't perform the Pink Panther theme that had made him famous. Plas even insisted on a car to take him from the Holiday Inn where he was staying to the James Brindley pub for a performance. Anyone familiar with the canalside area of Birmingham knows that on foot, this journey consists of walking across a side street.

The Bear was still performing valiantly for us, although Jim the landlord had left, to be replaced by a heavy drinker from Yorkshire and his equally heavy-drinking wife. The Hamsters, R Cajun and the Red Lemons could always be relied upon to pull a crowd. Joe Louis Walker was as good a draw as ever, as was Dave Kelly, while we found a great act called Lightning Willie & the Poorboys, from California and fronted by a Sioux Indian, who would do a three hour set without a break.

We also made the acquaintance of Howard McCrary, who had first arrived in Birmingham as part of Phil Upchurch's band at Ronnie Scott's in the city. Howard could sing like an angel and when he announced he loved Birmingham so much that he wanted to quit Los Angeles and move to the English Midlands we thought we'd got ourselves a star. Nobody stopped to think that anyone who was willing to trade California for Birmingham might have an ulterior motive.

It transpired that Howard's private life was tangled, to put it mildly, and California had become a bit unpleasant for him after his first marriage had failed. Howard could have been a big name; everyone loved him, he was massively talented and possessed charisma by the bucketload. He'd only been living in Birmingham a couple of months when he walked down the main New Street in the city centre one Saturday afternoon and virtually stopped the traffic. Unfortunately for all concerned, Howard fell between the stools of wanting to sing gospel, blues and pop. His second wife, Tammy, sister of soul singer Chaka Khan, didn't help with her overbearing attitude and the last I heard they were back in Los Angeles where Howard was singing in supper clubs and doing gospel shows.

By 1994 trade at the Bear was slowing down. The blues revival had fizzled out and bands that a couple of years earlier would have attracted 200 customers in a blizzard wouldn't pull in more than 80 even if we'd been giving away free beer. I'd got a job back in Tamworth, and with the World Cup coming up we decided to stop the club for the summer, as both Jim and I knew from experience that it was pointless trying to pull in a decent crowd when there was football on television.

We had plans to get things started again in the autumn, but never got round to it. Jim started putting blues acts on at the Birmingham franchise of Ronnie Scott's, where he had become a director. Ronnie's did well at times, although it never attracted enough customers throughout the week to run profitably, and their acts got increasingly mainstream. The club finally closed its doors, amidst rumours of dodgy financial dealings, in 2001. It's a lapdancing joint now.

By the time the Bear stopped I'd severed my ties with the jazz festival. Jim had never had much of a business brain and his insistence on cutting corners led to a strained relationship with all concerned. Bands thought he was ripping them off because he offered less than they were being paid elsewhere, employees would leave at the first opportunity and potential sponsors became harder to convince we were worthy of their support. The festival relied heavily on volunteer staff, who would often work twelve hours a day and more for no pay, yet Jim insisted on treating them the same as his (under-) paid employees and using them as scapegoats for his own failings. Many of them didn't last long and that left more work to be done by the rest of us. My wages weren't much compensation for the grief I was getting, so I walked away from Big Bear, and the music business, after the 1994 festival.

I was better off out of it. I'd settled down in Tamworth and that was more or less the end of my life in music. I had a brief moment in the spotlight when the Pistols reformed in 1996. The local Sunday Mercury interviewed me and I sold a few bits and pieces from those halcyon days at auction.

Then during 2001 I'd just been made redundant again so I got together with a steel guitarist named John Alderton and we went busking in Derby a few days before Christmas. We were doing well enough, then I noticed this big guy talking to three policemen and move towards us. Still being quick on the uptake, I thought "We're in trouble here," and he introduced himself. "I'm the town centre manager."

He handed over his business card and said, "Thanks for coming into the town and giving us some good music." I was waiting for the inevitable "but..." when he carried on. "We encourage quality buskers," and pointed out a better spot. He told us the best places to play and walked away, saying that if we had any problems we were to ring him. It was all a far cry from the days when Lord Longford was holding my band up as a threat to the moral fibre of the nation or Special Branch were staking out my house. John and I earned a few bob, had a good drink and enjoyed ourselves, which is what music should always be about, whether you're busking in Derby or headlining Wembley Stadium.

Over the years my children took it all for granted. They weren't phased by dad being in the music business and I didn't force my love of it onto them. Stuart, my son, was never bothered by the fact that the Sex Pistols had bounced him on their knees, it was just something that had happened. As they got older they came to the odd gig, but they never made a big deal out of it.

However, as they grew up it became clear that they had aptitudes for either music or the arts. Stuart was a natural musician. I gave him my old trumpet and he was getting a tune out of it within minutes, which was more than I'd managed in decades. He later went to Wycombe Art College, and is now a furniture designer. Terri, my eldest daughter, became a photographer, and her son, Matthew, works in a recording studio. Marie, my youngest, was a dancer for some time before giving me two grandchildren.

I've come full circle now, out of the music business and with a job at TNT Distribution in Tamworth. I get into conversations about music with people at work and they usually wonder what this old bloke knows about anything. One guy is a full-on punk and forever talking about the music, but I've never let on who I am, although word's got round a bit and a few of the people I work with are aware of my background. At least it's not like the time in High Wycombe when everyone thought I was loaded. Nobody in Tamworth thinks I've got a fortune stashed away and even if they do, they're wrong. The money I earned has gone on women and my children. Both have brought me plenty of enjoyment and I don't regret either.

I still get people contacting me now for interviews, wanting to know what Sid was like, or the 100 Club, or the British blues boom; Brian James of the Damned recently got in touch about some details from the early punk days. My two daughters nag me to get back into the business, because they'd like to be involved. And I still get the occasional act wanting to know if I'd book them. Who knows? Maybe the next Sex Pistols are out there, looking for a promoter. I'm still open to offers.

Chapter 25

What Do You Want From Life?

Just in case you're wondering what out of all the thousands of gigs I've witnessed were my personal favourites, here's my top dozen in no order at all:

Johnny Otis
100 Club – Summer 1971
This was when he played five times for me on the same tour, but the highlight was the first gig. Johnny and his band spent the afternoon rehearsing in the club while I tried to get some work done as I listened to them playing, joking and getting into shape with the consummate ease that befits professionals in any walk of life who know exactly what they're doing. Then they went and did it all over again that night, with a sell-out audience lapping it up. Every time his band played for me I'd try to have a word with the soloists because I'd have liked to put them on but Johnny, ever the businessman, always put a stop to that. They were his performers, and they worked for him.

Sly & The Family Stone
Isle of Wight Festival – August 1970
Roy Holly, one of the Pinions commune crowd from Wycombe, had somehow got hold of a car. He'd either found it or swapped it for something, but they were off to a wedding in Weymouth and I persuaded them to take me and Dave Morisoli, a friend of mine, to the ferry at Lymington. We were ushered straight onboard, then when we docked at Yarmouth there was a bus waiting to take us to the festival grounds, all without paying. When we arrived at the festival site I saw this kid who was starving and he had a mark on his hand that was obviously the pass-out. We bought him fish and chips and got him to rub the mark

onto our hands, which was enough to get us past the primitive security. I think that the organisers were glad we were going in semi-officially, because most of the people outside by this point were just breaking the fences down. To round off a cheap day out we'd gone into an off-licence and filled a box up with spirits, bottles of wine, beer and mixers. The owner was so far gone that I'd said, "This lot comes to thirty bob" and he'd agreed. I'd reckon that we had about a tenner's worth of booze, at least.

So there we were. We'd travelled from Wycombe, fed, and got into the festival with enough drink to last us the weekend and it had cost less than two quid between the pair of us. Things were going so well that we decided to see how far our luck could carry. We went straight to the press arena, made our way to the side of the stage and found ourselves in a private area, with deckchairs from where we could watch the music all night. The Who did well, the Doors were shambolic, but as dawn was breaking Sly and the Family Stone came on and they were magnificent. They were one of the few bands that bothered to put on a proper show; dancing, performing, great songs, the lot. Although their music was different, their attitude was similar to Brewer's Droop – a gig's about what you do as well as how you sound.

Fleetwood Mac
Thames Hotel, Windsor – round about 1968

It was a good venue, holding about 500, but no more than a quarter full although that didn't worry me too much because it wasn't my promotion. That was the thing in those days. With no advance ticket sales and more gigs than there are now, you could never be sure whether you would sell out or play to an empty room. More than once a promising night was ruined by bad weather or a bigger name playing in the next town. Fleetwood Mac were still in their early days, with Jeremy Spencer on slide guitar, and they were messing around all night, but whenever they got down to business they played some of the best blues I've ever heard. The audience were patient with them, because we all knew that however lightly they were taking things, they'd end up going back to the great stuff. Maybe it was the contrast as their set progressed that made it such a memorable night.

Lowell Fulson and BB King
100 Club – 1970

Lowell always put on a great show, but BB's appearance made this one the best of the lot. Things are always better for being unexpected.

Mississippi Fred McDowell and Jo-Ann Kelly
Mayfair Theatre – 1970

This may come as a surprise, but the venue was a theatre in Mayfair. It was an incongruous setting for a blues gig, but with plays not being performed on Sundays the theatre could be hired out for other performances. Again it wasn't my gig, although I'd brought Fred over and booked him with the promoter. I'd normally have the American bluesmen playing the opening nights of their tours in London, but this time round Fred had been playing for a few weeks, so by the time he rolled into town he was on top form. Jo-Ann opened the show, she was an old mate who'd been working the British blues circuit for years and played in America. She put on a great performance, then Fred went one better, and they finished the show with a duet. I had a great seat, upstairs in one of those lovely private boxes that West End theatres have, and Fred was knocked out by Jo-Ann's voice. Sadly, he died a couple of years later, and Jo-Ann died at an early age as well, in 1990.

Canned Heat
Ronnie Scott's – 1969

Chris Trimming and I were invited by United Artists, the band's record label. They were touring and put on this special show on a Wednesday afternoon for people in the music business. Free food, as much drink as we wanted and one of the top rocking boogie and blues bands in the world. Afterwards, Chris and I talked to the band's founders Al Wilson and Bob Hite, who were both great authorities on the music and told us about bluesmen from America we'd never heard of, but we certainly took notes to get them to tour. After all, you couldn't get much more of a recommendation than from Canned Heat in the late sixties. Al Wilson was a true blues nerd, the sort of bloke who never seemed to change his clothes or brush his teeth because he spent all his waking hours thinking about the blues. I went on to see Canned Heat a few times, but the intimacy of this gig made it such a special occasion.

Sex Pistols
100 Club – March 1976
This was the first time I promoted the Pistols, and the most memorable. I'd been hearing plenty about them in the weeks since I first saw them at High Wycombe, but I still didn't know what to expect. Then when they turned up with that attitude of theirs and the Bromley Contingent arrived, I knew they were going to be a force. The show might have only lasted about forty minutes including encores, but every second was full of energy, piss-taking and interaction with the audience. I knew I was onto a winner.

Johnny Thunder & the Heartbreakers
Nag's Head – March 1977
Word association time: Johnny Thunders. You're thinking of a junkie who could hardly stand up straight, correct? That might have been the image, and Johnny hardly made his addictions secret, but his band could play. I've rarely seen a band so together and those great New York punk songs that had got me interested in the first place kept coming. The Heartbreakers should have been one of the biggest bands of their era but the press were only interested in British stuff, even though the New York punks had been doing it all two years earlier and were much more talented than all but a handful of ours. Yet again the originators had been overlooked when a scene became fashionable.

Freddie King
100 Club – Summer 1975

This was Freddie at his best. He was always a rough and ready character, and that helped us to get on well. Freddie never got the acclaim that contemporaries such as his namesakes B.B. and Albert received, but he was getting there when he died on Boxing Day 1976. He always loved the 100 Club, and would insist on playing there even when he'd progressed to the big concert halls. Stan Webb used to follow Freddie around slavishly, and this night Freddie allowed Stan to sit in with him. There was always an air of excitement around the place every time Freddie played, even in the afternoon, before he turned up. He was a great big fat bloke but highly sexual, and he got into a fight with one of his roadies over a girl who Freddie had his eye on. Freddie had gone offstage during his set while his brother, the much under-rated bass player Benny, did a number, to find the roadie and the girl in the dressing room. A scuffle broke out, but fortunately it was all smoothed over later that night and everyone went home satisfied that another great night in the history of the 100 Club had taken place.

Brinsley Schwartz
Leicester University – 1973

Brewer's Drop were also on the bill, which was one of those university festival-type affairs where a host of different bands would be playing across the campus. We were performing in a bar while the Brinsleys were in a refrectory, where a temporary stage had been erected. They did a set, we played ours, and then they went on for their second half. I went through to watch them, and although there were only about a hundred people in the audience the band were on top form. I'd seen them loads of times, promoted them, seen them rehearsing at the Nag's and shared the same bill, but sitting there with a bottle of beer for company I realised just how good they were. They were doing a set of New Orleans r&b stuff, very soulful, instead of the country-rock that was their trademark and this was one night where they seemed to be playing for themselves rather than the audience. Seeing them on such neutral territory made me appreciate their abilities all the more. Brinsley Schwartz were talented enough to have been a big name but they were never quite in the right place at the right time, although of course Nick Lowe had a few hits in that immediate post-punk era when talent was briefly more important than fashion.

The Treniers
Slough Adelphi – 1956

The Adelphi was one of those cinemas that doubled as a concert venue in the rock'n'roll era and beyond. I was young, I was with my first real girlfriend and I was learning the wide-open mysteries of women and music. I was into their music and the four-man vocal line-up was extraordinary but the presentation of the show knocked me out. The drummer would be playing a basic shuffle beat, nothing out of the ordinary, then the rest of the band would form a line and dance backwards into a circle. These were the days when acts would stand rigid in front of a microphone, so watching guys who were getting off on their own act was something else. They were obviously enjoying themselves; one would go into a routine and the rest would look at him and laugh. Unfortunately, it also meant that the Treniers and other bands that followed them had limited appeal. Trendsetters in music have always been too precious about the whole business. As Johnny Rotten said during PiL's first gig, "Remember fun? You're supposed to enjoy yourself." Music gradually became less of a mystery to me, but understanding women never got any easier.

Count Basie with Jimmy Rushing
Hammersmith Odeon – 1966

Rushing had been with the Basie band way back when it began in the thirties. He'd spent some time solo, then rejoined in time for this gig and they were a joy to watch. It was a legendary combination and I was lucky enough to see them. Basie came onstage, started playing with his three-man rhythm section then BANG – the brass kicked in, it was as dramatic as any rock band intro; the audience was sitting, waiting for something to happen when we were suddenly rocked back in our seats. Basie had brought some of his finest-ever musicians – Eddie 'Lockjaw' Davis on sax and guitarist Freddie Green, together with some exciting new talents. I've been to many jazz gigs, but this one still stands out in my mind. Basie was a lot more powerful and slick than I'd expected, but then again, by this stage in their careers his band would have known every song they played forwards, backwards and through the floor.

Of course, nor everyone was a big fan of the Count. He wanted Jimmy Witherspoon in his band but they couldn't agree a fee. When Spoon played at Ronnie Scott's he was interspersing the lyrics to Kansas City with a few comments about the great orchestra leader that Fats Domino couldn't have imagined when he wrote the song:

"I'm going to Kansas City.
Count Basie wanted to bring me over.
Kansas City here I come.
But he'd only pay me 200 dollars.
Going to Kansas City
Cheating bastard
Kansas City here I come."

That's twelve, but there was another I had to put in, as performed by someone whose natural place would be to gatecrash a list like this.

Captain Beefheart & the Magic Band
Middle Earth – 1967

Middle Earth was a converted fruit and vegetable warehouse in a Covent Garden basement. Its origins were obvious – it was a bare, concrete basement that could hold about a thousand people, and it was half-full for the Captain. He came out and did a Howling Wolf number that in his style was as good as if it had been performed by the man himself. There was some weird stuff thrown into the set, but his blues was as good as anyone else was playing at that time. His record company tried to make Beefheart into a white blues act but he stuck to his guns and as a result he's kept his reputation for excellence to this day. Even though this was a hippy venue right at the height of the hippy era, there weren't as many of the audience floating away as you'd think. In fact I reckon that whole drug thing of the time was greatly exaggerated. I rarely saw anyone taking anything at that time and I certainly didn't go around with my eyes shut. There were other times when drugs played a much bigger part on the music scene.

HEROES PUBLISHING
PO Box 1703, Perry Barr, Birmingham, B42 1UZ
www.heroespublishing.com